THE LIFE & MUSIC OF
RANDY NEWMAN
MAYBE I'M DOING IT WRONG

THE LIFE & MUSIC OF
RANDY NEWMAN
MAYBE I'M DOING IT WRONG

DAVID & CAROLINE STAFFORD

OMNIBUS PRESS
London / New York / Paris / Sydney / Copenhagen / Berlin / Madrid / Tokyo

To Clemmie, Connie and Georgia

Copyright © 2016 Omnibus Press
(A Division of Music Sales Limited)

Cover designed by Fresh Lemon
Picture research by Sarah Datblygu
ISBN: 9.781.78305.553.1
Order No: OP55836

The Authors hereby asserts their right to be identified as the authors of this work in accordance with Sections 77 to 78 of the Copyright, Designs and Patents Act 1988.

All rights reserved. No part of this book may be reproduced in any form or by any electronic or mechanical means, including information storage or retrieval systems, without permission in writing from the publisher, except by a reviewer who may quote brief passages.

Exclusive Distributors
Music Sales Limited,
14/15 Berners Street,
London, W1T 3LJ.

Music Sales Corporation
180 Madison Avenue, 24th Floor,
New York,
NY 10016,
USA.

Alliance Distribution Services
9 Pioneer Avenue,
Tuggerah,
NSW 2259,
Australia

Every effort has been made to trace the copyright holders of the photographs in this book but one or two were unreachable. We would be grateful if the photographers concerned would contact us.

Printed in the EU

A catalogue record for this book is available from the British Library.

Visit Omnibus Press on the web at www.omnibuspress.com

Prologue

In 1945, Warner Brothers decided to make a biopic celebrating the life of the songwriter Cole Porter. They commissioned a couple of class writers to come up with a script. The writers had trouble. The rags-to-riches boilerplate that could usually be spun into something heart-warmingly American ("from the mean streets of the Lower East Side…") did not apply. Cole Porter was the grandson of the 'richest man in Indiana'. His professional life was an arrow-straight upward trajectory unruffled by setbacks. His personal life didn't hold much promise, either. His bisexuality was, according to the Hollywood conventions of the time, out of bounds, and 'Happily married to the same woman – a wealthy socialite – from the age of 28' was not the stuff from which a tale of tortured romance could be wrought. Even a terrible horse-riding accident, which left him in pain for the rest of his life, was difficult to work into a unified narrative: 'rich songwriter has hit after hit, then falls off a horse', though it has a tempting edge of *schadenfreude*, does not easily lend itself to a classic three act structure.

Orson Welles summed up the problem: "What will they use for a climax? The only suspense is: will he or won't he accumulate $10m?"

Randy Newman presents the biographer with a similar problem. His dad was a doctor, not madly rich but sufficiently in funds for the young Randy never to have been troubled by anything like a boxcar or blacking factory. He sold his first song in his late teens, released his first solo album as a singer-songwriter at 24, became a celebrated film composer and won truckloads of awards. He's been married twice, but the divorce was unremarkable. If he's ever tried man-on-man sex it didn't have enough appeal to make it a lifestyle choice. He's never been known to take a brisk gallop on a leg-shattering horse and, to stymie even Orson Welles' last resort, he made $10m a good few years ago.

Neither – another stalwart of the boilerplate biography – did he have to fight off the possibility of an alternative career. There never was a, "But I don't want to be a doctor like you, dad. Can't you see? I've got to sing. I've got to dance," moment. Music was the family business. Three of his uncles were Hollywood composers. Becoming a songwriter – an impossible dream for most kids – was for him no more than the line of least resistance, as easy as the heir to a shoe shop becoming a shoe salesman. If Randy had wanted to be a shoe salesman, *then* there might have been conflict and drama, but he didn't. And if you're looking for the really big, gritty, emotional stuff ("Though he regularly sang for the governor, Newman had a tough time in Alcatraz" or "then at the age of 62 he discovered that Stevie Wonder was actually his long lost half-brother"), you're howling for the moon.

Even if Randy Newman's time on earth had been fraught with cliff-hanging reversals and stomach-tightening dramatic tension, it's arguable whether the life would have had much impact on the art. He's often said he's not an 'autobiographical' or 'confessional' songwriter. Actually it's not true. Songs like 'Dixie Flyer' and 'I Miss You' contain enough biographical detail to put you in with a chance of accessing his online bank accounts. But, unlike many others, he's never been a 'cryptically' or 'elliptically' autobiographical songwriter. Joni Mitchell's 'Carey' is a song that many have assumed to be about her affair with James Taylor, although she herself insists it's about a man she knew in Crete. If Randy Newman were to write such a song he would banish all doubt by starting with a line like, "Once I knew a man in Crete, so I wrote this song about him," thereby rendering any literary forensics or psychoanalytical speculation redundant.

So, rather than spinning unpromising material into a rattling semi-fiction, it seems far better to present the reader with a *Companion To The Works* of Randy Newman, a crib sheet to the albums and movies, accompanied, where relevant, with biographical notes as well as historical background, anecdotes, thematic asides and illuminating diversions.

It should also be borne in mind that we, the writers, are British and this book is tailored, primarily, for British readers.

In his lyrics, Randy Newman reveals himself as a keenly perceptive psychogeographer who enjoys not just the sound of words like "Tuscaloosa", but the weight of nuance they carry – nuance that is, for the most part, lost on foreigners. While a born and bred citizen of the USA might assume that his or her understanding of the word "Tuscaloosa" is roughly the same as Mr Newman's, the current writers assume nothing of the sort, but rather accept that the psychogeographical, ethnological and socio-cultural research must be completed and the results reported.

There are other cultural stumbling blocks, too. What, for instance, goes on in Roxbury, Boston? Why a Lexus? Has the wood-block ever featured prominently on a Bruce Springsteen track? Are Korean parents really as good as they're cracked up to be?

Read on ...

Chapter One

To know about Randy Newman you have to know about the uncles, and to know about the uncles you have to know about Luba, and to know about Luba you have to know about the assassination of Alexander II, Emperor of all the Russias, and to know about the assassination of Alexander II, Emperor of all the Russias, you have to know about Vera Figner.

As Vera Figner sat in her St Petersburg apartment on that cold, damp night in February 1881, filling paraffin cans with gelignite, she can have had no inkling of the profound and lasting effect that she and her comrades were about to have on the history of American show business.

Vera was a ringleader of The People's Will, a revolutionary organisation whose avowed intent was to assassinate the Tsar and, thereby, inspire the people to rise against their oppressors.

A few days later, as the Tsar rode in his coach from the Mikhailovsky Palace, where he'd been reviewing his troops, to his home in the Winter Palace, Vera and her comrades flung their bombs. The first and second missed their mark, injuring horses and outriders. Alexander then made the mistake of climbing from his carriage to inspect the damage and comfort the wounded, at which point the third bomb, the fatal bomb, was thrown.

The spontaneous revolution that Vera had hoped for didn't happen. Instead, the secret police – the notorious 'Third Section' – quickly rounded up the usual suspects. Though Vera herself escaped, four of her comrades were hanged – one of them three times because the rope kept breaking. A fifth, Gesya Gelfman, was granted a stay of execution because she was pregnant. Gesya also happened to be Jewish.

Some rumours suggested that Alexander's death was divine retribution for the sin of marrying his mistress in unseemly haste after the death of his wife. The existence of Gesya Gelfman provided the loyalist press with an alternative explanation. God hadn't killed the Tsar. It was the Jews.

There had been anti-Jewish pogroms here and there in the Russian empire for 60 years or more. After Alexander's assassination they became more frequent, fiercer and – covertly at least – state sponsored.

Trouble started in Elisavetgrad (now called Kirovohrad), in Ukraine, a prosperous market town with a large and flourishing Jewish community which included Randy Newman's great-grandparents. Peasants from miles around, excited by the prospect of lucrative looting, rushed into town. Only one person was killed but 300 shops and 400 homes were destroyed.

The mayhem spread. There were more deaths, more damage. The government joined in, imposing draconian restrictions on Jewish property ownership, education and voting. As a result, over the next 15 years, somewhere between a fifth and a third of the Russian Jewish population emigrated, the vast majority of them ending up in the USA.

Irving Berlin and his family came over in 1893, about the same time as Mr and Mrs Gershwin, George and Ira's parents. Szmuel Geldfisz came over from Russian-controlled Warsaw, travelling alone while still in his teens. He stayed for a while in Birmingham, England, where he changed his name to Samuel Goldfish before fetching up in the USA, where he became Samuel Goldwyn and put the 'G' in MGM. Lazar Meir, who became Louis B. Mayer and put the second 'M' in MGM, came over from Minsk in 1887. Jack and Sam Warner, the Warner brothers, came over in 1888. The Karnovskys, coal merchants on South Rampart Street, New Orleans, who looked after the young Louis Armstrong as if he was one of their own and, according to some stories, loaned him money to buy his first cornet, came over from Lithuania in 1883.

Among the Ukrainian immigrants were Mr and Mrs Nimoy, whose son Leonard became science officer on the Starship Enterprise, Mr and Mrs Zimmerman, whose grandson Bob changed his name to Dylan, and Yale and Rossa Koskoff, great-grandparents of Randy Newman.

Maybe I'm Doing It Wrong

All this from one inexpertly packed paraffin can.

Yale and Rossa arrived in 1894 along with their 11 children and found their way to New Haven, in Connecticut. A couple of years later, they married their youngest daughter, Luba, off to Michael Nemorofsky, who'd arrived from the old country four years earlier and changed his name to Newman.

Michael Newman was a 'produce salesman', something on a sliding scale between fruit pedlar and greengrocer, more likely nearer the former than the latter. At the time of the marriage, Michael was 23: Luba was looking forward to her 14th birthday. Alfred Alan Newman, the first child – there were eventually ten – arrived five years later.

Luba had not come to America, land of opportunity, to watch her children chisel a living from the mark-up on apples, so when young Alfred showed a smattering of musical talent she empowered herself with all the grit, charm and persistence of the showbiz mamma and located a teacher prepared to show her wunderkind the rudiments for 25c a lesson – a sum she could just about afford as long as six-year-old Alfred was prepared to economise on fares by walking the ten miles to and from the lessons. For daily practice, she sent him round to a wealthier neighbour, who possessed an upright.

The boy did well, exceeding even Luba's hopes. A better teacher, Edward A. Parsons, was so impressed with the lad's potential that he took him on without charge as a 'scholarship student'. Alfred starting playing Beethoven for money which, squirreled away and added to a subscription raised by local music lovers, eventually provided the wherewithal to send him to study with the great Sigismund Stojowski in New York.

Stojowski, a Pole (not to be confused with Leopold Stokowski, the Polish/Irish conductor who had, if you look closely, an entirely different name), was a revered piano player and teacher. At that time, he was working at the Von Ende School of Music on West 85th Street.

In 1914, Alfred was awarded the Von Ende Silver Medal. In 1915, he got the Gold. To eke out his dwindling resources, he took a job at the newly opened Strand Theatre in Times Square, one of the first purpose-built movie theatres, to accompany the picture shows and provide entertainment in the intermissions as 'The Boy Wonder Pianist'.

A Newman was there at the start, among the earliest providers of music for the movies.

The need for cash became more urgent when dad, Michael Newman, walked out on the family, and 17-year-old Alfred became the man of the house, provider for mother and his nine siblings.

Learning that big bucks were, apparently, to be made in vaudeville, he shone up his smile and went on the road with Gus Edwards, composer of 'By The Light Of The Silvery Moon'. As part of Edwards' act, Alfred was required, allegedly and inexplicably, to dress as Little Lord Fauntleroy. Possibly to avoid this humiliation he soon found himself a better job as accompanist to the "Parisian cultivated voice" of Grace La Rue.

Grace was a former star of the *Ziegfeld Follies* and co-star, with Al Jolson, of *The Honeymoon Express,* which premiered her subsequent big hit, 'You Made Me Love You' ("I didn't want to do it, I didn't want to do it"). When Alfred joined her, she was a headline act on the Keith theatres – the number one vaudeville circuit.

Alfred took over her musical chores, providing accompaniment where needed (although sometimes she sang duets with Caruso's phonograph records) and keeping the audience entertained during her frequent costume changes.

It was a slog. The Keith circuit was the first to offer continuous entertainment, ten in the morning until ten at night, and though this meant most acts would only put on two or three shows over the course of the day, being on duty for 12 hours was still more wearing than the usual two shows nightly.

Grace's French-sounding name, by the way, and her previous experience with the *Ziegfeld Follies* – in which the costumes provided little in the way of warmth – have led some commentators to suggest that her act might have been a little *risqué* for one of Alfred's tender years and classical training. Be assured that nothing could be further from the truth. Every one of Benjamin Franklin Keith's theatres displayed a sign backstage warning that "vulgarity and suggestiveness in words action and costume" would lead to "instant discharge". And to make sure that no double-entendre could be attached even to the word "discharge", a Sunday school dignitary was on hand at every rehearsal, listening out for sniggers.

Anyway, it was the orchestra pit rather than the spotlight that mostly engaged Alfred's attention. He took a notion to become a conductor.

Back in New York, he got to know William Daly, the composer/conductor/orchestrator, who taught him the art of gently coaxing the violas with a wave of the hand and of quashing excessive brio in the trombone section with a single forbidding glance. Sometimes Daly even let him take the baton for matinées.

By 1919, Alfred was conducting the first of *George White's Scandals* at the Liberty Theatre. He palled up with George Gershwin – whose first big hit 'Swanee' was riding high in the sheet-music charts – and some of the other young hopefuls hanging around the Broadway music scene: that select group of individuals, mostly born, like him, around the turn of the century, who went on to write the 300 or so songs that constitute the Great American Songbook of 'standards'.

By the end of the 1920s, he'd worked on hit shows by the Gershwins, Cole Porter, Rodgers and Hart, Jerome Kern, Vincent Youmans and Sigmund Romberg and established a reputation as a safe pair of hands, a man who could bring discipline to the musical rabble that haunted the orchestra pits of New York.

Then, in 1930, the great Irving Berlin offered him a job in Hollywood as Musical Director on a Douglas Fairbanks/Bebe Daniels movie called *Reaching For The Moon*.

Alfred was reluctant to leave New York, but Hollywood money had the power to tear priests from their vocation and force high-brow novelists to shame themselves with shite. Alfred, too, yielded to its allure and got on the train to loony-land.

Reaching For The Moon was an inauspicious beginning. By the time of the preview, the director, unsympathetic to the musical-comedy genre, had cut most of Irving Berlin's songs and Irving, disgusted, walked off the project.

But Alfred came out smelling of roses. He was offered another job, then another. Darryl Zanuck, of Twentieth Century Pictures, put him on the payroll as general musical director. One of his first assignments was coming up with a few seconds of music to accompany the company's logo at the beginning of every film. When Twentieth Century merged with Fox, the new company used the same logo. Still do. Remember, each time you thrill to that familiar drum roll and fanfare – *drum drum ... drum drum ... drrrr-rrrr, drum drum ... pah, padadaaa, pa, pa, pa, pa, pa* ... and so on – that it is Randy Newman's Uncle Alfred who is making your pulses race.

The merger gave Alfred bigger budgets. He was able to hire the best talent around; a team of top composers and arrangers and a full-time orchestra of excellent musicians. The 'Newman Strings' were spoken of with awe. He developed the 'Newman System' by which a conductor could be cued to place the music correctly with five foot 'streamers' drawn diagonally with grease pencil across the projected film. He was, in the estimation of concert pianist, wit and star of film and TV, Oscar Levant, "the best conductor by far in Hollywood".

He worked, over the course of a 40-year career, on more than 300 films, 200 or so as composer. The roster includes *Song Of Bernadette*, *Wuthering Heights*, *How Green Was My Valley*, *How The West Was Won*, *The Robe*, *The Seven Year Itch*, *The Greatest Story Ever Told*, *Airport* and on and on. He received 45 Oscar nominations (four in 1940 alone) and won 9. He was also a first class studio executive, who ran his department efficiently, was adept at negotiation and knew about contracts and copyright.

He was never, by all accounts, an even-tempered man.

"Newman was of course talented," said Robert Tracey, an editor who worked with him without much relishing the experience. "He was also a little Caesar. He was brutal with an orchestra on the stage if they didn't perform precisely. He was very strict. He knew what he wanted and he wouldn't settle for anything less. His hours were the thing as disliked as anything, as I recall, because he never started recording until four in the afternoon and he would go on until four the next morning if he felt like it or if he didn't run out of J&B scotch."

The idea that Alfred ruled his department in the same way that Attila ruled subject territories is backed up by stories like that of Arthur Morton, an esteemed orchestrator and conductor, who, after ten years' loyal service with Fox, had the gall to ask Alfred for a raise. He was summarily fired.

Others suggest that Alfred's grip was maintained by respect rather than fear. "He was a very, very strict conductor, very meticulous, but at the same time he treated his musicians as though they were really musicians and not just a bunch of workaholics," Maurice Spivack, another contemporary said. "When Newman's orchestra worked late, as they often did, he would order dinner catered by Chasen's for everyone. But the price of this respect was high. Newman would not be spoken back to. He referred to anyone who displeased him as a 'lard-ass'."

High on Alfred's list of lard-asses was Charlie Chaplin, a one-man band who found delegation anathema. As well as starring in, writing and directing his movies, he also composed the score for many of them, including his 1936 satire *Modern Times*. Charlie played violin, but couldn't read or write dots, so worked with an amanuensis, in this case Israel Raskin, to get everything down on paper.

Maybe I'm Doing It Wrong

Alfred conducted the score. During the first session Charlie complained, accusing the orchestra of laziness. Alfred was allowed to call his musicians lard-asses, but nobody else was allowed to breathe a word of criticism, least of all an unlettered amateur. A row broke out. Alfred stormed off the podium swearing never to work with Chaplin again – a promise he kept. A lesser conductor took over the sessions. Watch the movie. Hear those sloppy woodwind ensembles and ragged tempo changes. That's what you get for pissing Alfred off.

Either the accounts of his late nights and harsh discipline are libellous or, with the passing of the years, he mellowed. By the time Randy was old enough to visit his uncle at the studio, the routine was more settled. Work invariably stopped at five, and not until then did the scotch appear.

From early childhood, Randy would visit Uncle Alfred and watch him work. Sometimes, Uncle Alfred would play him a piece and ask him what he thought.

"I might have inherited some of my attitude about composing music from my uncle," Randy, a composer perenially puzzled by self-doubt, told Paul Zollo, "because here was this guy who was the best movie composer there ever was, and he was asking me, when I was eight years old, 'What do you think of this?'"

Alfred always found time for an eventful love life. During the twenties he conducted a long affair with the Broadway actress Sascha Beaumont, who subsequently enjoyed an enduring marriage to his younger brother Robert. Alfred himself married three times: finally – from 1947 until his death in 1970 – to former model and actress, Martha Montgomery.

All of Luba's boys distinguished themselves, four of them, like many of the sons and daughters of her fellow immigrants, in show business. Nobody's ever come up with a satisfactory explanation of Jews' over-representation in show business and under-representation in, for instance, contact sports. Most likely it's a combination of many factors in which prejudice undoubtedly figures. Perhaps the question's incorrectly framed, anyway. Maybe a more sensible way of putting it is, rather than 'why are Jews over-represented in show business and under-represented in contact sports', to ask the more puzzling question, 'why are gentiles over-represented in contact sports, which involve running until you're out of breath and risking painful injury for no sensible reason, and under-represented in show business, which mostly involves being in the warm surrounded by people who are pretty for a living'.

Robert, the second child, was a producer and publicist, first on Broadway then in Hollywood. In New York, he was, for a while, close friends with the Mayor, the infamous Jimmy Walker, widely accused of corruption with hints of murder. Robert, the story goes, loaned his friend the money he needed to lie low in Europe when the heat was on. Nobody could blame Robert for this. Jimmy Walker – Beau Walker – was a man of charm so irresistible that, when his case came eventually to court, the judge warned the jury not to look him in the eye for fear that they too would fall immediately under his spell.

George, the third child, was even more wayward. When he was 11 – again according to legend – he was sent out to buy cigarettes and didn't return for ten years. When he did, he was driving a fancy car and carrying a gun, which he proudly showed to his younger brothers and sisters, claiming to be a detective. The following morning, he found a bum sleeping in the back seat of his car. George dragged him out and pistol-whipped him right there on the sidewalk. The brothers begged him to stop. Emil, the sixth child, vomited with shock and fear.

George later moved to Chicago where he lived next door to Tony Accardo, aka Joe Batters aka Big Tuna, former henchman of Al Capone, participant in the St Valentine's Day Massacre and subsequently boss of The Outfit, which ran Chicago as well as most of the West Coast rackets.

Emil the sixth and Lionel ninth children, followed Alfred's lead and became composers and musical directors.

"Lionel was very funny, but very vulgar too," Randy told Jon Ronson for *The Guardian*. "When he won an Oscar in the late sixties for [musical direction on] 'Hello, Dolly', the guy he won with had two Oscars in his hand, so Lionel sort of leered, 'Well, I'm glad I didn't do 'Portnoy's Complaint'. Orchestras were always complaining about him cursing, even under the most sacred of circumstances."

Emil could be difficult, too.

"All [of my uncles]," Randy said, "had massive, Greek, tragic flaws, whether with alcohol or women or gambling. But Emil had all of them."

On one occasion Emil didn't show up for work. He was supposed to be conducting a picture for Fox. The orchestra waited. And waited. He didn't answer his phone. Eventually an emissary was sent to to Emil's house. He found Emil, sitting on his front lawn in his bathrobe, smoking a cigarette. His house had burned down. He'd lost all his clothes in the fire, but nevertheless came to the studio in his dressing gown, got up on the podium and did a day's work.

Irving, the eighth child, Randy's dad, had a temper worse than Alfred's and nearly as bad as pistol-whipping George's. He, too, showed musical talent. He wrote songs and, in his teens, joined a band that Lionel had formed, playing clarinet and singing. For a time, they toured the Caribbean, playing the cruise ships as Newman's Society Orchestra, or sometimes The Newmaniacs. Irving played with Benny Goodman and Red Nichols, too, and could almost certainly have enjoyed a successful musical career were it not for his grades at school. They were good.

Irving was just two when Michael left and Alfred stepped into the dad role. Big brother took his family responsibilities seriously. He and Luba made plans for Irving. Maybe they had doubts about the eighth child's musical talent. Maybe they feared that the family was putting too many of its eggs in the show business basket. If the taste for entertainment were suddenly to wither and, simultaneously, brother George were to discover that the thing about crime not paying was absolutely right, they'd all be back peddling fruit.

Anyway, whatever the reason, they decided that Irving should take advantage of his good grades and become a doctor. Irving's reaction to the decision is not on record, and neither is there any evidence that George was invited to 'persuade' any opposition out of him, but somehow he got persuaded and enrolled at NYU to complete the qualifications required to sign up for medicine.

In the thirties it was tough for a Jew to get into medical school. Irving learned, however, that the State of Alabama, suffering from a shortage of doctors, was guaranteeing admission to the Medical College at Tuscaloosa to anybody who agreed subsequently to practice in the state.

Irving went south. He lasted less than a year.

One day, the Dean referred to him as a "Hebe". Irv could never overlook a racial slur. The red mist came down. He threw a punch. It connected. The Dean crumpled.

Irv came back from Alabama, possibly with a banjo on his knee and certainly with a black mark next to his name. He'd been expelled. Worse still, word had got round and he found himself barred from every medical school in the country.

Brother Robert, however, as we noted earlier, knew where the strings of power were kept and which ones to pull. His friendship with Mayor Jimmy Walker, had given him access to a good many politicians, including – possibly, facts are understandably shrouded – the outspoken hero of the poor, Huey Long, "The Kingfish", one-time Governor of Louisiana and United States Senator, a man who subsequently loomed large in Randy's imagination.

A nod, a wink, and Irv was squeezed into the newly opened Medical School of Louisiana State University in New Orleans. Miraculously, this time Irv managed to stay the course without recourse to violence. He finished second in his class. Perhaps love had something to do with it.

A fellow student at LSU was boarding with the Fuchs – a family who, for obvious reasons, had anglicised their name to Fox. Mr and Mrs Fox had a beautiful daughter called Adele. The friend bet Irving that he'd never get Adele to agree to a date. After several rebuttals, Irving agreed that his chances were zero and paid off the bet.

But later Irving and Adele ran into each other in the glamorous setting of a ball at the Roosevelt Hotel. The spark was kindled. Adele stopped rebutting and Irv was so pleased he even forgot to claim his money back from the friend.

Adele, Randy's mum, had been born in Brooklyn. The family moved to New Orleans when she was a toddler. Her dad was a barber, retired by the time Randy knew him. "I heard that he was allergic to hair," Randy said. "But he may have been allergic to something else – like allergic to work. He may have been a little off his head. He never said a word to me."

Adele was one of six children. One of her siblings was an artist, another an optician and some ran stores in Jackson, Mississippi, and, as we shall discover later, had a gentile friend who owned a green Hudson motor car.

After Irving graduated, he left New Orleans and went back to Luba and the rest of his family, who by this time had abandoned the winter snows of the East Coast and joined Alfred in Los Angeles. He got a job in a hospital and lived in.

Though a working doctor now, in his mid-twenties, with his own salary, Luba still thought he was too young to marry. But quietly, Adele, too, moved to LA and in 1939 the pair were secretly married in an orange grove in Santa Ana. They managed to keep it quiet for nearly a year before Luba found out.

Maybe I'm Doing It Wrong

Randal Stuart (Randy) Newman was born on November 28, 1943.

When the US joined the war, Irving Newman was sent to serve in Italy. He was not a model soldier. He refused to salute, he refused to march: he was there as a doctor and expected to be treated as such.

Randy has already written the next part of the story: "My poor little momma / Didn't know a soul in LA / So we went down to the Union Station and made our getaway / Got on the Dixie Flyer* bound for New Orleans."

Adele and Randy stayed in New Orleans for a couple of years and he returned for family vacations throughout his childhood. The place left an indelible mark.

He was two years old when he first saw his father. His reaction was the one adopted by many war babies on that first encounter. He bit him. Irving hurried his family back to Los Angeles.

But a seed had been planted. Those two formative events were all it takes, it seems, to make a man natural master of the New Orleans shuffle, the rolling left hand, the ruff, the Spanish tinge and the Texas boogie.

---

* The train in question would not, in fact, have been the Dixie Flyer, which ran from Chicago to Florida, but the Sunset Limited (most likely pulled by a GS-1 4-8-4 Golden State steam locomotive and featuring its own on board post office and barber shop), which ran from Los Angeles to New Orleans calling at Palm Springs, Yuma, Tucson, Benson, El Paso, San Antonio, Houston, Lake Charles and Lafayette. Not that it matters. Pedants who make a fuss about this sort of thing should probably just be led away and spoken to in a kind but firm way.

Chapter Two

A second son, Alan, was born to Dr and Mrs Newman in 1947. Adele lost the couple's only daughter after a difficult pregnancy.

As the fifties unfolded, the Newmans did a passable impersonation of an Eisenhower-era, *Saturday Evening Post* socio-economic unit. Dr Newman made good money and spent it on cars and appliances and a nice house in Pacific Palisades, a leafy suburb. The boys played Little League and shot hoops in the back yard.

They missed out on a couple of ticks in the White Anglo-Saxon Protestant boxes, but, in a town that boasts the fourth largest Jewish population in the world – just behind Tel Aviv, New York and Jerusalem – so did most of their friends and neighbours.

But the uncles could never do the *Saturday Evening Post* thing. One of Randy's early memories was of being driven to school by an unspecified uncle who occasionally took his hands from the wheel to take a pull at his breakfast of vodka and milk.

Irving had trouble, too. Apart from anything else, he punched nuns. Or rather just the one nun.

He was, at the time, attending a very sick young man in hospital. Fearing that the end could not be long coming, he suggested that the man's mother be called. The mother arrived and, on seeing her son, collapsed in helpless tears. A nurse arrived – a nun. She took in the scene and said, "We don't want any hysterical Jewish mothers in here."

Maybe I'm Doing It Wrong

So Irving punched her.

He was barred from the hospital, St John's in Santa Monica, for ever afterwards. Even when his niece fell ill in childbirth and was admitted, another doctor had to attend.

"I get my sense of humour from him," Randy told Erin Kaplan, "though I don't have his consistently bad temper, not to the point of being unreasonable. He treated a lot of famous people."

The roster of his celebrity clients eventually included Jerry Lewis, Oscar Levant, Pat Boone, Rod Stewart and Billy Joel.

"One of them was [televangelist and faith-healer] Oral Roberts, whom he liked very much, though my father actively grumbled about religion. He made fun of it. Once Oral called him in the middle of the night and said he had terrible haemorrhoids. My dad told him, 'Why are you calling me in the middle of the night? Why don't you stick your other finger up your ass and heal yourself?'"

Stories of Irv's fights are legion. There was the time he slugged it out with Nancy Reagan in the parking lot at Brentwood Country Mart. The time in the restroom at Hamburger Hamlet when he punched a guy who may or may not have called him a 'no good Jew'. Brentwood, it should be added, is a tame — give or take the odd OJ Simpson glitch — middle-class suburb with a village-in-a-town feel.

"[My father was] the kind of man who wouldn't let a child win a race," Randy told Barney Hoskyns. "I raced him when I was 13 and he was 43. He needed to beat me.

"My mother, she got squashed, in one sense. Between my father and my brother and me, she never got to the predicate of a sentence, because she talked slowly, and she ate slowly and my father ate really fast in case he got a medical call — that's what he said. And my brother and I consequently ate fast, so she'd just be dipping in and we'd be ready to leave the table.

"She kept her New Orleans accent her whole life, and she didn't have anything bad to say about anybody — unlike the rest of us. She was a soft person, unlike my father, who had a bad temper — and she was the victim of it sometimes."

Though most of Irving's outbursts were initiated by perceived racial and religious slurs, the Newmans were not a religious family. Irving was an "aggressive atheist" who never gave much thought to matters of roots or cultural identity.

In his teenage years, Randy was invited by a girl to a dance at a country club. The girl's father subsequently suffered the embarrassment of having to withdraw the invitation because the club didn't allow Jews. Puzzled, Randy went home and asked his dad, "What exactly is a Jew?"

The Newmans seemed plagued by health problems – maybe it's a common syndrome in doctors' families. Alan had asthma. Adele suffered migraines and often had to retire to a darkened room at which times Irving would try to preserve silence in the house by screaming at Randy to turn the TV down.

By the time he was four, it was clear that Randy had problems with his eyesight. He was severely cross-eyed. He had his first operation to try to correct the problem when he was only five.

School was a series of mild traumas. These were the days when 'anti-bullying initiatives' were as remote as interplanetary travel and Cherry Garcia. Randy was a cross-eyed Jewish kid with thick glasses. Survival at school would have required either iron fists, a rapier wit or a commanding personality. He had none of them.

Irving suggested that a lot of his problems were caused by his inability to look another kid straight in the eye.

At Paul Revere Junior High, he got his nose broken. He was standing in a queue for candy when another boy queue-jumped. Randy remonstrated. The boy reacted like Irving confronted by an anti-semitic nun. He punched him in the face.

"It was a brief fight," Randy said. "He hit me and I just bled on him. My friends said they were gonna get the guy. He got thrown out of school for a few days, and they said they would get him when he got back. I'm still waiting."

He did, however, have at least one more reliable friend.

Simon (Si) Waronker had once played violin in Alfred Newman's 20th Century Fox Orchestra. He'd gone on, in 1955, to found Liberty Records. Through his friendship with Alfred, he got to know Irving. His son, Lenny, though a couple of years older than Randy, eventually became a playmate.

"I must have met Lenny when I was one year old," Randy said. "By the time I was four I remember going to Roxbury Park with him."

Lenny had confidence, a spirit of adventure and a cavalier attitude towards his pal's well-being.

"[Lenny] would say, 'Let's ride on this tricycle.' He'd get on the back and I would pull him, and we'd fall off. I would get hurt and he wouldn't. I still have scars from that tricycle."

"Randy was always kinda quiet when he was younger," Lenny told Timothy White, "which is one of the reasons he didn't have a tremendous amount of friends. He read a lot, retreated to his room, was always drifting away. Early on, he started taking piano lessons, at seven or eight. I started at around the same time. He was encouraged, got a lot of encouragement when it came to that."

The encouragement came principally, and perhaps surprisingly given the generally competitive spirit, from Irving. "When I had some little talent, he was like, 'Oh, look what he can do, look at that, he can play a third,'" Randy said. "He was a doctor, but he thought his brothers – three of whom were composers – were the greatest thing ever. I think he wanted me to do what they did.

"A lot of them [the uncles] would play at parties – dirty songs and stuff. But it wasn't like we'd get together and make music. [Linda] Ronstadt told me how her family was very musical, always singing all the time. I like it, believe me. But composers are wary of having kids play for them – you know, music was work."

Randy was never a bad scholar, but doubts about the value of education came early. "What I remember about junior high," he said, "is some of the questions the teacher would ask. 'True or false – the Russian people are bad'."

After Paul Revere, he went on to University High on Texas Avenue in West LA, down towards Santa Monica.

Most of the people who later came to dominate the Los Angeles music and movie scene went either to University High or to nearby Fairfax High. Fairfax educated, at one time or another, PF Sloan, Phil Spector, Herb Alpert, Jerry Leiber and Slash of Guns'n'Roses. University High alumni include Marilyn Monroe, Judy Garland, *Partridge Family* heart-throb David Cassidy, Jan Berry and Dean Torrence of the surf duo Jan & Dean, Nancy Sinatra and her kid brother Frank Jr, Sandra Dee, star of *Gidget* celebrated in *Grease* ("look at me I'm Sandra Dee / lousy with virginity"), Bruce Johnston, songwriter and Beach Boy... and Randy Newman.

University High was a place of cliques, clubs and gangs. Economist and writer Alan Reynolds (Class of '59) gives us a taste: "These clubs varied in status, like fraternities and sororities. Jan & Dean were in a top group, the Barons. I belonged to a totally unsupervised lowbrow group, the Ladds, which was supposedly a car club except few of us had cars.

"The late fifties and early sixties was a time of rapid transformation in the definition of cool – in music, cars, clothes and hairstyles. Those with a sense of fashion, like Jan & Dean, were switching to khakis with a buckle in the back, while my friends were still wearing low-riding Levi's and rolled-up shirt sleeves. We listened to black R&B on Hunter Hancock's show (the Ladds' party favourite was 'High Blood Pressure' by Huey Piano Smith). Greased hair combed into a jellyroll (early Jan Berry) or waterfall (Dean), was on the way out. Shorter blonde hair, like Dean's later flattop, was on the way in."

The Ladds and the Barons, the jellyroll and waterfall, the khakis and Levi's, even breathing the same air that Marilyn and Judy had once breathed, left Randy disenchanted. "It was all so sullen and boring and small and vile," he told Bruce Pollock. "It was so seedy. You might have thought it was fun, but it was pretty grim, and not for me alone. God! The torment."

It was years before he discovered that the nameless longings, the vile isolation, the seething resentment were not Newman-specific at all. "I discovered that everybody was always scared all the time socially," he said, "whereas I thought that people were really together. No one was."

He did sports like a regular kid, Little League and so on, but still the feeling of alienation stubbornly persisted and persists. "I remember one time, I went to *Cats* here in London and I felt I was back in High School. I used to play sports and stuff, and when I'd go to a High School football game and people were jumping up and down, I just didn't give a shit, really. And *Cats* was the same experience. I felt I was from another galaxy, I just didn't get what they were liking up there and it was that same kind of feeling."

By the time he was in his teens Randy had had three or four operations on his eyes. He had to travel to a hospital in San Francisco for the last one – performed by one of the leading surgeons in the field who assured Randy that it would completely centre his eyes.

After the operation, his eyes were bandaged shut and he was moved to the blind ward. According to Irving, he was not a good patient. If the nurse was a little slow coming around with the bedpan, he'd feel his way around the room and piss in the sink. Or, if he couldn't find the sink, he'd piss in his shoe. "That's the way he was," Irving said. "He gave everybody his chance and then if help wasn't forthcoming he did it his own way."

The consequences of letting an occasional inmate of the blind ward – with a clinically flawed appreciation of parallax and perspective – get behind the wheel of a car should have been predictable but still, it seems, had the power to surprise and annoy.

When Randy was 12, his father allowed him to back the family car out of the garage. As he reversed, the bumper caught the spring of the garage door and bought it crumpling down on top of the car.

He failed his test twice. The first time he lost his temper with the examiner when he told him he had failed and swore at him. The examiner made a note on the system and ensured that he got to test him the second time. He failed him again. Randy detected a pattern emerging and booked his next test out of the area.

His first proper accident was on Melrose Avenue in 1959. Randy was 16. The other car was uninsured.

He owns up to about a dozen or so other car accidents in his teenage years, caused mostly by his defective vision, his offhand attitude and his taste for strong drink. "See, I have no control, I can't do anything in moderation," he told David Felton. "When I used to drink, even in high school and stuff, I always headed for oblivion, you know? I remember once, I drank six bottles of Ripple*, and the next thing I remember – I wasn't driving – I got in this big wreck."

The Ripple accident resulted in some fairly serious trauma surgery, including an operation just to get him breathing properly. In another traffic accident he suffered a slipped disk, and in another he broke his nose for the second time.

Drink helped him overcome his shyness, stopped him being so damned critical of everything and eased his hang-ups about the dividing line

---

* 'Ripple' (otherwise known as 'bum wine', 'street wine' and (in Glasgow) 'wreck the hoose joose') is a generic name for any cheap, strong wine, often with some flavouring added to disguise the underlying stink. Buckfast Tonic, made by monks, is a popular cause of many social problems in the UK. In the US, the equivalent would be something like Cisco, Night Train or Thunderbird ("an American classic").

between legal and illegal – his dad had to pick him up from police custody on more than one occasion. There was also the exciting possibility – unfounded as it turned out – that drink would help him get girls.

"I was so damned *shy* around girls," he told Timothy White. "I really didn't have many dates. I was strange looking – and I was a bad driver. I'd be trying to get my arm around a girl who didn't want to *know* about it while I drove the family car up on some sidewalk. We went to the movies, there was some parking at night, but I always did *bad*."

Between failing to make out with girls, totalling cars and getting drunk, he started writing songs.

Chapter Three

"He started writing at about 15," Randy's brother, Alan, said. "We were living in a big house in Pacific Palisades, and Randy had this brown upright piano in his bedroom that we later replaced with a baby grand Steinway. One of the first things I can recall him writing was a thing called 'Puppy Love' [no relation to the Paul Anka/Donny Osmond song of the same name]. He was a lonely guy, no girlfriends, was hard to get through to, and he'd work so hard on those songs."

When he'd written a song, almost invariably he'd play to his friend Lenny Waronker. "[Lenny's] instincts are better than mine, in some respects. He's always been, for me, the most crucial person to my career," Randy told Michael Hill. "When I was 16 or 17, Lenny was my backbone. I was too shy to play stuff for people and he was always the first person – in the first 25 years or so of my career life – I would play things for. Lenny was always there with enthusiasm or a suggestion and a drive I didn't have myself. I wanted to be the best I could be, but Lenny wanted me to be the best in the world, and I owe him a great deal."

After high school, Randy enrolled at UCLA (University of California, Los Angeles) majoring in music theory and composition. There's a 'Thelonious Monk Institute of Jazz Performance' at UCLA now, and a 'Herb Alpert School of Music'. When Randy went there in the early sixties, folk music had just about made it onto the syllabus and the

Department of Ethnomusicology was getting dangerously overexcited about Javanese gongs.

Some of the teachers were exciting, though. Distinguished European composers with a taste for sunshine and money often favoured the department with a master class or two. For a brief period during the thirties, Arnold Schoenberg, the 12-tone serial thriller, took up residence for a time. Hollywood's composers and orchestrators came to pay court. One of them, engaged in a tricky assignment, asked for his advice on writing 'airplane music'. "Just like music for big bees," replied the master. "Only louder."

In Randy's day the master in residence was Mario Castelnuovo-Tedesco, an Italian/Jewish composer of opera, violin and cello concerti and a huge body of work for the guitar, who, just as Schoenberg had escaped Hitler's Germany, had fled to California from Mussolini's fascism.

Randy was not a good student. Some days he'd drive to college and, if he couldn't find an easy parking space, would just keep driving.

Little brother Alan eventually joined him at UCLA. They took some of the same courses, or at least Alan took the courses and Randy read over his brother's lecture notes.

Meanwhile Lenny, two years older than Randy, had been studying business and "anything to get me through" at the University of Southern California. Since the age of 14 he'd also been helping out at his dad's record company.

In 1955, Si Waronker had borrowed $2,000 from a Los Angeles bank, using the furniture in his Pacific Palisades house as collateral, and set up his own record label, Liberty Records.

His friends the Newmans were involved in the project from the start. Among the label's first releases were Alfred's 'Theme From Captain From Castile' and Lionel's (under the name Bud Harvey) 'As if I Didn't Have A Thing On My Mind'.

The first big hit came from Julie London, a sultry torch singer Si had signed after seeing her at the 881 Club in Hollywood. An album, *Julie Is My Name*, produced by Bobby Troup (composer/lyricist of '[Get Your Kicks On] Route 66') who later married Julie, went to number two in the *Billboard Chart*. A magnificent single from the album, 'Cry Me A River', just Julie's voice accompanied by Barney Kessel on guitar and Ray Leatherwood on bass, sold a million.

Maybe I'm Doing It Wrong

A few months later, the label had another hit with 'Tonight You Belong To Me' by Patience and Prudence, the children (11 and 14) of Frank Sinatra's piano player.

A couple of follow-up singles from Patience and Prudence – including a UK minor hit with 'Gonna Get Along Without You Now' – kept things bubbling for a while. Then the company's fortunes began to slip downhill. Eventually Si considered filing for bankruptcy.

A joke release – half-expected to be the label's swansong – saved them. Rostom Bagdasarian, an American-Armenian who worked under the name of David Seville, wrote and recorded a dumb and arguably racist song, 'Witch Doctor', with an irritatingly catchy chorus that went, "Oo ee oo ah aah ting tang walla walla bing bang". It went to number one.

Later that year, Bagdasarian, intrigued by the sped-up tape effect he'd used in 'Witch Doctor', released 'The Chipmunk Song (Christmas Don't Be Late)' by the Chipmunks, advertised, as the name suggests, as a trio of singing Chipmunks. It sold 4.5m in seven weeks and won two Grammy Awards. The Chipmunks were named Alvin, Simon and Theodore after Liberty executives: Alvin Bennett (president), Simon Waronker (co-founder and chairman) and Ted (Theodore) Keep (co-founder and head of engineering).

Thankfully, by that time Liberty had also signed Eddie Cochran – so some semblance of decency was preserved – as well as Bobby Vee, Johnny Burnette, Jackie DeShannon, the Fleetwoods and Snuff Garrett.

Snuff was a DJ and Flagpole Squatter from Dallas, Texas. He worked for a while at station KDUB in Lubbock where he encountered and encouraged the young Buddy Holly and coined the catchphrase, "Come a-foggin' cowboy!" (still heard every day in Lubbock and surrounding districts). Then he moved on to KYSD in Wichita Falls. It was here that he revived the art of Flagpole Squatting, 1,600 years after St Simeon Stylites the Elder had first devised the stunt in ancient Antioch and 30 years after the height of the sport's popularity in the twenties.

When Snuff mounted his Wichita flagpole, the record of 71 days had not been broken since 1933. To vary the usual technique of just sitting atop the pole, and since the stunt was being sponsored by the local Renault dealer, Snuff hoisted a car up there and vowed to live in it, and broadcast from it, until the dealership had shifted 50 cars. It took a week. The first three days were spent in torrential rain, then some college kids tried to saw the flagpole down as a prank and finally a traffic cop served him with a ticket for prolonged parking.

When Snuff rocked up to Los Angeles, Alvin, Si and Theodore naturally had the good sense to offer him a job in promotion. Within a year he'd moved into production, creating hits for many of the label's roster.

Lenny Waronker, while he was still at college, worked occasionally as Snuff's gopher. He got to fetch coffee not just in LA but in New York and Nashville. He learned the business. By the time he'd graduated from USC, he was ready. "When my dad started the Liberty Company, I saw that it was a thing I could do," Lenny told Michael Kelly. "By getting involved in Liberty, I could be in music and didn't necessarily have to be a musician."

"Liberty was a company of young, aggressive, very together and forward looking people," Al Altman, who worked there at the time, said. "It was a good fraternity of people and a good many of them not only remained in the record business but have continued to be successful."

The company was growing fast. At the beginning of the sixties it had a staff of around 150 and a stable of hit-making stars under contract. The offices on Sunset Boulevard were impressively appointed with the latest technology. When Alvin Bennett, the company president, pressed a button on his desk, curtains would unfold to reveal a giant TV screen. He pushed another button and the TV came on. In 1962, this was more mind-blowing even than Moonships, or Sta-Prest trouser technology.

Liberty also opened its own publishing division, Metric Music, which signed Randy while he was still at college, for a sum which, at a time when the national average wage was around $100 a week, fell a good way short of derisory. Randy didn't think so: "$100 a month sounded great to me."

Metric and Liberty became a hangout for a bunch of disparate composers, musicians and singers, some under contract, some already well-established, others just looking to learn.

Sharon Sheeley, LA born and bred, was in the "well-established" category. She'd got her start when she tricked her ex-boyfriend, TV heartthrob Ricky Nelson, into recording a song she'd written. "Back then," she said, "the rock'n'roll business scene was dominated by men, all men. If I had told him [Ricky] that I had written a song that I wanted him to record, it would never have happened. So I made up a story. I told him that I knew this guy that had written a song for Elvis and Elvis had agreed to record it after he returned from Germany." Elvis was doing his military service at the time. "I told Rick that Elvis really loved the song. That did it. He believed he would be scooping Elvis."

The song, 'Poor Little Fool', was Ricky's first number one and the first ever US number one to have been written singlehandedly by a woman. "Oh, the shock of it when he found my friend was me. He would have never even considered it if he knew from the get go that a *girl*, a 16-year-old *girl*, had written this great song."

Later Sharon went out with Eddie Cochran, wrote 'Love Again', the B-side of 'Summertime Blues' and – a co-write with Eddie – 'Somethin' Else', the definitive anthem of teen longing. A year after that, she joined Eddie on a tour of the UK and was in the car, driving back to London from a gig at the Bristol Hippodrome, when it hit a lamp-post. Sharon, Eddie and Gene Vincent, who was also in the car, were ambulanced to St Martin's Hospital in Bath. Eddie died the following afternoon.

Sharon eventually limped back to California where she found her way to Metric and teamed up with an old friend, singer-songwriter Jackie DeShannon, a former child star who'd had her own radio show, back in Hazel, Kentucky at the age of 11. DeShannon and Sheeley songs turned up, mostly as B-sides and album tracks, for a disparate bunch of artists – The Kalin Twins, The Fleetwoods, Troy Shondell, The Ronettes. They had a stand-out hit with 'Dum Dum', a making out song which Brenda Lee took to number four ("Your ma's in the kitchen, your pa's next door / I wanna love you just a little bit more", the second phrase being half-spoken in a tone sultry enough to make adolescent boys drown in their own hormones).

Other regulars at Metric included David Gates and Russell Bridges, school friends from Tulsa, Oklahoma, Jim Smith and Glen Campbell. All of them would, by the end of the sixties, be farting through silk. David Gates, among other triumphs, formed the band Bread which charted 11 consecutive singles, all of which he wrote and produced. Russell Bridges changed his name to Leon Russell, played keyboards and guitar with Dylan, Clapton and Harrison, wrote 'Delta Lady' for Joe Cocker and generally made a legend of himself. Jim Smith changed his name to Jet Powers and then to PJ Proby (PJ after a Hollywood nightclub, Proby, suggested by Sharon Sheeley after Proby Benefill, an old boyfriend) relocated to the UK, scored three top ten hits and scandalised the British press by splitting his blue velvet trousers in Croydon, and then again in

Luton. Glen Campbell is and will forever be the Wichita Lineman and the Rhinestone Cowboy.

The glut of nascent talent meant that Metric could produce better than average demos. "Every demo I ever did for them had David on bass, Leon on piano, Glen on guitar. We all did falsetto backing vocals 'cos Liberty couldn't afford the girls," PJ Proby said. "You'd be surprised how high your voice can go for money."

Leon and Glen, together with drummer Hal Blaine, who also played on many of the Metric demos, became the core of first-call musicians that came to dominate and define the LA sound of the sixties; the floating team that, because they'd 'ruined' everything for the old-school big band jazzers, Blaine christened 'The Wrecking Crew' – although Phil Spector, the mad boy-genius homicidal producer, so far up himself that his sphincter eventually became his head, preferred to call them 'The Phil Spector Wall Of Sound Orchestra'.

Meanwhile, Randy's songwriting was progressing in fits and starts. Evenings and weekends, he and Lenny kicked around ideas for new songs and for inspiration that might turn old time standards into of-the-moment hits.

Approval was hard to come by. "People like Snuff [Garrett] thought he was too weird," Lenny said. "They kept saying, 'How's your weird friend?' and that's a painful thing to go through."

Lenny remained enthusiastic about his weird friend. Lenny's enthusiasm was a difficult force to resist.

Russ Titelman, later to become the producer of choice to rock royalty (Clapton, Paul Simon, George Harrison, Steve Winwood, Ry Cooder, Randy Newman etc., etc.), then a teenage kid hanging around, remembers Lenny as "this enthusiastic young song publisher/promo guy who always dressed in slacks, white shirts with the sleeves rolled up and the collar open, and a loosened necktie. He looked like a reporter! And he always sat on the back of chairs with his feet on the seat, leaning forward like he was going to jump off in excitement."

Gradually, the name R. Newman began to appear on record labels.

'They Tell Me It's Summer' was recorded in 1962 by the Fleetwoods – Gary, Gretchen and Barbara – who'd topped the singles chart a couple of years earlier with 'Come Softly To Me' and 'Mr Blue'. While Gary wonders why people tell him it's summer even though he can't see the sunshine because of the tears in his eyes, Gretchen and Barbara go "wo wo wo", "aaah" and "they tell me it's summer" with a persistence that, though admirable, eventually begins to grate. The sauntering melody, opening with a bold octave leap before settling into every comfort zone known to humankind, is enlivened by a leisurely variation on the riff used for the Everly Brothers' 'Walk Right Back' a year earlier, but played, with perhaps an almost imperceptible nod to Mexican sunshine, on the low notes of a xylophone or maybe a marimba. There's an even more imperceptible nod to the Caribbean in the second verse with the introduction of what sounds like the most politely played steel drum ever recorded. The track is nothing to phone home about, much less write, but on the good side it doesn't make you want to sue anybody for the 2'20" of your life it just consumed, which, in the pop climate of 1962 was a considerable achievement.

The record rose to number 36 in the singles chart, but unfortunately Randy's song was on the B-side. The A-side was a Neval Nader/John Gluck composition called 'Lovers By Night, Strangers By Day'.

All the same, Randy made $800 to supplement his $100 a month. "I should have earned more, but that's what I got, I think."

The Fleetwoods recorded other Newman songs, too. 'Who's Gonna Teach You About Love' didn't get released until it emerged on a compilation album, *Buried Treasure*, in 1983. It's credited as a family collaboration by A. [Alan] Newman, I. [Irving] Newman and R. [Randy] Newman.

Irving was always willing to pitch in, help out with a line, a rhyme, a turn of phrase. "And he was helpful, too," Randy said. "But old-fashioned. I got led down the road a time or two."

"Before you learned to swim / You had to sink", goes the 'Who's Gonna Teach You About Love' lyric. The line it's rhymed with, "Before you learned to speak / You had to think", could well be an example of this being 'led down the road' and would certainly be a matter of dispute among developmental psychologists and semioticians.

'Ask Him If He's Got A Friend For Me', also buried until the 1983 release, borrows its arrangement from the Everly's 'Crying In The Rain' and sets up a sort of morally corrective dialogue between the main and backing vocals – foreshadowing Randy's 'Shame' from the *Bad Love* album by nearly 40 years. When the lead vocal, for instance, requests the backing vocalists to ask their friend to find him a girl whose company will help assuage the pain of recent heartbreak, they chasten him with the accusation that he'd, "*use* some girl you'd never met / just to help you to forget." So that's him told.

'Lovers' Lullaby', which turned up on the 1963 album, *The Fleetwoods Sing For Lovers by Night*, could make the toes of a wooden leg curl.

The songs kept coming, though, and, in Lenny's eyes at least, Randy was on a roll. "He was on an uphill swing that was unbelievable," Lenny said. "I mean, literally every song I heard was a step up; there was just constant growth."

Pop songs in general were on an uphill swing.

Jerry Leiber and Mike Stoller, the acknowledged masters of the craft, had written or co-written 70 or so genre defining hits including – a truncated list with apologies for probably leaving out several of the reader's favourites – 'Hound Dog', 'Jailhouse Rock', 'Yakety Yak', 'On Broadway', 'Poison Ivy', 'Smokey Joe's Café', 'Spanish Harlem', 'Kansas City', '(You're So Square) Baby I Don't Care', 'Stand By Me' and 'I'm A Woman'.

In New York, Aldon Music, the publishing company formed by Al Nevins and Don Kirshner, had a small army of songwriters lodged in the Brill Building at 1619 Broadway, NY (actually more likely to be found just up the street at 1650 Broadway), each equipped with a tiny room, a piano, a desk and a typewriter, vying with each other to produce a bigger hit than the guys in the room next door. Neil Sedaka, Howard Greenfield, Carole King, Gerry Goffin, Neil Diamond, Paul Simon, Phil Spector, Barry Mann, Cynthia Weil and Jack Keller were all at one time or other churning out hits for Aldon.

Randy looked on their works and despaired. "What I did for years was I tried to be Carole King," he said. "When I started at 16, Carole King was just the greatest, I thought. And I still do."

While Carole King and her then husband Gerry Goffin were flooding the market with songs that, nearly 60 years later, still get covered, appear as star tracks on compilation albums and get used in ads for car spares and sanitary towels – 'Will You Love Me Tomorrow', 'Take Good Care Of My Baby', 'The Loco-Motion', 'Chains', 'It Might As Well Rain Until September', 'Up On The Roof', 'When My Little Girl Is Smiling' – Randy was providing an unbroken string of flops ('Looking For Me', 'Warm And Tender') for Vic Dana, a clean-cut singer-dancer from Buffalo, New York. And still Lenny Waronker thought he was on an 'uphill swing'.

Maybe I'm Doing It Wrong

Randy did not consider himself a singer (many critics still don't). He hated the sound of his own voice and never sang on his own demos, preferring to enjoy some of the glut of talent hanging around – his brother Alan, perhaps, or PJ Proby or Glen Campbell.

There was, however, an exception.

One of Irving's celebrity patients was Pat Boone, the all-American, all-Christian, white-bread, white-shoed singer who had made rock'n'roll 'acceptable' to the concerned parents of middle-America by ripping out the hearts, souls, lungs, livers and lights of Fats Domino's 'Ain't That A Shame', and Little Richard's 'Long Tall Sally' and 'Tutti Frutti'; then, having eviscerated the artistic heritage of black America, going on to do the same for Hispanic-America with 'Speedy Gonzales', a song about the drunken fecklessness of Mexicans.

Pat was constantly on the lookout for new material and was keen to extend his range by trying his hand at record production. Lenny encouraged Randy to come up with something. Half as a joke, he suggested that, as it was the start of the football season, Randy might try his hand at something sports-related.

'Golden Gridiron Boy'* is the plaint of a high-school geek, distraught because the object of his affection has eyes only for the Gridiron Boy ("when he makes a a touchdown, she goes wild with joy"). The poor sap is too small to make the team, and instead plays in the band. In keeping with the device established in 'Ask Him If He's Got A Friend For Me', the backing vocals rub salt in the wound with cries of "Touchdown!" and "Hero!" and "Yeah! Yeah!".

In a break with tradition, Randy, perhaps not wanting to bother one of the proper singers with such a trifle, sang on the demo that they handed over to Mr Boone. For some reason, the voice that critic Ellen Willis would later describe as making her think of "wet sand being eased out of a bottle" and William Tusher of *Variety* a "frightened bison", appealed to Pat.

"He heard my demos and he liked my voice," Randy later told *Billboard*. "One of the first humans to do so."

---

* Until the 1920s, the American football pitch was marked with a chess-board pattern of parallel lines – known as the 'Gridiron'. Though the pattern's since been replaced with side-to-side 'yard lines', and just two longitudinals dotted in, the name lingers.

Pat's enthusiasm was such that he used Randy on his re-recorded version of the song – the first written by/sung by Randy Newman record ever released.

The voice is not that of the mature Randy, resembling more an inept stab at a sort of Bobby Vee amicability. The song does have vague similarities to 'Stayin' In', the John D. Loudermilk composition that Bobby had released a couple of years before ('I punched my buddy on the nose after lunch / now I'm in trouble 'cos the Dean saw the punch / he was saying things that were not true about her / so I let him have it in the cafeteria'). And Randy does, just once or twice, interject the kind of tiger-cub growl that Vee had made his own.

But listen more closely and you know it's Randy in there. There's the mushy enunciation, a *Sprechstimme* abandonment of tonality on "game", a darkening of the vowels so that "talk" becomes "towk" and "one" becomes "worn". The sand's maybe wetter than it later became but the bottle's pretty much the same.

The guitar riff that runs through the B-side, 'Country Boy', sounds like a trial run for 'Old Kentucky Home', a track from Randy's *12 Songs* album released eight years later. The lyric tells the story of Mary, who comes down from Chicago to marry a country boy called Jack, and live in Jack's backwoods shack. But she soon tires of the country and pines for the city, so she goes back to Chicago leaving Jack alone in his backwoods shack. But then, one day, Jack's walking in the valley wondering if his broken heart will mend and he sees Mary coming over the mountain, returned from Chicago and declaring that she'll always love her country boy. And they all live happily ever after.

If the story sounds less than enthralling, remember that it's essentially the same deal as 'The Swiss Maid', a Roger Miller song recorded by Del Shannon (with novelty yodelling), that went to number one in the UK and you'll see that, given the state of the market at the time, Randy's tale of Jack's shack was quality product.

'Golden Gridiron Boy', released on Pat Boone's label, Dot, never became the novelty smash of 1962.

By this time Randy, still at college, was playing more and more with the big girls. Jackie DeShannon recorded his 'Did He Call Today, Mama?' as the B-side of her 'Needles And Pins', then collaborated with him on 'Hold Your Head High', a treatise on how to get dumped with dignity, comprising

Maybe I'm Doing It Wrong

a two-minute climax, with strings, horns and choir, underpinned by an urgent bolero beat.

Soldier songs, which had by this time all but vanished in the UK with the demise of National Service, were still big in the US where, even in the ten years of relative peace between the Korean and Vietnam wars, about 1.5m men were drafted into the military. A lot of these men were posted abroad, to Germany, Japan and England. This was, of course, a gift for songwriters, providing a ready market for 'you're far away but I still love you and can't wait until I come home' songs, often incorporating a bugle call, a rattling snare drum and a bravely contained sob.

Pat Boone's 'I'll Be Home', the Shirelles' 'Soldier Boy', Bobby Vinton's 'Mr Lonely' ("I'm a soldier, a lonely soldier" he sings in a falsetto voice suggesting that he's also suffered injuries of a personal nature) and hundreds of others got requested, played, bought, posted and maybe melted for novelty vases when the relationship petered out.

Randy, having done a football song, thought, "Why not?"

'Somebody's Waiting', a *sturm und drang meisterwerk* produced by Snuff Garrett with an arrangement stuffed to the brim with not just bugle calls and rattling snare drums, but also thundering tympani, cascading strings, ga-ga-ga triplets and the Johnny Mann Singers, was recorded by one of Liberty's most successful stars, Gene McDaniels.

Gene was an alumni of the University of Omaha Conservatory of Music and son of a Kansas minister. In 1961, he'd scored a monster hit with '100 Pounds Of Clay', a song describing the manner in which God had taken the 100 pounds of clay and with it "created a woman and a whole lot of lovin' for a man" – a theological interpretation which outraged the Bible belt but, oddly, brought not a peep from feminists, most likely because they'd temporarily been cowed into submission by Don Draper. Craig Douglas covered the song for the UK market, in the way that a wet towel covers a thrilling chip-pan fire.

A year later, though, Gene's career started to slump, and 'Spanish Lace' with Randy's military melodrama on the B-side, struggled to number 31 and slumped right back again. It was Gene McDaniels last visit to the top 40.

'Take Her', another of Randy's B-sides, recorded by Frankie Laine with Mann-Weill's 'I'm Gonna Be Strong' on the A-side, is worth mentioning for two reasons. First, Frankie Laine made the kind of records bought by people who think that bellowing is manly; the kind of records that made you stare at your record player astonished to see that the volume control was barely turned up to one. When he wasn't bellowing cowboy songs like the themes from 'Rawhide', 'High Noon' and 'Gunslinger', Frankie liked to bellow other kinds of song like 'Jezebel', 'Granada' and 'The Call Of The Wild Goose'.

The idea of him bellowing The Randy Newman Songbook – with hoof beats in 'I Think It's Gonna Rain Today' and whiplash effects punctuating 'In Germany Before The War' – might cause a moment or two of amusement. That's the first reason for mentioning 'Take Her'.

The second reason for mentioning 'Take Her' is that the circumstances of its recording bring together some of the transient themes explored in this chapter, thereby rounding it off in a satisfying way.

Terry Melcher, the son of professional virgin movie star Doris Day, produced the session. Jack Nitzsche, composer and arranger of many hits including some of Phil Spector's finest, was supervising the orchestrations. At the time Terry was romantically involved with Jackie DeShannon, who'd been providing some backing vocals.

Ominously, Phil Spector also had the hots for Jackie.

Just as the session was about to begin, Phil slipped into the control room – a silent spectre-Spector, death mask face and no-eyes glasses. He sat himself down and glared at Terry for six hours. Nobody tried to kick him out. It was Phil Spector. The fuss would be unbearable. Terry did his best to carry on producing. Frankie, in the studio, bellowed.

After the session, Spector warned Nitzsche and the other musicians that if they ever worked for Melcher again, they'd certainly never work for him and possibly never work at all.

Nobody took any notice.

The record, by the way, 'Take Her', was eventually recorded in Italian, Spanish and German as well as English, but didn't make any great impression in any of them.

But, with time, there was increasing evidence that Lenny's faith in his "weird friend" might be justified. In 1963, Erma Franklin recorded a thrilling version of Randy's 'Love Is Blind', but sadly never made it as big as her sister, Aretha (although she did provide backing vocals on 'Respect'). In the same year, Irma 'The Soul Queen of New Orleans' Thomas used his 'While The City Sleeps' as an album track, and took a single of his co-written 'Anyone Who Knows What Love Is (Will

Understand)', to number 52 in the *Billboard* chart. They're all records that can quickly restore your faith in pop's essential virtue.

At last, in the eyes even of people who weren't Lenny Waronker, Randy Newman was getting somewhere.

Chapter Four

On February 9, 1964, The Beatles made their first appearance on *The Ed Sullivan Show*. Across the USA, 73m people tuned in. Many senior Americans, their memories too fuddled these days to remember much about the Kennedy assassination, can with crystal clarity recall every moment of that show. By the end of the year, 11 singles in the *Billboard* top 40 were by British bands. Even crooner Matt Monro's 'Walk Away' was at number 45 and climbing.

The British Invasion did not, as more hysterical commentators have suggested, change the nature of music, lifestyle, politics and spiritual awareness *forever*, but it was a huge deal for the British agents, managers, record companies and sometimes even artists who, having only just got used to the idea of being able to walk into Dolcis and buy any pair of shoes they wanted, now discovered they could buy aeroplanes and countries. And it rattled the cage of the US music business.

There were, it seemed, two possible lines of defence: compete or co-operate.

The competition lobby tried launching a bunch of 'British-style' bands – or at least bands with British-sounding names: The Buckinghams, The Sir Douglas Quintet, The Beau Brummels. But they weren't fooling anybody.

Failure to find a home-grown Beatles inspired two ambitious film producers, Bob Rafelson and Bert Schneider, to invent one. In September

Maybe I'm Doing It Wrong

1965, they placed ads in the *Hollywood Reporter* and *Daily Variety:* "MADNESS!! AUDITIONS Folk & Roll Musicians-Singers for acting roles in new TV series. Running parts for four insane boys, age: 17-21." The new TV series was *The Monkees*.

Some 437 applicants tried out. The rumour that ritual serial killer Charles Manson was among their number has since been scotched, although references testifying to his status as an "insane boy" would have been impeccable. Harry Nilsson, Stephen Stills and Van Dyke Parks did audition. Randy wasn't tempted and, anyway, would have baulked at the idea of being too busy singing to put anybody down. People should *make* time for that sort of thing.

The parts eventually went to two former child stars – Davy Jones and Micky Dolenz – and two aspiring folk musicians – Peter Tork and Mike Nesmith. They Monkeed around for 58 episodes and released a string of top quality singles, including two number ones, 'I'm A Believer' and 'Last Train To Clarksville', the former written by Neil Diamond. They weren't The Beatles, but they captured a moment when to be young, agile, single, white and possess even a modicum of musical ability was the dream of America's youth.

Meanwhile, Randy, probably more by luck than judgement, found himself trying the second strategy: co-operate. He took coals to Newcastle, sold songs to British acts and, as a result, enjoyed a string of unqualified A-side, certified hits.

He quit college in 1965, one semester before he was supposed to graduate. Sometimes he says it was because the staff objected to his singing like Fats Domino at his required performance. Sometimes, more cryptically, he says it was because, "some housewife blew me out on the gongs in orchestra. It crushed me," – suggesting that, contrary to expectations, Gamelan can foster a dangerously competitive spirit.

Who needed paper qualifications anyway? By this time, he was a working musician.

Things were changing in Hollywood. The breaking up of the old studio system and the Musicians' Union strike of 1958 had led to the studios scrapping their in-house orchestras. Instead they'd assemble freelance musicians as and when they were needed, or, worse, record in Europe or, worse still, use 'library music'.

Uncle Alfred went freelance himself, leaving his job at 20th Century Fox in the capable hands of Uncle Lionel, who eventually became Vice President in charge of Television and Feature Music. Sometimes he was able to put a bit of work Randy's way.

Randy pretty much worked his way through college at the 20th Century Fox music mill. His first full score was for *The Many Loves of Dobie Gillis*, a teen-angled sitcom aired on CBS. As well as the romantically inclined lead character of the title, it featured a bongo-playing beatnik character called Maynard G. Krebs, so was as hip as CBS could be.

Newcomers Warren Beatty and Tuesday Weld both cropped up in the first series. Randy worked on just one episode, and 'score' would be something of an overstatement for his collection of short stings and links.

He went on to write and orchestrate bits and bobs for shows like *Peyton Place*, *Lost In Space* and *Voyage To The Bottom Of The Sea*. He even did some feature film work, and once got a whole tune with a title and everything – 'Galaxy A-Go-Go' – onto the soundtrack of the spy-spoof movie *Our Man Flint*.

Even after he'd started having top ten hits, he'd put in a few hours now and then for Uncle Lionel.

One day, George Martin, The Beatles' producer, once came to visit him.

"I knew that he was related to Alfred Newman, a great film writer," said George, "and that Lionel Newman, head of music at 20th Century Fox, was his uncle. So I went first to see Lionel, whom I knew, and he told me: 'Randy's working in the arranging and copying department. You'll find him over there.' 'Over there' was a building that was just part of the whole township of a typical Hollywood studio. The music section was a vast area like a typing-pool, with men sitting at anonymous desks writing music. At one of these was a little dark-haired chap who had glasses and a slight squint. This was Randy Newman.

"We introduced ourselves and I told him how much I liked his work. But at the same time, I was wondering to myself what on earth he was doing in this place when he had such talent. Then, glancing along the rows of desks, I spotted an English writer I knew, who had done a lot of music for Tony Newley and Leslie Bricusse. I was astonished. Of course, they were earning a good living at it, but it was so tedious: exactly like a typing-pool, a musical factory production line. They would be asked to write 17 seconds of car-chase music, or $45^{3}/_{5}$ seconds of music for moonlight romance. Sometimes they would not know what film they were writing for."

According to Randy, when George Martin came to visit, his job in fact was more menial still. He wasn't writing anything at all, just operating the 'thermostatic copying machine'.

Maybe Randy would have stayed there, fetching toner cartridges or whatever thermostatic copiers used, writing the 17 seconds of car chase music, rising up the hierarchy, maybe one day getting to be an executive like his uncles, were it not for his friend Lenny, who had other plans.

Lenny was building contacts. From time to time he would take Randy to see the big guns of the industry and play them the demos.

People liked what they heard. "Jesus, this kid's good," Jerry Leiber said, after hearing a couple of songs.

One of the demos found its way across the Atlantic.

In April 1965, Cilla Black released her sixth UK single. Produced by George Martin and recorded at Abbey Road, 'I've Been Wrong Before', Randy's song, weaves a lush melody around a stark, single-line piano riff that relentlessly negotiates the various modulations and triplets, never giving up. The lyric's a simple idea – a new love that feels right but 'I've Been Wrong Before'. The piano riff serves the lyric in the same way that the repeated riff from Mike Oldfield's 'Tubular Bells' served *The Exorcist*. It's creepy. It raised the emotional stakes. The fear that everyone feels at the start of a new love affair is, in this case, a breathless terror.

The record went to number 17 in the UK at a time when playing the Brits at their own game and scoring was something to crow about. A couple of months later, Dusty Springfield released her own version of the song as an album track on *Everything's Coming Up Dusty*. Many people, including Randy, regard Cilla's version as the definitive interpretation, but Dusty can't half do haunted. And petrified. She inhabits the song.

"When we'd finished the recording," said Ivor Raymonde, Musical Director on the session, "Dusty rushed out of the studio for some reason or other and I popped out to see if the recording had gone well. And there was Dusty with all her famous mascara trickling down her cheeks. She'd really been very, very moved by the lyric, which really is very beautiful. And it had just broken her up completely. That to me is the sign of a fabulous artist."

There's maybe even a hint of the bunny boiler in Dusty's interpretation; a suggestion that she murdered the ex-lover, the one she was 'wrong' about, the one who so cruelly disappointed her. But if she stood in the witness box and sang Randy's song, there's not a jury in the world would convict.

Other Brit sales followed.

'I Don't Want To Hear It Anymore' was never a screaming hit but had a long shelf-life. Close in musical style to the sort of thing Burt Bacharach was producing (and, like Randy, selling to the Brits), it's a drama about a man who has learned about his partner's infidelity by hearing the neighbours gossiping through the thin walls of his apartment. "'Lord, ain't it sad,' said the woman cross the hall, 'that when a nice boy like that falls in love, hey, it's just too bad that he had to go and fall for a girl that doesn't care for him at all.'"

Jerry Butler released it as a single that sneaked momentarily into the *Billboard* Hot Hundred. Then the Walker Brothers, a Los Angeles trio who had travelled to Swinging London to seek their fortune and taken Burt Bacharach and Hal David's 'Make It Easy On Yourself' to number one, stuck it on their first album. Later, Scott Walker, divorced from his 'brothers', released it as a single.

Then the song crossed the Atlantic again when Jerry Wexler, co-boss of Atlantic Records, imported Dusty Springfield to make an album at the American Sound Studio in Memphis. Dusty, described by Jerry as "one of the most insecure singers in the world, all raw nerves and neuroses," was picky about material. Jerry sat with her "ass deep in albums and acetates" sorting through possible contenders. "An artist of her fragile sensitivity, had to be selective," he said tactfully. "To say yes to one song was seen as a lifetime commitment after months of agonising evaluation."

Two of Randy's songs survive the agony – 'Just One Smile' and 'I Don't Want To Hear It Anymore'. The album, *Dusty In Memphis*, was released in April 1969. "Everybody loved it," said Jerry, "except the damn public."

Since then, of course, it has become such a revered classic that many older pop fans lie shamelessly, claiming that their treasured first editions are original purchases and not bought on eBay at ruinous expense at all. 'I Don't Want To Hear It Anymore' was Dusty's favourite track.

Maybe I'm Doing It Wrong

Gene Pitney was a nicely turned out singer-songwriter from Hartford, Connecticut who'd been scoring hits since writing, singing and playing most of the instruments on '(I Wanna) Love My Life Away' in 1961.

As a singer, he'd recorded the Oscar nominated 'Town Without Pity', the arguably definitive version of Bacharach and David's '24 Hours From Tulsa' and the paradoxically jaunty 'It Hurts To Be In Love'. He'd also covered 'I'm Gonna Be Strong', the A-side that Frankie Laine had recorded at the fraught Terry Melcher/Phil Spector session. Where Frankie bellowed, Gene whined.

As a writer, he'd come up with 'He's A Rebel' for Phil Spector and the Crystals, 'Rubber Ball' for Bobby Vee and 'Hello Mary Lou' for Ricky Nelson. He'd also been credited with playing on some early Rolling Stones sessions, along with Phil Spector. On the sleeve notes, they're referred to as 'Uncle Phil and Uncle Gene'.

To be completist about his enviable credentials, it should be mentioned that 'Uncle Gene' also had a brief affair with Marianne Faithfull.

Pitney recorded two of Randy's songs. 'Nobody Needs Your Love', never released in the US, went to number two in the UK. It is a song of stirring misery – at this stage in his career Randy seemed incapable of writing a song about anything except exquisite torture. "Why can't it be like before, don't you need me anymore?", Gene sings, and "if you don't want me I don't want to live". Journalist Tony Parsons described the record, with some accuracy, as a "suicide note", but then again, Gene Pitney could have made 'Happy Birthday To You' sound like a cry for help.

Later in the year, Gene took another one of Randy's heartbreakers to number eight in the UK and 51 in the US.

'Just One Smile' is the plaint of a crushed soul, so reduced in self-esteem that the glimpse of a single smile is all he dare ask of his faithless lover ("one little dream to build my world upon"); or, to put it another way, it's the scream of the 'bottom' in a co-dependent SM relationship. Either way, you listen and, even as your heart aches with empathy for the poor unfortunate's plight, the sensible part of your brain is thinking "you need to end this relationship and get out of the house. No second thoughts. Just do it. Now, I know that's hard, but I'm going to give you some phone numbers of organisations that can offer you counselling and practical advice."

Then the empathy returns and by the end of the song, you're drowning in your own tears.

Scott Walker also recorded a magnificent version of 'Just One Smile', but unless you're of a particularly strong emotional constitution you're advised never to listen to the Dusty Springfield version. It's Track 1, Side 2 of *Dusty In Memphis*. Reggie Young's hesitant guitar intro is enough to set you off. Then Dusty comes in with a rabbit-in-the-headlights vulnerability and builds to a sort of hopeless, helpless defiance. Temazepam can help, but make sure you've got the Samaritans' phone number handy, too.

Three hits in 12 months, albeit in a tiny country 5,500 miles away from LA, was a big step up from Vic Dana B-sides. Randy, it seemed, had cracked it.

"When I wrote 'I've Been Wrong Before' and 'Just One Smile' and 'Nobody Needs Your Love'," Randy said, "my publisher at the time, Aaron Schroeder [also Gene Pitney's manager], was so happy, because they were songs with hooks and it looked like I would go on to earn some money. But I didn't continue doing it.

"I'm not saying that I could have written millions of hit songs if I'd decided to; that's a talent that I may not have. Burt Bacharach has it: he knows where the gold is. My uncle Lionel used to say Burt Bacharach songs sound like third oboe parts. He was rough! But when Bacharach gets his hook, he knows it's there. I've come to appreciate him."

One of Randy's less successful British releases had the distinction of being the first single released by Deram, the label that would later release records by Procol Harum, the Moody Blues, David Bowie, Cat Stevens and Whistling Jack Smith.

The song 'Happy New Year' was sung by Beverley Kutner, billed merely as 'Beverley'. Later Ms Kutner met and married the charismatic John Martyn with whom she made a couple of albums as John and Beverley Martyn. 'Happy New Year' is also notable for featuring half of Led Zeppelin, a near-Beatle and a near-Rolling Stone – the musicians on the session being Jimmy Page and John Paul Jones, drummer Andy White (who'd once played on a Beatles' session while Ringo sulked and smacked a tambourine) and Nicky Hopkins (pianist on a slew of Stones' tracks as well as many by the Kinks).

Maybe I'm Doing It Wrong

It's an 'everybody's having fun at this New Year party except me and I'm really cross about it' song. "A cheer of new year spirit / Dies on the still night air/ I shout but you can't hear me / And you don't care," Beverley snarls.

It failed to chart. Maybe because it was released in September.

Chapter Five

At this point the narrative – inasmuch as it can be called a narrative – needs to take a fairly lengthy diversion to provide some historical and cultural context.

To the average British, male pop fan of the early sixties – stunted, pasty-faced, staring at the faded pictures of hamburger travesties in a Wimpy Bar before putting a Pac-A-Mac over his C&A 'jeans', going out to face the drizzle and gazing in despair at the junk-strewn 'beaches' of Rhyll, Swanage, Bridlington or Largs, California was a place as alien as attack ships on fire off the shoulder of Orion and as desirable as sex.

Out there in California, there were two girls for every boy and the boys, young men, the same age as you, owned cars and knew how to drive them; their skin was tanned, their hair was blonde, their shirts were striped, their jeans were white, their chests were not consumptively sunken and sunshine was never hazy. At home, where their mums and dads often smiled, they had special jars for 'cookies' (like biscuits, apparently, but bigger). They also did something called 'surfing', the unfeasibility of which suggested that those Pacific waters had a different viscosity to the ones at Rhyll, Swanage, Bridlington and Largs. Or maybe they'd turned the gravity down over there.

It has to be said that many Americans from other (lesser) states, even if they already had cookie jars, felt that same sense of envy – or aspiration, as it's sometimes known. Indeed, so did most Californians.

The privileged few spent all day on the beach, then went on to the Rendezvous Ballroom at Balbao with its 12,000 sq. ft. dance floor and 64 ft. soda fountain, to dance the Surfer Stomp to the hot sounds of Dick Dale, the Chantays, the Chancellors or the Surfaris, then on maybe to a house party crammed with blonde girls with long tanned legs. Party all night and start again the following morning. The ballroom and bands varied up and down the coast, but the routine stayed roughly the same.

By 1961, the year of Dick Dale's 'Let's Go Trippin'', Jan & Dean's 'Heart and Soul' and the Beach Boys 'Surfin'', surf music was acknowledged on both sides of the Atlantic as the sound of paradise.

Gradually, though, some of those outside the surfing community, and even some of the sharper thinkers within it, began modestly to raise a questioning index finger and say, 'Er ...' They noticed, for instance, that an elite of blonde, strong, healthy white boys staking out beaches and dance-halls as their rightful *lebensraum* had uncomfortable parallels with events in another place and another time.

Stephen Wayne Hull, surfer, sociologist and author of *A Sociological Study Of The Surfing Subculture In The Santa Cruz Area*, noted that though the California surfing community was possibly three or four hundred thousand strong, "in the author's 13 years of surfing, only six to eight African-American surfers have been observed."

Percentages of black to white in the music business were about the same as those on the beaches. Though Randy had worked with Gene McDaniels, Erma Franklin and Irma Thomas, and Phil Spector with the Crystals, Darlene Love and the Ronettes, away from the vocal mic segregation – albeit of an unconscious, innocent and thus more insidious nature – was more apparent at Sunset Sound, Gold Star and Capitol Studios than it was even at Stax in Memphis, Tennessee.

The floating population of 60 or so studio musicians who constituted the 'Wrecking Crew', for instance, was about 91% white and 98% male. Behind the glass, the control rooms and production offices were white ghettos.

The picture was radically different at Sam Cooke's SAR records on Hollywood Boulevard and at Tamla when it began to relocate to LA, but the 'separate but equal' doctrine had, theoretically at least, been overturned years before.

Racial segregation, in other words, even after it had been legally proscribed in Alabama, Georgia and Arkansas, was still a matter of everyday life on the beaches of Santa Cruz, San Clemente and Malibu, the recording studios of Hollywood and Burbank, and on the streets of Los Angeles, San Diego and San Francisco.

In the thirties and forties, Los Angeles had seen fire bombings when black people dared to move into white neighbourhoods. It had seen crosses burning on lawns in South Gate and Huntington Park. White gangs roamed 'white' neighbourhoods, daring outsiders to set foot on their turf. Though nominal measures had been taken to address the problem, in practice the suburbs of Los Angeles remained white preserves, leaving the East and South of the city, places like Watts and Compton, rapidly turning into ghettos.

In September 1965, riots broke in the Watts area. The National Guard was brought in, martial law declared and a cordon put around South Central Los Angeles. The riots continued for six days. There were 34 deaths, 1,032 injuries, 3,438 arrests, and over $40m in property damage.

Randy later described the riots as "the biggest shock to me and the biggest inequity in this country [...] I always felt that the race situation was worse here than anywhere."

Randy's contemporaries, not long before preoccupied with nothing more vexing than their jellyrolls and waterfalls, their khakis and Levi's, had begun to look around and see there was real stuff to worry about, some of which had a very direct impact on their own lives.

In 1965, 200,000 US troops were deployed in Vietnam. Just under 2,000 of them were killed. By 1966, the numbers engaged in combat had pretty much doubled and the deaths tripled. The draft was tightened up. At the medical board, tanned, well-muscled surfers didn't have a hope of exemption.

At colleges, there were protests, demos and sit-ins, about Civil Rights, about Student Rights, about the war.

Pop music was growing up along with its demographic. Though the 'kids' were still catered for – The Monkees alone, in the early days at least, were, singlehandedly, giving the under-16s all the perky poppiness they could handle – people in their late teens and twenties, rather than putting away childish things and switching to jazz, 'the classics' or EZ-listening, the way they were supposed to, were sticking with variations on the basic themes of pop and rock'n'roll. Pop became more intelligent/pretentious/ arty/farty/relevant/up itself/subtle/smug/complex/delusional depending on your point of view.

Maybe I'm Doing It Wrong

In January 1965, the Byrds fused Dylan's 'Mr Tambourine Man' with the George Harrison sound of a sparkly Rickenbacker 12-string and – according at least to the simplified GCSE history of pop – invented 'folk-rock'. The record went top ten on both sides of the Atlantic. In the same year, Dylan switched his Martin for a Stratocaster, scored his first US top ten hits and, in the eyes of many, betrayed Christ. On *Rubber Soul*, the Beatles abandoned all pretence of being harmless and wrote songs about revenge arson, existential alienation and homicidal fantasies. They indulged in rude backing vocals and had the nerve to sing in French.

'Protest', a less media-alarming description of what had for centuries usually been called something like 'political' or 'satirical' song, became chart material. PF Sloan's 'Eve Of Destruction', recorded by Barry McGuire, a scatter-gun condemnation of all that was hypocritical and bad in the world ("Think of all the hate there is in Red China / Then take a look around to Selma, Alabama / You may leave here for four days in space / But when you return it's the same old place") went to number one on both sides of the Atlantic.

The change was never seismic. Though the new, 'more mature' songs made the occasional dent in the charts, Herman's Hermits' 'Mrs. Brown You've Got A Lovely Daughter', Freddie & the Dreamers' 'I'm Telling You Now', Vic Dana's (a hit at last but unfortunately not with a Randy song) 'Red Roses For A Blue Lady', and the soundtrack album from *Mary Poppins* still more than held their own.

In jerks and judders, though, pop was opening up to new ideas. Gradually executives and A&R men were coming round to the idea that a song that moved too far from a I, iv, IV, V chord structure, or wasn't about love, or contained hard words, wasn't *ipso facto* uncommercial.

In other words, the world, in so many different ways, was preparing itself for the flowering of Randy Newman.

One must never underestimate the importance in all this – the importance in everything – of Frank Sinatra, who was riding high in a permanent April with no prospect of ever being shot down in May and whose charted course, inevitably, given his omniscience and omnipotence, intersected Randy's largely uncharted one in many curious ways.

Mr Sinatra did not like rock'n'roll and never had. "Rock'n'roll smells phony and false," he said. "It is sung, played and written for the most part by cretinous goons." He went on to rail against its "imbecilic reiteration" and "sly, lewd, in plain fact, dirty lyrics."

His disdain was confirmed when a top rock'n'roller was involved in a heinous outrage against his family, the circumstances of which, though they are of relevance to Randy Newman only inasmuch as they involved his school mates, nevertheless beg to be told.

In 1963, Jan & Dean – Jan Berry and Dean Torrence – who'd been a couple or three years ahead of Randy at University High, scored a number one with the ultimate surf anthem, 'Surf City' ("two girls for every boy"), a song written by Brian Wilson of the Beach Boys and recorded on Liberty, Randy's best friend's dad's label.

Then, one day, Dean's old school friend, Barry Keenan, down on his luck, decided to kidnap Frank Sinatra's 19-year-old son, Frank Jr – another Uni High alumni – and hold him to ransom. He discussed the plan with Dean.

Frank Jr was following in dad's footsteps, crooning with a revamped Tommy Dorsey Orchestra at Harrah's Club at Lake Tahoe. Barry Keenan and his accomplices drove up there and snatched him at gunpoint from his motel room.

"As the drama continued to unfold," said *Time* magazine, "there were rumours that it was all a publicity stunt or some other sort of hoax, and indeed that was one of the first avenues of investigation probed by the FBI. Then, too, there was the matter of Frank Sr's genial flirtation with a kind of shadow Clan of his own, consisting of high-echelon hoods. No one figured out the connection, if any, but many were prepared to view the kidnapping as something less than the real thing. They were wrong."

Frank Sr paid the $240,000 that was demanded (even though he had offered a million dollars reward for the return of his son) and Frank Jr was dropped off near his mother's house. But one of Keenan's accomplices boasted to his family about what they had done. He was later picked up by the police, and Keenan himself soon after.

During the trial, Dean initially testified that he had no prior knowledge of the plan. But then he came clean and admitted that Barry Keenan had told him all about it. He also explained how, after the kidnap, Keenan had brought a paper sack containing $25,000 and left it in his shower.

Keenan received a life sentence, but thanks to the far more liberal parole system of the sixties, walked out of prison after serving just under five years. Though no charges were pressed against Dean Torrence, he did not remain unscathed. He had, after all, got on the wrong side of Mr Sinatra.

"Not many people in show business want to incur the wrath of Frank Sinatra Sr," said journalist Dorothy Kilgallen in her *Voice of Broadway* column. "His tentacles reach into too many branches of the industry, from movies to records and you-name-it."

Jan & Dean had provided the title song for *Ride The Wild Surf*, a movie starring Fabian and Tab Hunter. Originally they were scheduled to appear in the film, too, but Dean's contract was summarily terminated. "I think," he said, "they thought another one of my friends might try to kidnap Fabian."

Two years later, Jan Berry lost control of his Corvette in Beverly Hills. He was in a coma for a month and suffered brain damage and partial paralysis. Nobody's ever suggested that Frank Sinatra Sr was in any way implicated in the accident, but, as Dorothy Kilgallen said, he did have tentacles.

And Mr Sinatra's tentacles, in a more productive way, eventually touched the lives of Lenny Waronker and Randy Newman.

By 1960, Mr Sinatra had been with Capitol Records for seven years and had proved himself, time and time again, the label's most lucrative asset. Of 12 albums released on the label, 11 had gone top ten and two to number one.

Indeed, he'd made so much money for Capitol that he felt it was time he got a bigger cut, control of his copyrights and more creative say. He suggested forming his own label, under the Capitol banner, and splitting the take 50-50. Capitol demurred. Negotiations, grew heated. "I'm going to destroy that round building," Frank screamed, referring to Capitol's distinctive HQ on Vine Street. "I'll tear it down." Or maybe he said something a bit like that, but in a much quieter voice. Versions of the story vary.

Finally, Frank ploughed $200,000 of his own money into a new label, which he called Reprise. He became 'The Chairman of The Board' and, to take care of the day-to-day running of the label, poached Mo Ostin from Verve records to be the label's Vice-President.

Mo, of whom we shall hear a great deal more as Randy's career progresses, was generally known to be a sound and adventurous businessman and fierce negotiator who was also blessed with excellent ears and impeccable taste.

To grace his new label, Frank signed his rat-pack pals Dean Martin and Sammy Davis Jr, a roster of jazzers like Ben Webster, Barney Kessel and Shorty Rodgers, and even found room in the catalogue for delights like *The Passionate Valentino Tangos* by Francisco Cazador & His Barcelona Caballeros and *The Ol' Calliope Man At The Fair* by The Sande & Greene Fun-Time Band.

The label scored hits for Sammy Davis Jr and for Frank himself, but profitability was not quite as exciting as initial projections had promised. Accordingly, in 1963, Frank sold two-thirds of the company to Warner Bros. This gave Mo Ostin a little more leeway and independence.

Not sharing Frank's "cretinous goons" assessment of rock'n'roll, he signed British acts – the Kinks and Sandie Shaw – and steered Frank's daughter Nancy to number one with 'These Boots Are Made For Walking'. In April 1967, he brought Arlo Guthrie and Jimi Hendrix to the label and, over the next few years signed Joni Mitchell, Neil Young, Van Morrison, Jethro Tull, James Taylor and Deep Purple.

He also hired the freshest production and A&R talent in town including Richard Perry, Ted Templeman, Russ Titelman, Andrew Wickham and, in April 1966, Lenny Waronker.

So, to summarise, the world had moved on from surf-worship to protest and politics, music had moved on from "Oo ee oo ah aah ting tang walla walla bing bang" to "You don't need a weatherman to know which way the wind blows", and Lenny Waronker and his childhood friend Randy Newman at last found themselves in position to make their assault on the very summit of pop superstardom, or thereabouts.

Chapter Six

A month after Lenny arrived at Warner-Reprise, Brian Wilson and the Beach Boys released their masterwork, *Pet Sounds*, and Dylan released his double album *Blonde On Blonde*. Three months later the Beatles released *Revolver*. Around the same time there were first albums by the Doors, Cream, Jefferson Airplane, the Small Faces, Tim Hardin, Tim Buckley, Buffalo Springfield and the Grateful Dead. Pop was being reinvented by the hour.

"To an extent," Randy told Mike Greenblatt, "we knew what we did as popular songwriters wasn't exactly high art, but everything was competitive. We were all wondering what the next thing was going to be. We would all wait there, afraid to commit.

"I reached a point where I was writing relatively conventional songs. Musically they were all right, but it wasn't what I was responding to in literature and television and comedy."

"At that time Randy was really writing tunes more than lyrics," said Lenny Waronker. "He was much more tune conscious. Then out of the blue he wrote a batch of songs that were completely different, titles like 'Mama Told Me Not to Come', 'Bet No One Ever Hurt This Bad' and 'I Think It's Going to Rain Today'. It was great, like a beautiful fusion of words and music."

"It was resistance on my part to doing 'I love you / Why don't you love me?' lyrics," Randy said. "One day I just didn't want to do that any more. Other people did it better: Rodgers & Hart, Carole King, Leiber & Stoller. My literary sensibility was more than that, just as Paul Simon's is. I wanted to write what I was interested in."

The first noticeable public outing of the new style came in 1966. Judy Collins, a classical pianist turned folk singer, had been recording since the early sixties – mostly standard folk-club fare and songs by Dylan, Phil Ochs, Woody Guthrie and Pete Seeger. Her 1966 album, *In My Life*, featured a more eclectic selection: the Lennon-McCartney song of the title, Brecht-Weill's 'Pirate Jenny', Donovan's 'Sunny Goodge Street', a couple of songs by the then little-known Leonard Cohen and Randy Newman's 'I Think It's Going To Rain Today'. The album wasn't a huge hit, but Judy featured the song on a couple of TV shows. People got to know it.

It's since been covered 20 or 30 times by everybody from Nina Simone to Leonard Nimoy and from Dave Van Ronk to Chris Barber and his Dixieland Jazz Band. Bette Midler's done it. Peggy Lee's done it. Streisand's done it. Dusty nailed it.

It is a song about alienation and loneliness, built out of movie-montage images, sung to a bleak pentatonic tune so simple it could be a nursery rhyme for morose kiddies – until the bridge section, which takes off for a moment, like a sob, before the desperate self-control reasserts itself. Many rate it as his best song ever. Randy was never so keen.

"I don't like its image-laden quality with the broken windows and empty hallways," he told Margaret Daly. All the same, it must have paid a few bills down the years.

One of Lenny's first jobs at Warner-Reprise was to look after a roster of artists acquired by a takeover of the Autumn label, which included a San Francisco band called the Mojo Men and a surf/Britbeat band called the Tikis.

Lenny matched the Mojo Men with a cover of Stephen Stills' 'Sit Down I Think I Love You', hired Van Dyke Parks to come up with an arrangement and Randy to play piano. Despite the presence on the record of something that sounds like a hammered dulcimer which has tuning issues that made many buyers fear for the integrity of the idler wheel on their Dansettes, it went top 40.

The Tikis were given Paul Simon's '59th Street Song (Feelin' Groovy)'. Lenny changed the band's name to Harpers Bizarre and hired

Maybe I'm Doing It Wrong

Leon Russell (Van Dyke Parks is sometimes credited, but it's Russell's name on the record label) to come up with a multi-layered vocal arrangement in the manner of Les Swingle Singers, a French group that scat sang Bach Fugues and Preludes in a way that impressed the kind of people who were impressed by that sort of thing – *dooo-doo-pee-doo-pee-dooo* they went, often on the *Two Ronnies*, while viewers put the kettle on.

It was the right thing to do. '59th Street Song (Feelin' Groovy)' by Harpers Bizarre (*doo-pee-doo-doo*) was bang on trend. The record was released in April 1967, the spring before the Summer of Love. All across the nation kaftans were being aired, flowers grown, ties-dyed, beads threaded, bells tuned and acid taken by the tankerload.

In Laurel Canyon, ten miles and seven spiritual dimensions away from the breadhead toxicity of Hollywood, Beverly Hills and Pacific Palisades, the folk/acid/rock splifferati were bonding and parting like quarks in an atom smasher, moving into fancy bungalows and dreaming of a white picket kid and maybe a couple of fences running around the yard, getting their shit together, putting it to music, singing it in high harmony and learning to rodeo-ride the frequent bouts of paranoid hysteria like they were unbroken lizards.

It was the spring of Sunshine Pop: the Turtles 'Happy Together', the Mamas and the Papas' 'Dedicated To The One I Love', the Hollies 'On A Carousel', even the Beatles' 'Penny Lane' – with its Bach trumpet and 'ba-da-ba-daahs' – qualified as Sunshine Pop.

Harpers Bizarre were perhaps a little too straight, a little too polite, a little too Four Freshmen, a little too – dare one say it – Swingle Singers truly to rank with the open throats of the Turtles, the Mamas and the Papas and the soaring, nutrient-starved adenoids of the Moptops. They clearly washed a lot, too, wore suits and ties and smiled in a "what I want you to ask yourself, good buddy, is can you really afford not to?" salesman way rather than the 1967-approved "I seem to have lost the use of my facial muscles" way. And they worked with the likes of Lenny Waronker and Randy Newman, neither of whom were Laurel Canyon people. Lenny liked his shirts to be ironed. Randy wore the wrong kind of glasses.

Nevertheless, the record was close enough to the sound of the moment to peak at 13 in the *Billboard* singles chart. So then Lenny and his posse had two top 40 hits to their names.

A couple of Harpers Bizarre albums, *Feelin' Groovy* and *Anything Goes*, followed. As well as Rodgers & Hammerstein's 'Happy Talk' and songs from Van Dyke Parks, Leon Russell and Sergei Prokofiev, the first album had no less than three tracks by Randy Newman – 'Happyland', 'Simon Smith And The Amazing Dancing Bear' and 'The Debutante's Ball' – and the second album two tracks – 'Snow' and 'The Biggest Night Of Her Life'.

Three out of the five songs are unexceptional. 'Snow' is about the white stuff that falls from the sky and buries our lost loves – a sort of 'Crying In The Rain' but colder. 'The Debutante's Ball' is about a party where, "No one gets stoned, it's all chaperoned and it's just good clean fun". 'The Biggest Night Of Her Life' is a Carnaby Street jauntalong with a risqué lyric about a teenage girl about to lose her virginity: "Susie's going out tonight to a promise she must keep / She thought about it all last night and she was too excited to sleep / And you can bet it will be the biggest night of her life."

'Happyland' and 'Simon Smith', on the other hand, are unmistakably new-style Randy Newman. 'Happyland' is a Sunshine-Pop-twee eulogy for lost childhood: a place, seen from the grey skies of adulthood, where there were "apples on a stick" and "big old jars with gumdrops in them". "I was much better off when I was pretending: everything's far too real." The retreat from the adult world into infantilism (or a 'child-*like*' not 'child-*ish*' take on reality, as its proponents insisted), was big in 1967, and easily achieved with the right dosage. Traffic – Dave Mason and Steve Winwood's band – rode on the back of a giant albatross to a place where music played ever so loudly. "A.B.C.D, can I bring my friend to tea?" sang the Beatles. "When we were at school our games were simple, I played the janitor, you played the monitor," sang the Hollies, describing, perhaps, a variation on Doctors and Nurses for the educationally disadvantaged.

But there's something other than straightforward infantilism going on on 'Happyland'. There's an edge. After the first couple of lines, the tune takes a left when it should take a right and negotiates a couple of acrobatic swoops before returning to land. At the same time the woodwind, providing the accompaniment, switches to horror movie harmony, as if a rag doll just opened its eyes and looked around for someone to eat. The lyrics are light, the theme dark. It's not a song you'd want on your iPod: it's not even a particularly good song, but, in prototype form, there's no doubt it's a Randy Newman song.

Maybe I'm Doing It Wrong

'Simon Smith And The Amazing Dancing Bear' is one that Randy still performs in his live act to thunderous applause. He'd had the song hanging around in one form or another for a couple of years before Harpers recorded it, and the demo had found its way around the world. He credits it as being the first song he wrote that properly engaged his intelligence as well as his craft – "the first time I wasn't trying to be Carole King." "I don't know where that song came from. It was the first one like that."

It started life as a romantic song about a girl called Susie which wasn't going anywhere. "I did the tune quick, it was really quick," he told Michael Wale for the London *Times*, "but I couldn't get the lyric. I was thinking of a rhyme for 'where' and I came across 'bear'."

So he wrote a song about a bear instead. It was a liberating experience that made him realise that writing conventional pop songs had been a constraint. "I know more words than that," he said.

Alan Price, former keyboard player with The Animals, took a single of 'Simon Smith' (inconsequentially retitled 'Simon Smith And *His* Amazing Dancing Bear') to number four in the UK charts. Price had become something of a champion of Randy's work, using no less than seven of his songs on his LP, *A Price On His Head*, most of which later re-emerged on Randy's own albums. The lyrical playfulness and old-time country/vaudeville musical style of Price's own songwriting shows that Randy's influence had gone deep (compare and contrast Price's 'The House That Jack Built' with Newman's 'My Old Kentucky Home').

His former bandmate, Eric Burdon, shared the *aficion* and put three of Randy's new "I know more words than that" songs on his first solo album *Eric Is Here*: 'I Think It's Going To Rain Today', 'Mama Told Me Not To Come', more of which later, and 'Wait Till Next Year', in which the excitement of "more words that that" carries Randy away to the uncharacteristic clumsy cleverness of lines like, "the world is restricted and I've been evicted / Condemned and convicted for being myself."

Some of the more obsessive pop fans in the UK, and even one or two observant journalists, began to register a new and important songwriter.

In August 1968, Geoffrey Wansell wrote a piece for the *Times* asking: "Which are the popular songs that will last?" He mentions works by Bacharach & David, Lennon & McCartney, Henry Mancini, Bob Dylan,

Tony Hatch and Jim (*sic*) Webb, and added, "Another slightly shadowy figure is the American Randy Newman, who provided the Alan Price Set with their best record to date, 'Simon Smith And His Amazing Dancing Bear.'"

Alan Price's reading of 'Simon Smith', like the Harpers Bizarre version – and, incidentally, the Scooter and Fozzie Bear *Muppet Show* version – is relentlessly cheerful. But everyone who came across the song spotted that there were traces of blood in the kiddies' sandpit. "A lot of children like it, but a lot of messed-up liberals like it, too," Alan said in an interview with Dawn Eden, "because they read all sorts of social whatchamacallit into it. I never even thought of it."

Randy came across the social whatchamacallit, too. "Someone once told me he thought 'Simon Smith And The Amazing Dancing Bear' was about Sammy Davis Jr," he told Mat Snow. "He's fairly likeable: he realizes with his gimmick that he can get into where he couldn't otherwise. So that makes sense."

He wonders, even, whether the song was unconsciously autobiographical. "I feel like an outsider, a little bit, looking in. I always try to be like everybody else, but I don't think I ever quite succeeded. It's not exceptionalism in the small sense of being exceptional. I just couldn't seem to do simple things. I don't feel absolutely comfortable on the planet."

Getting married helped him feel a bit more comfortable.

He'd known Roswitha Schmale a couple of years. She was over from Germany, working for the Bank of America, staying in a building where a college friend of Randy's also had an apartment. The first time Randy saw her, she was sunning herself next to the pool.

"She was real pretty," he told Christopher Connelly. "It kind of threw me when I saw her. I jumped into the pool with my glasses on."

He asked her out. They went to a Peter Sellers film. They hit it off.

Roswitha was grounded and practical. She made the business of everyday living – a knack Randy has never quite managed to master – much more palatable. It was largely thanks to her that the distractions that had bothered his uncles – drink, drugs, gambling, inappropriate sexual liaisons and so on – were, for the most part, kept under control.

"I'm glad I married who I married," Randy told Timothy White. "Especially when I think how I could have ended up, with the lack of control I've had in terms of drugs and everything else. Speed, mainly, was the one I could control least. I just have never had any moderation about whatever I'm doing."

"It's good to have her, I'm telling you," he said. "Ask Lenny – I could have married somebody like me."

Randy and Roswitha stayed together for 18 years. They made a home in one of the leafy turnings off Mandeville Canyon Road, not far from where Randy was brought up, and raised three boys, Amos, Eric and John.

"He was maturing in a funny way, I guess," said Lenny Waronker. "He had a certain offbeat sense of humour that was becoming more obvious to people. His personality developed in a queer way. He was becoming a character – not a jokester or a jester, but almost Holden Caulfield-esque in humour."

Holden Caulfield is the principal character in JD Salinger's *Catcher In The Rye*, a novel that's found immense popularity in the serial-killing community.

On the strength of his two top 40 hits and respectable album sales, Lenny was rising up the corporate ladder. He had his own office by this time, and a secretary. He felt easy enough to spread his wings. "One hit will do wonders," he said. "Two allows to you take chances."

A couple of months after Randy's wedding, Lenny offered his friend a deal. He wanted to sign him to Warner-Reprise to make his own album as a singer-songwriter. The customary advance against royalties, however, was not on the table. Randy's initial answer was "Fuck you."

At around the same time, A&M Records had offered Randy a $10,000 advance. He decided to take the money. Lenny wasn't pleased. "I think he thought, somehow ... he often thought somehow that I didn't have to make a living," Randy said. "He never considered that side of things. The way I wrote, and have written all my life, it sounds like I haven't thought about it either. But I guessed they matched the offer or something, and I signed with Warners. Luckily."

Lenny also signed Van Dyke Parks.

"Inevitably you will want to use the word 'eccentric' in your writing about me – if you run out of 'quirky'," Van Dyke Parks told Dorian Lynskey for the *Guardian*. Other words frequently used to describe Mr Parks include "elfin" and "brilliant".

"Compressed quotes can't give the full flavour of Parks' raconteurish charm; his fondness for looping tangents, pungent opinions, historical trivia, useful quotes, deadpan puns, colourful aphorisms and mischievous asides," Lynskey said.

Born into a two-piano household in Hattiesburg, Mississippi, son of a psychiatrist/musician and a Hebraic scholar, Van Dyke had been a boy soprano with, allegedly, a five octave range. He studied singing and piano at the Columbus Boychoir (later the American Boychoir School) in Princeton and worked as a child actor in a string of TV shows and movies including the sitcom *Bonino*, *The Swan* with Grace Kelly and Alec Guinness, and *A Gift For Heidi**. Once, possibly while carol singing (there are many versions of the story), Van Dyke encountered Albert Einstein and sang in German while Albert accompanied him on violin.

For a time he worked as a folk-duo with his brother Carson and hung out with the folkies of Seal Beach where "you had women in leotards discussing Karl Marx and the industrial revolution by candlelight [...] waiting for Leonard Cohen to show up."

In the mid-sixties, he made a couple of singles for MGM. The first, 'Number Nine', was released into a pop world not yet ready for a folk-rock version of Beethoven's Choral Symphony sung in German. The second, 'Come To The Sunshine', despite being an impeccable example of Sunshine Pop, did no better.

He worked with Brian Wilson on the ill-fated album *Smile* and got recording dates with the Byrds, and Paul Revere & the Raiders: "a session pianist negotiating Hollywood atop a Yamaha scooter." For a very short space of time, he even linked up with Frank Zappa's Mothers Of Invention but left because he didn't like being screamed at.

He was initially suspicious of Lenny Waronker, too, regarding him as a 'filthy rich kid'. As the son of a psychiatrist, when he began to work with Lenny and Randy, it was inevitable that he would spend some time figuring out the psychodynamics between the three of them.

"I knew he [Randy] was very bright," Van Dyke told Richard Henderson. "He had been hired to do some scoring on a television series called *Peyton Place*. I could see he was bored and I fed off his competition

---

* In which he played Peter – mischievously entered into a singing competition by teasing Heidi. The film also featured, as Mr Binder, the great Austrian actor Rolf Wanka.

with Lenny Waronker which was residual of their adolescence together. That and Dr Newman's medicine cabinet became central to the propulsion of what became a very symbiotic triangulated regard; three people and all of us with different abilities. I came in, I think, because Lenny Waronker wanted Randy to be troubled by somebody who was as gifted as I was on the piano. That's all. I could play the piano real good."

Parks and Newman were the same age, both spent some of their formative years down South, both were classically trained musicians, both wore spectacles and both were partial to amphetamines – hence the reference to 'Dr Newman's medicine cabinet'. It was a time when the medical profession had no compunction about prescribing valium to calm you down, barbiturates to help you sleep and amphetamines to keep you awake. "Can they be habit-forming, doctor?" "To a degree, yes, but no more so than smoking. Here, have one of mine."

In 2008, Randy, on BBC Radio 4's *Desert Island Discs* spoke fondly of the time his father had given him amphetamines to help him write. Only half joking, he told a shocked British nation how Irving had loved the "magic" that medicines could do and how he always made sure that Randy took his pills so as not to fall behind the other boys.

Brian Wilson was another great advocate of the pills' efficacy, impressed by the way no more than a handful or so enabled him and Van Dyke to work on the *Smile* songs throughout the night and into the following week.

Lenny saw that Randy and Van Dyke shared certain values he admired: "They weren't old school guys. They were modern characters but they had old school values regarding certain records that needed to be made, certain artists who needed to be heard."

They were both interested in the craft of music – what Van Dyke called "diligence". Their reference points were encyclopaedic. Whereas other popsters might be able to compare and contrast the works of Bobby Vee and Bobby Vinton, they knew about Wagner and Jelly Roll Morton, Gene Autrey and Alban Berg, Hopi Indian chants and DeSylva, Brown and Henderson. They knew ragtime. They knew about consecutive fifths and flattened ninths. Van Dyke Parks' love of the Great American Songbook – the 'standards' of the twenties, thirties and forties – would have made Mr Sinatra's seem no more than a casual infatuation.

And now Lenny had signed him and Randy to make albums of their own. More than that, Lenny was ready to "take chances". "Van Dyke's musical genius just killed me," he said. "I didn't think people could be that smart when it came to music."

"There's no sure thing," he advised the genius. "Go in with a good song and weird it out."

Van Dyke's album *Song Cycle*, released in December 1967, didn't half heed that brief. It is a complex work, recorded using a then state-of-the-art eight-track tape machine and anything up to 25 string players, 13 woodwind and a 10-strong choir, complemented by balalaikas, accordions, harp and percussion.

Here's a bit of backstory to the session, not strictly relevant, but worth mentioning as an indication of how close the LA music community was.

Norman Botnick was a viola player in the orchestra at Republic Pictures. In 1958, when Republic folded, he and his wife opened a hardware store and, for a time in the early sixties, Van Dyke and his brother Carson lived in a room upstairs. Norman's sons, Bruce Botnick and his little brother Doug, both became superlative engineers and producers in the Hollywood studios. Look at the credits on your favourite albums and chances are you'll see their names. They both worked on *Song Cycle*, and on many of Randy's and Lenny's subsequent albums. Bruce invented an effect especially for Van Dyke, which they called 'farkle'. It added a kind of flanging effect to some of the string passages. So – Norman played viola, Si played viola, Van Dyke lived with Norman, Norman's sons engineered for Si's son on Van Dyke's album, on which Si's conductor nephew, Randy, also worked: all part of the big, happy LA family.

On December 23, 1967, a full-page ad in *Billboard* screamed: "Van Dyke Parks is generic… the first in a decade since Dylan and the Beatles! Already there is speculation among record critics, commentators and cognoscenti as to how and to what extent his emergence will influence tomorrow's tastes and trends. No matter what your age, musical preferences or sociological point-of-view, it is uncommonly predictable, inevitable, inescapable: you are about to become involved with Van Dyke Parks."

Times had changed. Nobody had ever discussed the sociological point-of-view of Francisco Cazador & His Barcelona Caballeros or wondered to what extent Vic Dana's emergence would influence tomorrow's tastes and trends. Not in *Billboard*, anyway.

Those who bought *Song Cycle* – few in number – found that far from being inevitable and inescapable, it was uncommonly difficult to become involved with Van Dyke Parks. Confronted by a dense and apparently random collage of music and lyrics, the usual reaction was either to wish you'd bought the new one by the Temptations instead, to increase the dosage and go with it, or, intrigued, to begin to analyse every note and nuance. Those who chose the third option are, at the time of writing, coming to the end of the initial period of research and hope to publish their findings within the next 30 or 40 years.

The lyrics are an allusion-rich stream-of-consciousness that sound as if they could have escaped from James Joyce's *Finnegan's Wake* or the mind of a stroke victim. It's hard to quote a 'typical' example but "I'm guessing this is called civil, regrettably strife / So lessen your appalled pall mall and middle life / Long last a hymn to Him to help you on your way" from the track 'Widows' gives some indication of the size of the problem. Even in the context of "Tangerine trees and marmalade skies", "Oom-pah oom-pah stick it up yer jum-pah", and "Turn off your mind, relax and float downstream", it was considered puzzling.

There's no doubt, however, that there is a major talent at work here, a prodigious, if unhinged – but that's never a bad thing – musical and verbal imagination.

"I was learning how to make a record and I made every mistake I could possibly make," said Van Dyke, looking back. "It's good work for a 24-year-old boy. We're not talking Bach here but then again it's not Andrew Lloyd-Webber. It's an entirely individual effort, and I think terrifically entertaining, but you can hear that it's highly troubled."

All the tracks on *Song Cycle* were written by Van Dyke, apart from 'Donovan's Colours', an instrumental version of – as the title suggests – Donovan's 'Colours', and the opening track 'Vine Street', written by Randy Newman especially for the album.

'Vine Street', like 'Happyland', is a nostalgia song: a song that looks back to an imaginary time when the singer and his pals used to live on Vine Street. They had a group in which the singer played third guitar and they'd play right there on the street while 'she' – a mother, sister or wife – would "make perfume in the back of the room" (which could be a drug reference but, if it is, the only reason one can think of for not saying, "make drugs in the back of the room" instead in those drug-addled times is scansion).

Musically, it's a collage of what one eventually came to know as Randy Newman trademarks: lush strings, ragtime harmonies with the suspensions and resolutions moving in and out like breathing, relaxed tempo, unseemly leaps of aching and longing in the melody, and a cinematic climax in the middle (best summarised as 'dawn comes up, a shark appears, dusk folds a blanket over the scene').

In keeping with the rest of the album, there's even a couple of quotes from Beethoven's Choral Symphony (the 'Number Nine' of Van Dyke's first single) and Scott Joplin's 'The Entertainer'. It's a song with a lot of listening in it.

The album received some stunning reviews. *New York* magazine called it "a milestone in pop"; *Jazz And Pop* "the most important, creative, and advanced pop recording since *Sgt Pepper*"; *The Free Press* "a high flying ear trip"; *Women's Wear Daily,* "a startling musical and artistic experience". It even got a couple of nominations for album of the year, but it "moved out of stores like a stone unable to roll."

Accordingly, Stan Cornyn, head of Warner-Reprise's Creative Services Department, hoping perhaps to generate a few sales by some sort of reverse psychology, took an ad in the *Billboard*: "How we lost $35,509.50 on 'The Album of the Year' (Dammit)", below which he quotes all of the above reviews and subtly suggests that the reason it didn't sell was because only really cool people were hip enough to dig it.

The ad did nothing to boost sales, so a couple of weeks later, Stan took out another ad announcing a "one cent sale" – anybody who sent in a copy of *Song Cycle* would receive two new copies – one to keep and one to give to a friend, thereby spreading the word.

The ads still had no effect on sales, but they didn't half piss Van Dyke Parks off: "I believe the music was beyond Warner Bros.' comprehension, and flippancy was the only conclusion that they could come to. And it hurt."

Chapter Seven

Lenny, Randy and Van Dyke were getting a reputation around Warner-Reprise.

"Being in Lenny's Corps was like you're in high school and you're over in the corner of the library with a couple of other geeky kids," said Stan Cornyn. "You all wear glasses, and you're memorizing what you're studying, and can only dream of Friday night, of dating that cheer leader over there.

"Lenny's fastidiously produced albums were respected, but not shoved out front when it was time for Sales Demo meetings. The public for his/their albums was hard to find. Radio and record stores were hard to impress. *Rolling Stone* was not yet even published, [in fact it was ... just] so any reviews of this 'listen carefully' style mostly showed up in obscure, once-a-week freebie papers with names like *The Independent* or *Free Press*."

Commercially, *Song Cycle* had struck out. Now it was Randy's turn to step up to the plate.

As always, Lenny was in the changing room and on the field, ready with the pep talks, geeing him up, getting him match perfect.

"What it really boils down to, I think, is that I had a much clearer picture of his potential than he did," Lenny said. "I think my enthusiasm eventually wore him down, though he fiercely resisted it. Let's face it, you can't shield yourself indefinitely from someone relentlessly reminding you of your greatness. You want to hear it."

'Lenny's Corps' – Randy singing and playing, Lenny and Van Dyke producing – went into the studio to make an album to be called *Randy Newman Creates Something New Under The Sun*. The title was a little overheated. Nothing about the album was hugely innovatory, but the arrangements were extraordinary, the singing unique and the lyrics stunning.

Seventy-five musicians were involved in its creation, including Wrecking Crew stalwarts like Carol Kaye, Plas Johnson and Tommy Tedesco, countrybilly guitarist James Burton, who played with Elvis' TCB Band and Emmylou Harris' Hot Band, jazz guitarist Herb Ellis of the Oscar Peterson Trio, Sal Valentino of the Beau Brummels on guitar and vocals and, on drums, Jim Gordon, who later worked with Delaney & Bonnie and Eric Clapton's Derek & the Dominos before the voices, which told him to kill his mother with a hammer and a knife, led him to the California Medical Facility.

The album touched on themes that Randy would continue to visit for the next half century – race, love, ageing, fathers and sons, religion and death.

'Love Story', the first track, tells a tale of an unadventurous couple, and covers, in just under three-and-a-half minutes, their courtship, marriage, parenthood, old age and demise. "It's about someone with a dream so modest that it hardly counts as a dream," Randy said in 1999. "Listening to it now – I'm 30 years older now – it seems like a lot to ask for."

The sweetness of the verse, with featherlite strings floating above the troubled aspirations, ("We'll have a kid / or maybe we'll rent one / he's got to be straight / we don't want a bent one"*) is intermittently, and violently smashed by the insistence of the chorus, hammering the line

---

* Recent critics have cited this line as a shocking example of homophobia. It should be noted, however, that most slang dictionaries, even now, cite 'homosexual' as one of the more uncommon meanings of 'bent' and some suggest that it is primarily a British usage. In 1968, 'straight' had many associations – as it still has. It was used far more frequently to suggest the opposite of 'hip' (a 'straight' cigarette, 'straight' society') than anything to do with sexual orientation. A 'straight' child would have been an upright citizen. Contrasting it with 'bent' also suggests that 'straight' might have been used in its mundane geometric sense rather than 'conforming to society's norms' – a comic juxtaposition. It's a joke.

"You and me, you and ME babe" against a Phil Spector wall of sound. And when the unexciting couple get old, their children will send them "To a little home in Florida / We'll play checkers all day/ Until we pass away."

'Bet No One Hurt This Bad' is a festival of competitive, self-aggrandising misery in which the singer invites the listener to appreciate the utter despair he's in – possibly a deeper despair than any human being has ever experienced. This is not someone to whom you'd want to say, "Yeah, that's exactly how *I* felt when my wife left me". He'd bite your head off. Musically it's akin to 'Spinning Wheel', the Blood, Sweat & Tears track of a year or so later, the chords running the cycle of fourths – always a favourite ride of Randy's – round and round, like the singer's trajectory as he swirls into the dismal whirlpool of his self-imposed misery.

'Living Without You' acts as a sort of commentary on the track before. It's a song of heartbreak that has developed into genuine clinical depression and begins, like 'I Think It's Going To Rain Today', with a sequence of cinematic images: "The milk-truck hauls the sun up / The paper hits the door / The subway shakes my floor / And I think about you". He can't get out of bed to face the day. "Nothing's gonna happen, Nothing's gonna change". The bleakness swells and peaks in a howl "so hard living without you".

Two unsettling verses and choruses and that's it, leaving you with the gnawing music-box glockenspiel that's underscored the whole thing.

'Linda' – the heroine of the last track on side one – has stood up the narrator, leaving him on a pier listening to the carousel playing. On cue, the orchestra kicks in with a tipsy fairground motif, which can't help but sound sinister. The thing with Linda never really sounded viable anyway.

Few songwriters have addressed the baffled, stumbling relationship that exists between fathers and sons as comprehensively as Randy. In 'So Long Dad', the son comes home after many years and attempts to square things with his dad, because, maybe, the dad's dying. The song isn't clear about what it is that needs to be squared. Maybe sons always need to square things with their dads, or dads need to square things with their sons.

The stumbling sentiments are set against an intermittently huge orchestral arrangement built on a New Orleans shuffle – loping piano and whisk-broom drums. It's a lazy style which, in a Randy Newman song, usually carries with it a hint of offhand cruelty so casual as to be cosy.

Whatever, the shuffle was to remain his default setting – his by birth, by taste and by temperament.

"I was so influenced by Fats Domino," he told Jim Beviglia in 2012, "that it's still hard for me to write a song that's not a New Orleans shuffle."

Most of his albums feature a religious song of some sort. In 'I Think He's Hiding', Randy considers God with the awestruck wonder of a congenital atheist. It wonders as much about pea-brained religious certainty as it does about God. He warns that the 'Big Boy', like Santa Claus, is coming to town, and apologises for humankind's shortcomings, excusing them on the grounds that we could only work with "what You gave us". Sung in the strangulated voice of a man who's been drinking whisky steadily for at least 48 hours, he rounds the song off with: "Now I've heard it said / That our Big Boy's dead / But I think he's hiding…"

This is followed by a cowboy song called 'Cowboy'. Every boy brought up in the fifties is half cowboy. Back then, kids used cowboy hats, waistcoats and gunbelts as daywear. The diet at the movies and on TV was intense and continuous: *Hopalong Cassidy*, *Cisco Kid*, *Roy Rogers*, *Gun Law*, *Sugarfoot*, *Cheyenne*, *Bronco*, *Wagon Train*, *Maverick*, *Wells Fargo* and on and on, drilling the cowboy code and the pioneer lifestyle deep into the psyche until the Ponderosa was the happy place and a night without a dream of sage brush and tumbleweed was considered sleepless.

The young cowboy's reaction to this obsession in later life is complex. Most manage to put it behind them as a childish thing, of course they do, but still it lingers and worries, providing simultaneous shame (because you know at heart you're still in thrall to that shit) and dignity (because you'll ride tall in the saddle and die with your boots on). Randy wrote some terrific cowboy songs, all of them sown with the seed of their own unmaking.

'Cowboy' was inspired by *Lonely Are The Brave*, the Kirk Douglas film about a cowboy trying to adapt to a modern world of traffic jams and helicopters, and was originally written for the Dustin Hoffman/Jon Voight/John Schlesinger film *Midnight Cowboy*, a tale of two losers in a hostile world. It's not in the film.

'The Beehive State' is a half-formed song, not quite there, which gives account of a discussion in Congress, maybe, about the needs of Kansas and Utah (the Beehive State). The representatives of those two states make their modest demands. Kansas needs a firehouse in Topeka. Utah

Maybe I'm Doing It Wrong

needs to irrigate the desert. That's pretty much it. "It should have been longer," Randy said, "but I couldn't think of any more to say".

The orchestra in 'Laughing Boy' plays a desperate, sledgehammer riff, something along the line of 'Twelfth Street Rag' played by the inmates of a ghost prison, while the singer goes, 'Ya-da-da-da-da-da-da – laughing boy keep moving.' Then there is a pause for thought.

The thought is self-referential and goes, "An unprincipled and uncommitted clown can hardly be permitted to sit around and laugh at what the decent people try to do." Which, it could be argued, is exactly what Randy is doing on much of the rest of the album – and, indeed, continued to do on subsequent albums.

"This guy wrote me a letter saying his friend had just killed himself, and he left 'Laughing Boy' on the CD to play over and over and over and over," Randy told Jon Ronson in a 1999 *Guardian* interview. "Kind of a compliment, you know? I wrote back saying, 'Thank you. Great compliment.'"

This leads on to Randy's own version of the much-covered 'I Think It's Going To Rain Today'. He mumbles the lyric to a sparse piano accompaniment played at a tempo so slow you could soft boil an egg in the first verse alone. In the second verse it's as if he can't raise the energy even to play piano any more and the strings have to take over. We aren't privy to what has brought the singer down so low but it's implied: "Tin can at my feet / think I'll kick it down the street / That's the way to treat a friend." In 'Davy The Fat Boy', the narrator promises Davy's dying parents that he will always care for Davy, to whom he's been close since childhood. It's a touching scene. Then Randy breaks out the rinky-dink piano as the narrator cashes in on his vulnerable friend's size issues. He puts him into a freak show. Passers-by are invited to guess his weight. And if that isn't humiliating enough, the orchestra starts a slower, wheedling theme: "I think we can persuade him to do / The famous Fat Boy Dance for you".

"I never get tired of doing 'Davy'," he said years later. "It depresses me that I wrote it so long ago. I don't know that I've written stuff much better than that."

Randy was a stickler in the studio.

"Randy did three different versions of 'Davy The Fat Boy' and five introductions for 'So Long Dad'," Lenny told David Felton. "Eventually we have to kind of trap him. We know he'll always show up once the musicians are booked, so I'll casually ask him something like, 'Well, if we went with *this* version, what musicians would you use?' And as soon as he tells me I'll run out and book them, and that's that.

"When we were recording 'Cowboy', he kept commenting on how it should sound like it was outdoors [...] His need to create a three dimensional reality in his songs is a constant. We were always asking ourselves 'How do we capture the idea of the song and make it interesting and keep it musical?'"

The album, *Randy Newman* (with, in much smaller print, *Creates Something New Under The Sun*) was released in June 1968.

There were some good records around that year, debut albums from Leonard Cohen, Joni Mitchell, James Taylor, The Band, Simon & Garfunkel's *Bookends*, Van Morrison's *Astral Weeks*, the Byrds' *Sweethearts Of The Rodeo*. Tough competition. The smarter critics recognised that Randy was something special.

"Newman is fascinated with the vocabulary of insensitivity and has mastered it completely, to the point where he can compose searingly revealing stanzas out of straight quotes," Clive James said, in a review for *Creem* magazine headlined "The Hoarse Foreman Of The Apocalypse."

Rex Reed, in *Stereo Review*, wrote: "Randy Newman is either an outrageous put on or he is really something new under the sun to which we should all pay very close attention. If you have the patience to listen to this album more than once, you may agree that he is not putting us on. [...] Musically he is reminiscent of Bernstein and Blitzstein. I suspect there is the making of another *West Side Story* in Randy Newman – only this time it won't have to be based on some old story by Shakespeare. He has the guts to tell it like it is today."

Robert Shelton in the *New York Times* said: "Mr Newman is a droll and cunning song-writer with a style vaguely reminiscent of Hoagy Carmichael's, in which he smears phrases as if finger painting. But Mr Newman, to continue the art images, is a sort of Jacob Epstein of Silly Putty, building most intriguing statuary."

It could have been his bill matter: "Randy Newman – the Epstein, Bernstein And Blitzstein Of Tell It Like It Is Today Pop."

The album delivered smart songs for smart people who had felt for a while that pop, even at the clever end, had ceased to serve them. It hit the spot like an untipped Senior Service or something peaty from the Isle of

Maybe I'm Doing It Wrong

Jura: songs that amused, horrified, saddened and made you laugh all at the same time, while providing toe-tapping melodies, challenging harmonies and a rewarding sense of intellectual superiority.

This last appeal came primarily from Randy's use of irony – a word which... one can almost hear it happening... causes the ears of pedants to prick up and their hackles to raise. HF Fowler, joint author of *The King's English* and *The Concise Oxford Dictionary* and sole author of *Modern English Usage*, the widely accepted authority on such matters, has this to say: "Irony is a form of utterance that postulates a double audience, consisting of one party that hearing shall hear and not understand, and another party that, when more is meant than meets the ear, is aware both of that more and of the outsiders' incomprehension."

In other words, the smart, who believed that they appreciated the 'jokes' and the dense layers of meaning and contradiction and self-reference going on in Randy's songs, had extra reason to be smug because these layers and levels were not apparent to the wider public. The exclusivity of the coterie to which the Randy-understanders belonged was satisfyingly confirmed by the initial sales of the record: 4,700 copies.

If all the copies that were sold of Michael Jackson's *Thriller* were laid end to end, they would stretch half way round the world. If all the copies that were sold of *Randy Newman* on its first release were laid end to end, they'd stretch from your house to the shops. Or to be more geographically precise, from the Greenwich Meridian to the Ryman's by the traffic lights on Montpelier Vale.

The album slipped away. Robert Wilonsky of the *Dallas Observer* called it a soundtrack without a film. In retrospect many wondered whether the lavish orchestral backing had been a mistake, overpowering Randy's frail and mumbled vocals and masking the quality of the songwriting.

In May 1969, almost a year after the release, Stan Cornyn, the man who'd pissed off Van Dyke Parks with his "How we lost $35,509.50" campaign, tried to bump up sales by placing another of his 'special' ads.

This one said, in huge type surrounded by inches of white: "Once you get used to it, his voice is really something."

Then, in tiny type at the bottom of the page: "Apparently, it's taking longer than we thought to get used to that voice. We put out *Randy Newman* almost a year ago. Not much happened in the record stores. When we asked him about that, our Mr Sherman, who heads up Reprise's sales department, started changing the subject and asking when we'd be ready with the next Sinatra album."

The copy goes on to say, "The occasion for this advertisement is that now Mr Thrasher, our art director, has just put a new cover on the album, hoping that'll help."

The ad includes images of "The Old Cover" with a cross through it, and "The New Cover".

The original cover was a shot of Randy wearing a lemon yellow turtleneck and slacks, no glasses, his wayward curls slicked down and blue skies behind him – "like an insurance salesman trying to look hip, but in his attempt he just underlines that he is as square as a breeze block."

The revised cover was a much murkier and moodier close shot of his face – sardonic mouth, intense sideways gaze.

But the repackaging did nothing to improve sales. Worried that the public might start getting the idea that Warner-Reprise was a label for losers, the company launched another ad, claiming that crappy sales, far from being a cause of shame, was proof of integrity.

"It wasn't luck that made them [Warners] get behind Van Dyke Parks and Randy Newman when Lenny brought these extremely unusual and seemingly uncommercial composers into the company. Warner Bros. for the last year has been absolutely fearless about giving people who were known by reputation to be creative absolute artistic freedom and the money and equipment and support to make that freedom meaningful."

The company boasted of its 'family' atmosphere. To a degree it was true. Warner-Reprise artists did play together nicely. When Gordon Lightfoot made his first Reprise album, for instance, Randy provided some string arrangements, Van Dyke added harmonium and John Sebastian (another signee) chipped in with some slide guitar.

Randy went along with the family ethos... up to a point. "Whenever a mystique forms around a corporation," he said in Warren Zanes' 2008 book celebrating 50 years of Warner records, "as it has with Apple or Microsoft, and as it did around Warner-Reprise, I always think it's excessive, because it's still a corporation. And when you dealt with Warners on business, you may as well have been dealing with a mortgage broker. They were tough. Mo [Ostin], Joe Smith, whomever you dealt with. Though not on record budgets... I never heard that I couldn't use an orchestra, for instance. The main thing about the label, though, is that they gave you the chance to fail. They put up with you if what you were doing was good in, let's say, an aesthetic way. There was no A&R department that passed judgment. If it felt like somebody was doing something, they'd let you fail, and fail again, and fail again."

The Warner 'integrity' ad might have started a face-saving exercise to cover their lousy sales, but in time it drew genuine dividends.

Lenny Waronker always knew that in the long term building a brand can be more important than short-term gains, and Randy and Van Dyke and other low-sales artists who followed were solid brand-builders. "If you're doing something good, good things follow. Artists would come to the label because of those records. The creative community recognises when something is going on musically whether it's selling or not."

Ry Cooder, the singer/guitar player/musicologist, released his first album for the company in 1970. When it languished in the record stores, he was initially confused – relieved but confused – that the company came back for more. But gradually he began to get it. "I went, 'I see. I don't make money and I don't sell records, but there's a service I'm able to provide somehow'."

The 'service' was that Randy, Van Dyke and Ry worked as bait, luring other artists in with their example of creative freedom uncompromised by anything as sordid as sales.

James Taylor, who'd been with the Beatles' Apple label, practically begged Warner-Reprise to sign him: "Lee Herschberg, the engineer, and Lenny Waronker and Russ Titleman were all staff people at Warner Bros. Russ and Lenny had produced Ry Cooder and Randy Newman and I was crazy about both artists, so I asked Russ and Lenny to take me on."

Even years later, Elvis Costello, who in 1988 signed a five album deal with Warners, saw the label as special: "I was quite proud to be signed to Warner Bros.," he said. "In my time as a record buyer and music fan, Warner Bros., more conspicuously than any other label, was a supporter of artists who elsewhere wouldn't have gotten anything like a shot – people like Randy Newman, Ry Cooder and Van Dyke Parks, especially who, to say the least, would be regarded as uncommercial by some other labels."

Make three loss leaders, wait 20 years, reel in Elvis Costello. The plan worked.

Early in 1968, before he'd started recording the album, Randy got a meeting about a movie score. It would have been his first, except he blew it. The film's producer asked him to play something. Randy had just finished writing 'Davy The Fat Boy'. It was fresh in his mind, a piece of work he was proud of. He decided to try it out, forgetting for a moment that the producer weighed more than 300 pounds.

"About halfway through," Randy told David Felton, "the absurdity of my singing this song about a fat kid for this overweight producer suddenly hit me. When I finished, he said, 'That's wonderful; do you have any songs about blind people or bald men?'"

Chapter Eight

Randy spent most of his first two years in New Orleans and went back there for occasional family vacations. It was, as he frequently pointed out, enough. It left its mark.

"New Orleans is all kinds of unfathomable…" it says in *Unfathomable City*, a historo-geo-cultural guide to the place, "… a city of amorphous boundaries where land is forever turning into water, water devours land, and a thousand degrees of marshy muddy oozing in-between exist; where lines that elsewhere seem firm-drawn are blurry; where whatever you say required more elaboration; where most rules are full of exceptions the way most land here is full of water."

A "place where lines that elsewhere seem firm-drawn are blurry; where whatever you say requires more elaboration" is, of course, a natural home to Randy Newman.

The pace of the South suits him, too. In Memphis airport, he once discovered: "I was part of a stream of people moving at the same speed I was," he said. "In New York, old people, cripples all walk faster than you. In the South, I finally found my people, my planet."

The dead cannot be buried in New Orleans. The soil is too soft and often so sodden that the coffins float back up again. Even when you lock the coffins up in sturdy mausoleums, the floods are liable to come and float them back out into the streets. When the line between even life and death is nebulous, everything's up for grabs.

The city's past and its culture are more Caribbean than American. Founded by the French, it then passed to the Spanish, then back to the French and was finally sold to the USA by Napoleon in 1803. One legacy of this patchwork history is an attitude towards race slightly more nuanced, not to say confusing, than the binary apartheid that held sway in the rest of the South. A class of mixed-race 'free people of colour', often educated and wealthy, had rights and status that in Georgia or Alabama would have been considered an outrage to decency. Distinctions of caste were invested in language, too: people might speak English, French, Louisiana French, Cajun French, Spanish or combinations thereof and the picture was further confused when Jews came to settle and Irish, Chinese, and more recently Hondurans and Vietnamese.

It's always been a wicked town. Seafood and stickiness aren't the only things that make the air smell of sex – sex itself makes a sizeable contribution, too. It is – it's often been said – the place where the Bible belt is loosened and the sin from all ten states washed by the Mississippi comes to settle.

Sin and music always went hand in hand. In 1918, the *Picayune Times* described 'jass' music as an "indecent story syncopated and counterpointed" and though its practitioners – King Oliver, Kid Ory, Sidney Bechet, Louis Armstrong, Jelly Roll Morton and the rest – took their music north and eventually all the way to Carnegie Hall, it was a good long time before 'jass' lost its USP as top-quality rutting music.

Rock'n'roll was alive and well in New Orleans long before it got named. In 1945, Cosimo Matassa, a dropout from Tulane University, opened a studio – J&M Recordings – at the back of a record shop on the corner of South Rampart Street and Dumaine and started recording local acts. There were plenty to choose from. After the Second World War, there was a taste in the clubs for heavy-on-the-left hand boogie-woogie piano players and small, raucous bands playing jump jive. The Caledonia Inn was featuring the pianist Roy Byrd aka Professor Longhair, with Apeman Black on sax, Big Stick on drums and Walter 'Papoose' Nelson on guitar. The Hideaway in the Ninth Ward had Antoine 'Fats' Domino playing with Billy Diamond's band.

Seven years before Elvis recorded 'That's All Right' at Sun Studio in Memphis, four years before Jackie Brenston & His Delta Cats recorded 'Rocket 88', often regarded as the first rock'n'roll record, Roy Brown

Maybe I'm Doing It Wrong

recorded 'Good Rocking Tonight', the song later covered by Elvis, at J&M.

Eight years later, in 1955, Robert "Bumps" Blackwell, of Specialty Records, brought Richard Penniman to record at J&M. The musicians assembled for the session stood open mouthed as the young man introduced himself and later said they "didn't know whether to call him he or she". After a few false starts, he sang them a sensational song that was unreleasable because its lyrics rhymed "your mamma turns tricks" with "your daddy sucks dicks", kicked off with "a wop bob aloobop a good god damn", and had, as its chorus, "Tutti-Frutti, good booty". Local lyricist Dorothy La Bostrie was hastily summoned to clean up the words and the sanitised version, with Penniman credited as 'Little Richard', went to number two in the *Billboard* R&B chart.

Antoine "Fats" Domino cut his first singles at J&M, too. 'The Fat Man' went to number six in the *Billboard* R&B chart. 'Goin' Home' made number one. During the fifties, Fats enjoyed a string of hits – 'Blue Monday', 'Ain't That A Shame', 'Blueberry Hill', 'I'm Walkin'', 'Walking To New Orleans', that made his sales second only to Elvis'. And Randy Newman absorbed them into his DNA.

In 1968, Randy had one of those opportunities kids dream about – like Pelé coming round your house and saying he was putting a team together with Diego Maradona and Bobby Charlton and was just wondering...

Fats' career had been stranded up a backwater. He'd had label trouble. His glory days with Imperial Records in the fifties were long gone. He was signed for a while to ABC-Paramount and flirted with Mercury and Broadmoor with little to show for it. Now Mo Ostin had persuaded him to make a comeback album with Reprise. He'd got a young-gun hot-shot producer, Richard Perry, who'd just done the honours on Captain Beefheart's *Safe As Milk*; he'd got a line-up of the Wrecking Crew's finest ready, willing and able, together with King Curtis on sax; he'd got together an exciting list of possible songs, but... here's the thing... the fat man, for reasons lost to history, had decided he didn't want to play piano on the album, so ...

Randy didn't get the gig.

Instead they hired James Booker, the 'Black Liberace', described by Mac Rebennack (Dr John) as "the best black, gay, one-eyed junkie piano genius New Orleans has ever produced".

Randy did however get to arrange the horn parts on eight of the tracks, including Fats' cover of the Beatles' 'Lady Madonna'. It was a sort of homecoming for a song which, as Paul McCartney has pointed out, had been heavily influenced by Fats Domino in the first place.

In the event, Randy's work, on that track at least, was more in the nature of transcribing rather than arranging: the Fats record copies the Beatles' faithfully enough to be a karaoke version, down to the backing vocals and the bright piano sound.

Fats also recorded one of Randy's own songs, an unrestrained version of 'Have You Seen My Baby' – a song about an innocent looking for his love, unable quite to appreciate the significance of her having been seen with the milkman and the gypsies in the wood. It was released as a B-side in 1970 and features two pianos, acoustic and electric, having a wonderful time, and, though it's uncredited anywhere, what sounds like Ry Cooder swooping around on slide guitar.

At around the same time, Ry and Randy got involved with a movie. Donald Cammell, a painter who'd become a 'face' on the London scene, was getting into film production and had come up with an idea for a pop-romp initially called *The Performers*. As the project developed it got darker. And darker. Nick Roeg, then a cameraman who'd worked on *Lawrence Of Arabia* and Truffaut's *Fahrenheit 451* came on board to shoot the film and co-direct with Cammell.

Mick Jagger was coaxed into the cast, along with Anita Pallenberg – Keith Richards' girlfriend – and James Fox (Harrow School, Coldstream Guards, *The Servant*, *King Rat*, *Thoroughly Modern Millie*). The film by now had acquired a new title, *Performance*, and been laced with ultra-violence, troilism, hallucinogens and a stench of brimstone.

When he was a kid, Cammell had known Aleister Crowley, Initiate of the Order of the Golden Dawn, Prophet of the Aeon of Horus, author of *The Book Of Lies* and advocate of 'sex-magick'. In the year the film went into production, the Stones released *Their Satanic Majesties Request*, and 'Sympathy For The Devil'. "Oooh," they sang, "Ooooooh."

Originally, the Stones were supposed to provide the score for the film but, as production of the film got underway, the group's personal dynamic began to malfunction. Keith suspected that the sex scenes in the movie between Mick Jagger and Anita Pallenberg didn't involve much in the way of 'acting'. He took to sitting in his car outside the house where the film was being shot, and spent his days in poisonous brooding.

There could have been some substance to Keith's suspicions. After the film had been released, Sanford Leiberson, the producer, took ten minutes of out-takes, retitled *Performance Trim*, to the Amsterdam Wet-Dream Film Festival, a showplace for Europe's finest pornography. Though much appreciated, it failed to win an award.

A distribution deal had been put together with Warner Bros. movies. Jack Nitzsche was signed to Warner-Reprise, he'd worked with the Stones, he'd worked in movies, he took drugs: perfectly qualified, then, to take over the *Performance* score. Ry Cooder was one of the musicians he hired.

"He [Nitzsche] went through an important door, which involved pop music in film, and was a really good arranger with interesting compositional abilities," Cooder said. "In those days, movie people looked askance at the idea of pop music in films – of drums and bass – it was all wrong as far as film theory was concerned. But Nitzsche got the job. The idea of world music had occurred to him. [Drummer] Milt Holland could play the table. [Singer-songwriter] Buffy Sainte-Marie came in with her mouth bow. He brought in [actor/singer/psychodrama pioneer] Roy Hart. Some great people who could play some crazy things. Nitzsche had a really good idea there."

"What was fortuitous was the group of friends Nitzsche assembled to work with him," says Paul Buck in, *Performance: The Biography Of A 60s Masterpiece*. "Randy Newman, who would later make his own contribution to film music, opens the soundtrack with 'Gone Dead Train', written by Nitzsche with Russ Titelman. Newman is not known for his blues singing, but this up-tempo rock song benefits from his gravel-tired voice. Randy was the core of the band, along with Cooder and Titelman. Though the song was based on King Solomon Hill's 'Gone Dead Train', it was so loose that it bears little resemblance. The original lyrics were to do with an actual train, a Death Train, which was probably part of the reason for its inclusion at the head, and its reprise at the end of the film."

A lot of the score was improvised. "They'd screen the film – projected in those days – and the director would wave his arms and talk in aphorisms, like English people do sometimes, trying to get you to know what he wanted you to feel and play," said Cooder. "It worked pretty good.

"I used to go home from these sessions with a splitting headache, thinking, 'What's the world coming to? This is about the nastiest looking thing I've ever seen, this film.' It scared me. It made me ill."

It had its effect on others, too. After making the film, James Fox had a breakdown and gave up acting for 15 years. It made the execs at Warners go a bit wobbly. They shelved its release for two years. It was never destined to be a blockbuster – despite Jagger's name – and, when it was finally released in 1970, it received a mixed critical reception.

Nevertheless, a single from the soundtrack album, 'Memo From Turner'/'Natural Magic' (conducted by Randy Newman) went top 40 in the UK.

In 1969, Randy got an entire film score to himself. This one dispensed with the troilism and ultra-violence and dealt instead with the curse of nicotine.

Cold Turkey, produced, directed and co-written by Norman Lear, starred Dick Van Dyke, Bob Newhart and, in his last ever role, an 83-year-old Edward Everett Horton. It's a comedy about a town that accepts a $25m challenge to give up smoking for 30 days. Though there's not much music, what there is raises the tone. Xylophone and wah-wah trumpet gags get treated instead to sweeping Americana with a result that's more classy than it is incongruous.

The film also features a theme song. In keeping with Dick Van Dyke's role as a minister, it's a hymn called 'He Gives Us All His Love'. The tune is vaguely reminiscent of 'He's Got The Whole World In His Hands'. The lyric is – ostensibly at least – inoffensive enough to be included in *Hymns Ancient And Modern* without raising eyebrows. It's about what a great guy God is, sitting up there in heaven watching the babies crying and old folks dying and giving us all his love. And we can talk to him any time we want to and he'll listen.

In a different context, which it found on Randy's fourth album *Sail Away*, you realise that the God of the song – and maybe in lots of other songs that talk about God, even the ones in *Hymns Ancient And Modern* – is strangely ineffectual. He sees pain, grief, hardship and disease, he listens to our prayers, but never actually does anything but smile on us – a benign but pointless presence.

It's a mistake to try and pinpoint a specific 'message' in any Randy Newman song. Like Shakespeare's plays or the Old Testament, they're open to a good deal of interpretation. But one possible interpretation of 'He Gives Us All His Love' is that whether you believe in God or not, whether he exists or not, it doesn't really make a lot of difference.

This film, too, was shelved by the distributors for a couple of years (during which time Edward Everett Horton died), eventually doing a respectable, if unspectacular, $5.5m at the box office.

Between the making of *Performance* in 1968 and the release of *Cold Turkey* in 1971, the world of rock'n'roll went crazy.

The shape of things to come was perhaps first sketched out at the Northern California Folk-Rock Festival, at Santa Clara in May 1968. The Grateful Dead, Big Brother & the Holding Company and Jefferson Airplane were on the bill.

A man and a woman calling themselves Hog Man and Hog Woman wandered through the crowd, distributing orange pills. Then the woman jumped on stage, grabbed the mic, shouted "We're all on hog" and instructed everyone to take their pills. Two dozen were subsequently hospitalised with acute sickness and diarrhoea.

"We are stardust," Joni Mitchell sang about another festival a year later, "we are golden, and we've got to get ourselves back to the garden" – because the queue for the chemical toilets is half a million strong and we're all on hog.

The hog incident was a small thing, but a warning. The collapse of stupid hippie hope into vile insanity when it came, came quickly.

Brian Jones drowned in his swimming pool. Jimi Hendrix overdosed. Janis Joplin overdosed. Judy Garland overdosed. Frankie Lymon (of Frankie Lymon & the Teenagers) overdosed. Tony Hancock (British comedian) overdosed. Alan "Blind Owl" Wilson (of Canned Heat) overdosed. Mary Ann Gànser (of the Shangri-Las) possibly overdosed. Brian Epstein overdosed and The Beatles split up and sued the arses off each other.

"It's very hard to get rich and famous at a young age and handle it well," Randy told Dorian Lynskey. "I can't think of anyone who did. Some of them got through it and now they're fine, and some of them died, and some of them are assholes, and some of them don't have money any more. But no one was the same person. [...] Fortunately I wrote stuff that people didn't like. I dodged a bullet there."

Outside pop, the world turned viler still.

Charles Manson and his gang massacred Sharon Tate and six others at Terry Melcher's old house on Cielo Drive. At the Altamont Free Festival starring the Rolling Stones, Jefferson Airplane and Crosby, Stills, Nash &

Young, one man was stabbed to death by Hells Angels, one drowned and two were run over by cars and died*.

In 1968, the Viet Cong launched the Tet Offensive, which led to some of the bloodiest engagements in the war, and US troops indiscriminately murdered and raped hundreds of civilians in the village of My Lai.

Martin Luther King was murdered. Robert Kennedy was murdered.

The 'Prague Spring' came to an end when Russian tanks rolled into Czechoslovakia.

Following the Battle of the Bogside, British troops were deployed in Northern Ireland.

Hundreds of thousands died and millions starved as a result of the Nigerian Civil War.

And so on ...

The generalised optimism that had been around in the sixties, the feeling that a corner had been turned, that this might – regardless of your scepticism towards Astrology – be the dawning of the age of Aquarius, had crashed and burned. And all those trippy notions – that drugs were pretty good, that if you asked "War, what is it good for?" Lyndon Johnson might think, "good point" and stop the bombing, that there was nowhere you can be that isn't where you're meant to be – were now greeted with howls of derisive laughter.

The 'Sunshine Pop' of Harpers Bizarre was so inappropriate to the new zeitgeist that it was almost bad taste. The laconic, detached pessimism of Randy Newman, on the other hand – songs about "broken windows and empty hallways", about the casual abuse of fat people, about God sniggering at the human condition – seemed to fit the times like a latex glove.

Randy had never been much of a sixties person, anyway.

"Most people I knew weren't married at the same time I was," he told the *Houston Chronicle*. "So I ran around and did bad things, and there were drugs and all that. But for me it was more centred on the not bad

---

* Fans of conspiracy theories might like to know that, after Altamont – according to a former FBI agent – members of the Hells Angels conspired to murder Mick Jagger in retribution for his lack of support after the stabbing, and would have done so were it not for a sudden and mysterious storm which sank a boat they used to approach a Long Island house in which Jagger was staying.

Maybe I'm Doing It Wrong

things. I was never a part of any group. It's partly shyness. A streak of anti-sociality."

His position in the rock'n'roll community was never entirely secure.

"I was talking one time to Paul McCartney on the phone," he said. "He called me to do something for [Welsh folk singer] Mary Hopkin – and I was saying, 'I'm trying to write… Jesus, it's a drag.' And he says: 'Well, you really don't have that much to live up to anyway, do you?' And I replied, all meek and mild, 'Oh yeah, I guess not', but I was thinking, 'Who're you, shithead?' I never forgot that."

(Years later, Randy met Paul again at a party. By this time he was one Oscar up on the Beatles and McCartney had clearly revised his opinion because he jumped over a sofa to get to talk to Randy. Randy was impressed, not by the change in his standing and reputation, but that Paul McCartney could still jump over a sofa at his age.)

More discerning members of the music community rated Randy's work very highly indeed.

Harry Nilsson, the sweet voiced singer-songwriter, chose Randy's 'Simon Smith And The Amazing Dancing Bear' as the last track on his 1969 album *Harry*. Alan Price had beefed up the song with a brass section and a kick in the rhythm. Nilsson went the other way with a modest tent-show pit band arrangement: brushes on the drums, fiddle and button harmonica.

The lyrics, inside the album sleeve, were illustrated with appropriate photographs, including two of Harry and a bear. The bear was played by his sometimes writing partner, Bill Martin, appropriately disguised.

"It was the only bear suit in town, and it was made from an actual bear," Bill said. "I was inside the bear looking out through these rows of teeth, and Harry's in an overcoat and a muffler, but it was 103 degrees up in Laurel Canyon. Dean Torrence [from Uni High, Jan & Dean and the Frank Sinatra kidnap case] was doing the photography, and we're both sweating like pigs. Then the bear seemed to return back to life after about 15 minutes. I could see the steam coming out from the bear's mouth. I smelled like a bear for three days."

Harry Nilsson was from Brooklyn. His dad disappeared before his first birthday. His paternal grandparents, according to his mum, were circus performers working under the name 'Nilsson's Aerial Ballet'. "And they had another act," Harry said, "called Nilsson's Luminous Butterfly ….", an assertion that comes with a reminder that Harry's mother was fond of a drink, and the potency of drugs in the late sixties was a hit and miss affair.

He was an extraordinary singer and mysterious songwriter whose musical head seemed stuck in some empty, echoing theatre in 1932, or maybe just beneath the canvas roof of a circus tent at the turn of the twentieth century, smelling the rosin and elephants, with the sound of a rattling orchestra and the astonished crowd far, far below. He was smart, shy, funny, didn't know how to be hip and, on the right day in the right place, delightful company.

He and Randy started hanging out, getting together for the odd game of ping-pong. Then Harry decided that, for his next project, he wanted to make an entire album of Randy Newman songs.

"I did those songs actually because I consciously felt at the time they were the best songs to record," Harry told Stuart Grundy in a 1977 BBC interview. "I had, like, five songs and instead of doing five of my own, I thought, 'Wait a minute, Randy Newman's got a bunch of songs.' This was in the early days before he was known at all. I thought, 'Why not do a unique album, an album of somebody else's songs? That hasn't been done for a while has it?' And, you know, the idea was to go with just him playing the piano and me singing, no orchestra.'"

"I think that he really admired [my songs]," Randy said. "He was enormously decent, and open minded about other people's work, which is the case very rarely today. And I think he just wanted to show people my songs."

Randy acknowledged that maybe he and Harry were out of time, carrying on an older tradition that pop was still to absorb. "It was a funny time," Randy said. "You know, like we really believed it was an art form. [...] The records Harry made and the first records I made, it was like we didn't know that the Rolling Stones existed."

Both used song as a medium for storytelling and comedy and both had an affinity with showbiz – a wary affinity maybe, but one that all the same pushed them a bit too close to the greasepaint and footlights to be truly rock'n'roll.

On August 20, 1969, the two of them repaired to RCA's West Coast studios and started rehearsing and recording. Harry worked hard, insisting that he had to get inside the songs, to know them as well as Randy knew them.

"Randy was tired of the album before we finished making it," Harry said in the liner notes. "Because for him it was just doing piano and voice, voice and piano, over and over and over."

Harry, by contrast, was manic. He had discovered a way never to get tired. "Harry was using a lot of cocaine and I had never seen him using it before," his then wife Diane Nilsson told Alyn Shipton. "Now I don't know if he used it before those sessions, but maybe that's why he was adding so many things. Because it's a stimulant. And he just didn't seem to be able to stop."

The 'so many things' he was adding were principally layer upon layer of his voice. Apart from a little guitar and drums used for effect only on the first track, and an occasional sparse use of other instruments they perhaps found lying around the studio – there's a vibraphone on one track, an organ on another and a wind machine used on 'Cowboy' – it's all Randy on piano and Harry on vocals and Harry on vocals and Harry on vocals; sometimes layer upon layer to make a choir of Harry Nilssons, causing one of the record-company staff to chide him for neglecting to credit the backing singers.

From time to time, in the middles of tracks, we hear Harry giving incongruous instructions to the engineer behind the glass, "actually I need more of the current voice" he says, from the middle of massed overdubs on 'So Long Dad'. You could write a doctoral thesis on this. About the way he 'disrupts the narrative' or 'breaks the text' in order to invite examination of the political and cultural assumptions that underlie the 'album' as an artifice and artefact and ultimately a commodity for capitalist exploitation. Or you could go out and have a couple of drinks. The choice is yours.

Five of the tracks had already been released on Randy's first album: another would be released on his second album, and one had been used on Van Dyke Parks' album. Randy wrote just one new song, 'Caroline', especially for Harry's album.

"I've never recorded it myself," he said. "No one else, I think, has ever recorded it. It was pretty and it was a type of nonsense; 'When… daylight surrounds you, there's no one around you but me…' But he could make it work. I didn't have the type of voice to be a tenor, a romantic. That's maybe why it's written like that. But I mean he could do it. And did. It's one of my favourite things on that album. Damn good."

Nilsson Sings Newman was released in February 1970. *Stereo Review* nominated it the album of the year, expressing the opinion that Nilsson "seems the very best choice to sing Newman's songs," and adding, "after all, someone has got to do it, because Newman's voice drives too many people up the wall."

Sales weren't spectacular, but not so bad as to make Stan Cornyn start with the jokey ads.

In 1968, Jerry Leiber and Mike Stoller were planning an album with Peggy Lee. Like a lot of the band singers from the forties, Peggy had seen her sales dip since the advent of rock'n'roll. Her last top ten entry had been 'Fever' back in 1957.

The songs Leiber and Stoller wrote for her were a brave departure. 'Ready To Begin Again', for instance, was written from the point of view of a woman, about the same age as Peggy, who takes her teeth from a glass by the bed and her hair from a drawer before she can face the day. 'Tango' is all steamy sadomasochism: "The tango is done with a thin black moustache, a wide scarlet sash, black boots and a whip."

'Is That All There Is?', is an answer to the question, 'How jaded can a human being become before she spontaneously implodes with *ennui*?' It had a pre-war Berlin *Kabarett*/Kurt Weill feel to it. They approached Randy for an arrangement.

It was Peggy who first suggested Randy's name. "We went to LA to have our initial meeting with Peggy at her home on Tower Grove," said Mike Stoller in the Leiber & Stoller biography *Hound Dog*. "She wanted us to hear a debut album by a musician she liked, Randy Newman. Jerry and I loved Newman's work and thought it would be a great idea if he did the chart for 'Is That All There Is?' We heard in Randy's work an irony and theatricality that we thought appropriate for our song. We were right. Randy's contributions went beyond the scope of what arrangers and orchestrators normally do. I'll be forever grateful to him."

"Randy Newman went to work," James Gavin said in his biography of Peggy Lee. "He thought the song needed something in the front besides the rote and undramatic chords Stoller had written. He threw them out, along with the barroom jauntiness of the demo. As Peggy Lee spoke about watching "the whole world go up in flames" an eerily childlike waltz would play behind her. And when she told of the circus visit that had left her cold, the horn section would play a sinister countermelody in the background. Before they recorded, Newman went to her house to talk things through. Finally, he met Peggy Lee – a singer tarnished by life, faltering commercially, and hoping against hope that his work would save her."

On January 24, 1969, Randy went with Stoller to conduct the orchestra at a night-time recording session at United Studios in Hollywood. Peggy came a day or so later to overdub her vocal. Many artists dress down for recording sessions in rehearsal clothes, something loose and comfortable. Peggy wore a black silk dress, elaborate maquillage and high heels. In her bag she had a bottle of brandy.

"I'll do three takes," she said, "and no more."

When the three takes were in the can, she seemed unable to remember her stipulation, so another take was suggested, then another, and another.

Somewhere around take 15 the bottle came out.

Eventually she reached "an almost 'zen' state" and gave a performance of detached, sublime ennui.

Take 36 was "pure magic". They turned to the engineer and asked for a playback. After a long pause, the engineer spoke the worst seven words anybody can say in a recording studio.

"I forgot to hit the record button."

"What do you mean you forgot to hit the record button?" Jerry screamed.

"This has to be a fuckin' prank. No one forgets to hit the record button. This was the greatest take in the history of takes. Stop joking! Let's hear it! Play the goddam thing!"

But there was no goddam thing to play. Peggy took the news philosophically, either from loyalty to the code of the show business trooper or because she was very, very drunk.

"Guess I'll have to sing it again," she said.

"Take 37 was nothing short of marvellous," Jerry said. "But it's not, nor will it ever be, take 36."

Capitol, the record company, were not overly enthusiastic about the track. Though they released it on a single, they pressed just 1,500 copies. On the label it said, "arranged and conducted by Randy Newman."

Then Peggy sang it on the Joey Bishop show. It took off. By November 8, 1969, it had climbed to number 11 in the *Billboard* Hot 100. It went all the way to the top of the 'Adult Contemporary' Chart and it won Peggy Lee a Grammy for Best Female Pop Vocal Performance.

"I didn't get anything for it," Randy said, "but I never thought it would come out after we did it. I didn't think anything of it."

Chapter Nine

Compared with the first, Randy's second album, *12 Songs*, was a stripped down affair – no orchestra, just a horn section and a small group of favoured musicians including Randy on piano, guitarists Ry Cooder and Clarence White (of the Kentucky Colonels and the Byrds), and drummers/multi-instrumentalists Gene Parsons (of the Byrds) and Jim Gordon (who in that same year was also featured on George Harrison's *All Things Must Pass* and Derek & the Dominos' *Layla And Other Assorted Love Songs*, most memorably playing piano on 'Layla').

Lenny Waronker produced. Van Dyke Parks stepped back from this one. "I know Randy is going to be successful in many vast and important ways," he said, "and it's just natural that I should withdraw from participation with him." It's a statement that can mean a lot of different things, so it's probably best to take it at face value and move quietly on.

Many of the *12 Songs* are steeped in the spirit of Fats Domino, others are straight down the line rhythm and blues. All of them are laden with what Randy liked to call "snide, third person shit."

Rob Burt and Patsy North, in their book *West Coast Story*, describe the songs as being set in suburbia, but not in "the suburbia of Mr and Mrs Jones, the typical suburban couple with two kids and a mortgage to keep", this is "the suburbia of the misfit, the peeping tom, the dropout, the neighbourhood drunkard."

The album essentially covers two meaty themes: racism, and toxic sex.

It opens with the most well-adjusted of the sex songs: 'Have You Seen My Baby', the B-side released by Fats Domino. 'Let's Burn Down The Cornfield', the second track, is a twisted tale of sex and arson. It's also one of Bob Dylan's favourite Randy Newman songs.

"'Burn Down the Cornfield' is where Randy Newman kept it simple," Bob said. "His style is deceiving. He's so laid back that you kind of forget he's saying important things."

'Mama Told Me Not To Come', in which a young innocent finds himself astonished by the sights sounds and smells of a grown-up party, is a song that had appeared three years earlier on Eric Burdon's album. Randy's version is easier to believe. Eric Burdon had looked dissipated since he was about 12. The idea of his being shocked by the appearance of a 'jazz cigarette' or alarmed by the smell of stale perfume was never entirely plausible.* The scant handful of people who'd seen the picture of Randy on the sleeve of his first album – the first picture, with the yellow jumper – could well believe that this man had not done a lot of parties. He sounds terrified even of Ry Cooder's guitar, which is, admittedly, very dirty indeed.

'Suzanne' is a stalker song. "It's my Leonard Cohen but on a lower, immoral level," he said. The protagonist, unlike the one in Cohen's 'tea and oranges' saga, has no interest at all in touching anybody's 'perfect body' with just his 'mind'. He has found Suzanne's name and number in a telephone booth, tracked down her address and now he's "gonna wait in the shadows / for you to come by/ and then I'll jump from the shadows". It's not a song Randy often performs live. "It puts kind of a chill on a show and it's hard to laugh," he said, "although the audience still does, at least a little bit."

'Lover's Prayer' is a nasty version of 'Mr Sandman' ("bring me a dream / make her complexion like peaches and cream") in which the protagonist is a jerk who tailors his needs accordingly: "Don't send me nobody with glasses / Don't want no one above me / Don't send nobody takin' night-classes / Send me somebody to love me."

---

* The French version of the song, 'Maman Viens Me Chercher', recorded by Patrick Topaloff in 1971, sounds like Jean Paul Sartre addressing the *Ecole Doctorale* at the Sorbonne.

'Lucinda' is a death song sung by the girl's bereaved boyfriend. The doomed Lucinda, having celebrated her graduation perhaps a little too much, lies down on the beach and gets, literally, swept away by the beach-cleaning man and his beach-cleaning machine. "It actually happened," Randy said. "A girl got run over by a beach-cleaning truck at the beach I used to go to."

It's another of Bob Dylan's favourites. Bob showed up at one of Randy's early live shows and came backstage afterwards. The two exchanged compliments. Bob mentioned he was thinking of relocating. "I'm thinking of moving out to California," he said. "That song about the beach cleaning... do you think I could write a song like that?"

Randy wondered whether Dylan was taking the piss, but there's no reason to believe he was. Dylan writes some weird shit sometimes.

'Underneath The Harlem Moon' is a problem song in every way imaginable.

By 1970, some of the Civil Rights battles in the US seemed to have been won. Laws had been passed and in some places enforced. But all the laws in the world weren't going to change attitudes and perceptions.

The Black Pride movement had made it clear that equality did not necessarily mean that African-Americans would become nice middle-class white people give or take a skin tone. White kids at the time – the cool ones anyway – understood this perfectly. They didn't want to become nice middle-class white people either.

However, once the initial hurdle of 'we're all one race – the human race' had been vaulted, people of all ethnicities found themselves beset by mini-hurdles, trip-wires and snares. That old standby, "They're just like us, really" was no longer an acceptable liberal position. Who is 'us'? Who is 'they'? How can I respect this 'otherness' without stereotyping it or patronising it. How can I express my own identity without reinforcing the stereotypes? Does it matter?

And, in the white liberal conscience, all this confusion was overseasoned with unhelpful guilt and anxiety. Does saying, 'Elvin Jones is a terrific drummer', make me a racist inasmuch as it might contain within it a suggestion of the stereotype that all people of African descent have 'natural rhythm' – possibly (and this is where the racism gets really offensive) because they are more 'primitive' than whites? If I invite the guy from the next apartment to my party will

I be accused of tokenism? Will he think I'm patronising him? *Will* I be patronising him?

In a 2009 episode of the US sitcom *30 Rock*, Jack Donaghy (Alec Baldwin) is speaking to his mother's Puerto Rican carer Elisa (Salma Hayek). Elisa fears that mother dislikes her. Jack tries to reassure her ...

"It's not because you're a... I'm sorry, what do you call yourself?"

"A Puerto Rican," says Elisa.

"No," says Jack. "I know *you* can say that, but what do *I* call you?"

"A Puerto Rican."

"Wow," says Jack, confused, "that does not sound right."

Back in 1970, the twenty-something college kids and graduates – Randy's demographic – sitting in coffee-houses and seminars were painfully aware that if they weren't part of the solution they were part of the problem. Four or five years before, when they'd marched and maybe seen Doctor King speak, they'd felt part of the solution. But now they were crippled with doubt: and growing increasingly aware that 'crippled' isn't a good thing to say, either. Even being worried was a worry. What did they have to worry about? They weren't single mothers on welfare in the projects.

And then Randy Newman – one of them – drops 'Underneath The Harlem Moon' on them.

It's one of the few covers that Randy ever recorded, written in 1932 by Mack Gordon, a Warsaw-born New York Jew, who also wrote, or co-wrote, 'Chattanooga Choo-Choo', 'The More I See You' and 'There Will Never Be Another You'. At the time it would have passed as an anti-racist song, explaining how people in Harlem had happily left behind the miseries of the past, "They don't live in cabins like the old folks used to do / Their cabin is a penthouse up on Lennox Avenue."

Nevertheless, the bridge, "They just live for dancing / They're never blue or forlorn / It ain't no sin to laugh and grin / That's why darkies were born" – a reference to the song, 'That's Why Darkies Were Born' from *The George White Scandals Of 1931* – inevitably brings a barely-restrained splutter to the liberal throat. It wouldn't be so bad if it wasn't such a seductive bloody tune, sung and played to turn every blue note and augmented fifth into a source of exquisite guilt. The issue is further clouded by the knowledge that many of the records of these apparently racist songs were made by proud black performers. Paul Robeson, the bass-baritone Civil Rights activist who was blacklisted for his Communist sympathies, had a hit with 'That's Why Darkies Were Born'. Billie Holiday sang it, too.

Putting a song like that on a record like this sung by a man like that is a tease and a provocation. It might provoke a nervous laugh of complex understanding and self-recognition: it might provoke utter condemnation from perfectly decent people; it might provoke enthusiastic support from the Ku Klux Klan. At one time or another it's probably provoked all three.

According to Paul Colby, owner of the Bitter End, one night Randy was beaten up outside the club by somebody who took particularly strong exception to his inclusion of the song in his set list. He never had this trouble when he was writing songs for Vic Dana.

'Yellow Man', the first track on side two, rehearses the clichés of racism against a shuffle that makes you know that this racism really is the casual kind. Even the pentatonic intro, doubled at the fourth (*cf.* David Bowie's 'China Girl' and Carl Douglas and Biddu Appaiah's 'Kung Fu Fighting') is a racist cliché. The 'Yellow Man' is "eating rice all day, while the children play". "They say they were there before we were here", Randy sings with an air of sceptical surprise.

It's a little song, thrown away, hardly bothering to engage with the issues it's addressing. It doesn't need to. At the time, the US Air Force was dropping tens of thousands of tons of cluster-bombs and napalm – the incendiary that sticks as it burns – on Vietnamese and Cambodian targets. General William Westmoreland, US Army Chief of Staff, said, "The oriental doesn't put the same high price on life as the westerner. Life is plentiful, life is cheap in the orient, and, as the philosophy of the orient expresses it, life is not important."

In which context, 'Yellow Man' needed no more than a nod in the right direction to make its point. Less is more.

The next track, 'Old Kentucky Home' is potentially another tricky one. It borrows its title and chorus from Stephen Foster's 1853 hit 'My Old Kentucky Home, Good Night'. Foster's original is allegedly an anti-slavery song, but this time Randy is kind enough to replace Foster's line 'Tis summer, the darkies are gay' with 'And the young folks roll on the floor'.

The verses, though, are Randy's own and present vignettes of a delightfully dysfunctional family, told with a sort of tall-tale, front-porch, Mark Twain, mountain humour.

'Rosemary' is disturbing. On paper it could be Romeo singing to his Juliet: he's out on the street, she's up there in her room. It's a standard romantic situation, except the tempo's wrong and the sentiments are suspect in the same way that every elegant line that Romeo gushes, every impulsive action he makes, would be sinister if his thing with Juliet wasn't consensual. You don't actually learn that Randy's protagonist's thing with Rosemary isn't consensual: it's just that he wants her to take her shoes off and come to a place he knows in the park where it's "nice and dark / and I'll hold yours, baby, and you'll hold mine / I'm thinking about you all the time."

'If You Need Oil' – probably the only love song ever written from the point of view of a gas station attendant – is just good old-fashioned *double entendre* in the tradition that goes back to blues singers squeezing lemons and Kenneth Williams going up the Khyber. "I'll wipe your windshield clean," sings the pump monkey. "And I'll fill your tank with gasoline."

'Uncle Bob's Midnight Blues' is a straightforward 12-bar in which the 'third person' is an old drunk, rambling because "That shit that I been using sure confuse my thinking". In the second verse he decides to buy a goat. Along the way, he refers, for no clear reason to other songs, 'Please Don't Talk About Me When I'm Gone', 'When The Blue Of The Night Meets The Gold Of The Day' and 'The Old Chisholm Trail'. It's not a song you'd learn for a party piece.

When he had finished the album, Randy had a massive crisis of self-confidence. He hated it and everything about it. He hated the songs, he hated his voice. His negativity became infectious. Lenny Waronker said he was bringing everybody down so much he had to have him "thrown out of the building".

"Two weeks later he calls up and says, 'Hey, you know? It's not bad.'"

Randy's cousin Tony did the shots for the artwork. The album sleeve is a black and white picture of a house with a wooden fence, a TV set on the lawn, a rocking chair and a child-sized chair in the foreground. On the back, there's a colour shot of Randy and Roswitha, half in shadow with the bright light of a supermarket behind. Randy's carrying groceries. Roswitha's carrying baby Amos. Christmas is coming. The supermarket

"Once you get used to it, his voice is really something."

The Fleetwoods: "While Gary wondered why people told him it was summer Gretchen and Barbara went 'wo' 'wo' 'wo'."
MICHAEL OCHS ARCHIVES/GETTY IMAGES

Harpers Bizarre: Sunshine Pop's "Apples on a stick".
RB/REDFERNS

ene Pitney and Dusty discussing which of them sounded more clinically depressed on Randy's 'Just One Smile'.
IRIS WARE/KEYSTONE FEATURES/GETTY IMAGES

arry Nilsson: "Damned good."
AN MEAGHER/DAILY EXPRESS/HULTON ARCHIVE/GETTY IMAGES

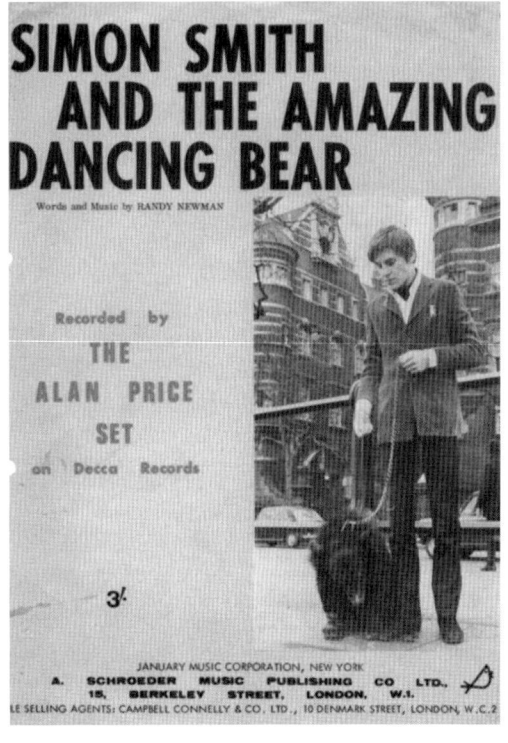

Alan Price: "A lot of children liked it, but so did a lot of messed up Liberals." AUTHORS COLLECTION

Alfred Newman: "All my uncles had massive, Greek, tragic flaws – alcohol or women or gambling...."
BOB LANDRY/THE LIFE IMAGES COLLECTION/GETTY IMAGES

"... Emil had all of them." EVERETT/REX/SHUTTERSTOCK

"The songs are becoming darker," Lenny Waronker said, "a little more grim, perhaps." DICK BARNATT/REDFERNS

Lenny Waronker and Van Dyke Parks: "Go in with a good song and weird it out." MICHAEL OCHS ARCHIVES/GETTY IMAGES

"I want Shea Stadium." EVERETT/REX/SHUTTERSTOCK

ewman gropes down into diseased souls…" VCAEM/GIJSBERT HANEKROOT/REDFERNS

"I do not know if his discoveries frighten him, but they terrify me."
EPARD SHERBELL/CORBIS SABA

Randy, Roswitha and their two oldest boys: "She's real good to me." THE LIFE PICTURE COLLECTION/GETTY IMAGES

1981, the first of Randy's many, many … many Oscar nominations. GEORGE ROSE/GETTY IMAGES

has special offer booze in a fake, snow-covered cottage – "Holiday Parties Start Here!" says the sign.

"I'm interested in that stuff – how people live," Randy said, "And that market, with the fluorescent light, has such a sick, lonely feeling to it, you know?"

In April 1970, when the album was released, the critics stood up to applaud.

"The best I've heard since the Band," said one.

"The full emergence of a leading innovator in rock'n'roll," said another.

"Hopefully, with the release of this album, Randy Newman will no longer have to worry about being misunderstood," said a third.

"While the material is not always as strong as on the first record," said Bruce Grimes in *Rolling Stone*, "*12 Songs* is by far the more successful album. The subtle nuances of the music and the unique phrasing of the singer require careful listening, and Randy's performance is much more effective without complicated orchestration."

Boosted by the reception, Warner Bros. confidently told the press, "Randy Newman is about to become truly famous."

The album bombed.

There were consolations. A month after the album's release, Randy had his first US number one with Three Dog Night's version of 'Mamma Told Me Not To Come'. Three Dog Night, rather than faking the innocence, sing it as though they're terribly glad they ignored Mamma's advice and, far from being alarmed by the orgiastic sights, sounds and smells of the party, join in to the extent that by the end of the song they're practically the life and soul. It stayed in the top ten for nine weeks.

"At first I didn't like the way that they did the song," Randy said. "But when the royalty cheques started drifting in, I figured they might be able to send my son to Harvard."

In June 1970, Randy appeared on NBC's *Liza Minnelli Special*. He sang 'Love Story' from his first album and then sang a duet with Liza on 'So Long Dad'. They didn't seem to bond.

At the studio, Randy watched Ms Minnelli rehearse a dance number. When she'd finished, she asked him if he liked it. He told her she was "a real Mitzi Gaynor out there".

Mitzi Gaynor is a popular singer and dancer, best known for her stunning performance as Nellie Forbush in the film of Rodgers & Hammerstein's

South Pacific. She's 15 years older than Liza. Liza was apparently not impressed by the comparison.

"But I always liked Mitzi Gaynor," Randy said.

Later that year, Randy decided to bite the bullet and play live. Just him and a piano.

"I kinda figured that I might regret it if I didn't try," he told Steve Turner for *Beat International*. "It's kinda nice to hear an audience appreciating what you do. Y'know, the mystique of the floodlights and all that stuff. It's an unusual thing for a human being to be doing, playing in front of a bunch of people, particularly with just a piano.

"But it also makes you lazy in a sense. When you write, you're radical in your way of thinking, you want to keep changing. But when you perform it tends to make you more conservative, like you'll tend to say something that people laugh at and you're so exposed up there that you'll say it again at every concert. There's a degree of artifice involved."

He was booked into smallish venues: The Lion's Share in San Anselmo, north of San Francisco; The Troubadour in Los Angeles; Philadelphia's Main Point; and the Bitter End in New York.

Randy discovered he was good on stage and maybe even enjoyed it. "The first time, I found it difficult. I took some speed. I was playing in a little club up in Northern California and never faced the audience. I was totally paranoid. I gave a horribly repressed performance on my first show because of the stuff I took. After that I didn't find it particularly difficult. Not as hard as writing."

As well as songs from his own two albums and from *Nilsson Sings Newman*, he did Arthur Alexander's 'You Better Move On', Fats Domino's 'Blue Monday' and treated the audience to a couple of his own songs that had never been recorded.

'Lonely At The Top' was a song that Randy had originally written for Frank Sinatra, maybe as a follow up to Frank's big 1969 hit, 'My Way'. "Yeah, it's amazing that I thought he'd do it, and I actually played it for him," he told *Mojo* magazine.

It's about a superstar at the top of his game, complaining that even though he's "been around the world" and had his "pick of any girl" he's nevertheless unhappy. "Listen all you fools out there / Go on love me – I don't care / Oh, it's lonely at the top."

Frank declined.

"I think he was intelligent enough to laugh at the whole premise," Randy said.

So there was never any chance of sleeping with the fishes. But, all the same, it was a pity. "He could have truly got it if he had a sense of humour and he actually was leaning against a lamppost, looking forlorn."

"I played it for Streisand and she said, 'Well ha ha...'. She liked it but thought people would believe she meant it. And it suddenly dawned on me – that's why I'll never exactly win the love of the American public. They want artists to mean what they say."

'Living Without You' is probably one of the starkest, bleakest manifestations of loneliness ever written. It's almost callous. It could make a penthouse-full of tail-wagging puppies throw themselves off the balcony.

'Tickle Me' – a song of toxic sex – is just as bleak in a different way. "What can you do to amuse me, now that there's nothing to do?" asks the lover and answers the question himself. "Why don't you tickle me? ... what a perfect way to kill some time." The subtext being, "You bore me, but I might as well have sex with you, anyway."

'Maybe I'm Doing It Wrong' is a song of sexual anxiety and over-analysis that could be an early Woody Allen routine set to music. "Sometimes I throw off a good one, least I think it is, no, I know it is ... But I shouldn't be thinking at all."

'Last Night I Had A Dream' is a nightmare in a brooding minor-key. There's a vampire and a ghost, but, "you scared me the most" – possibly qualifying it as another song of sexual anxiety. He'd recorded it back when he was doing the first album in 1968 and promo copies of a single were pressed with 'I Think He's Hiding' on the B-side. It was never released.

Russ Titelman and Lenny recorded three nights' worth of performances at the Bitter End.

Mark Trueblood, technician at the Fedco Audio Labs who worked on the recording, said: "I remember Randy Newman coming out to the Fedco truck in a black leather jacket. He introduced himself, met everyone, and talked to the audio engineer a bit. This rarely happened on the other gigs, where the band we were recording would stay holed up in their dressing room with their groupies between sets."

Randy Newman

Oddly, what worked well in the US did not translate to the UK. In October he played the trendy Revolution Club in Bruton Place, Mayfair. He got through 'Lover's Prayer', 'Yellow Man' and 'I Think It's Going To Rain Today', then, dismayed by the lack of response, said goodnight, quietly closed the lid of the piano and left the stage.

Chapter Ten

Sometime, maybe in 1971, a nebulous idea for a movie, or rather a series of short movies strung together, was mooted. The details are hazy. Randy Newman and others – maybe Elton John, maybe Kris Kristofferson – would each be given a ten-minute section to do with as they pleased.

Randy came up with a seafaring saga. He would play a huckster, an old-time carpetbagger, in white suit and dark glasses – "sort of a Warren Beatty brooding part".

His ship would set sail and cross the broad Atlantic to the coast of Africa. There'd be a band on board and when the ship made landfall, the musicians would disembark, set up their instruments and play something cheerful to gather a crowd – something like 'Take Me Out To The Ball Game'.

An entertainment would follow. A tenor would sing 'Does Your Mother Come From Ireland', then the band would go into 'Camptown Races' and the assembled audience would be encouraged to join in with the "doo-dah, doo-dah".

And when they were pumped up with fun and excitement, Randy, the huckster, would make his pitch, encouraging them to set out on a big adventure "across the mighty ocean to the Charleston Bay".

He was recruiting them for the slave trade. He promised them Jesus, watermelon and wine in a land free of lions and mamba snakes.

"In America every man is free to take care of his home and his family," he'd tell them, neglecting the exclusion clauses in the small print.

The movie was never made but the song was not forgotten.

Early in 1972, Randy went into the studio with Lenny Waronker, Russ Titelman and a 45-piece orchestra supervised by Uncle Emil, and they began to make *Sail Away*, certainly his best album to date. Many still regard it as his best ever.

Rolling Stone journalist David Felton was invited into the studio and witnessed Uncle Emil conducting an orchestral piece that sounded, Felton said, like a "Navy hymn or a Mormon Tabernacle spiritual."

The intro to the album's title track, 'Sail Away', could indeed have come from a hymnal, or it could be the love theme from a sanctimonious cowboy movie, with evocations of 'Abide With Me' and the *Largo* (the Hovis bread tune) from Dvorak's 'New World Symphony'. It's airy, healthy outdoor, music.

Then the piano comes in with a repeated nine note riff and Randy sings his huckster slave-trader song, laying on the hard-sell, callously unconscious of history or humanity.

Like 'Underneath The Harlem Moon,' it's a challenge to the liberal sensibilities of his audience and to the knee-jerk, agitprop approach that directed most 'protest' songs. The contradictions pile up – of sense and meaning and consequence and comedy and horror and significance and what the music's doing to your spirit and what the lyrics are doing to your brain: and though the song constantly threatens to collapse into an amorphous mess of pointless insensitivity, miraculously it stays up there, and the listener stays with it, simultaneously uplifted and outraged: 'Springtime For Hitler' but so much more insidious.

The song takes on yet another level of meaning in some of the cover versions. Ray Charles sings it in the weary voice of a 120-year old slave, looking back. Sonny Terry and Brownie McGhee radically reinterpret the song, adding thumb piano and banjo as well as Terry's mouth-harp, and singing with quiet, chilling dignity.

"The songs are becoming darker," Lenny Waronker said, "a little more grim, perhaps. But, you know, that's just where he is at the time."

The working process was as fraught as ever. Randy had frequent crises of confidence and would phone in the middle of the night to cancel the next day's sessions. He would come down with mysterious flu viruses. He would arrange a song, tear it up, write it again, tear it up – over and over.

Lenny and Russ, as well as being producers, had to take on the roles of cheerleader, psychiatrist, bully and mom.

"We have to coax him," Lenny said. "Going over to his house and dragging him out of bed, telling him things like, 'Think of your kids, think of me, think of the company, but do something."

Progress was so slow that to keep product coming Lenny and Russ suggested releasing the Bitter End recordings as a live album. Randy was reluctant. Lenny and Russ accordingly put it out as a promo album, not for sale. It went out to DJs and was an instant hit on FM radio. Some stations played the entire album uninterrupted. Pop fans were outraged that Warner-Reprise were holding back. Randy, reassured, gave it his blessing.

The reviews were rapturous. "Randy has the deepest, most consistent, most original comic vision to be found in pop music today," said *Rolling Stone*.

The plaudits provided encouragement to carry on with the new album, and somehow *Sail Away* got finished.

It opens with the majestic 'Sail Away', followed by 'Lonely At The Top', a studio version of the 'Frank Sinatra' song from his *Live* LP, boosted by tuba, banjo, woodwind and brass.

'He Gives Us All His Love', the song from *Cold Turkey*, is sung with the fond intimacy of a mom telling bedtime stories about Jesus and then, in the choruses, getting carried away by the glory of it all.

'Last Night I Had A Dream', the scary one from the *Live* album, is given added spookiness by Ry Cooder's guitar.

'Simon Smith And The Amazing Dancing Bear' is his own take on the song, just him and piano, sung with a curious glee that could be disguising an infinite cosmic despair.

The first side closes with 'Old Man', a father and son song and a fine example of Randy's command of 'the vocabulary of insensitivity'. The protagonist conspicuously fails to say the right things to his dad – like Irving, a confirmed atheist – at his deathbed. What are the right things to say to a dying atheist, anyway? "Won't be no God to comfort you / You taught me not to believe that lie."

It would be another 18 years before Randy was called upon to visit Irving on his deathbed, at which point the song became more autobiographical than he'd intended it to be.

For comedy fans, and many critics, the stand out track of the album is 'Political Science', which advances the argument that the world would be a much better place if America were to nuke most of it. "It's almost closer to Tom Lehrer type songs that I like to get," Randy told Michael Wale of the London *Times* in 1972. "Oddly enough, I've had that song three or four years and I had never played it till six months ago. I didn't think of it because I felt it was too obvious."

Tom Lehrer is a Mathematics professor, who, in 1958, created something of a stir with his co-written *The Distribution Of The Number Of Locally Maximal Elements In A Random Sample* published in the *Annals of Mathematical Statistics*.

On the side, he was also a pianist and singer who wrote some of the funniest songs ever heard, including 'The Masochism Tango' ("you can raise welts / like nobody else"), 'I Wanna Go Back To Dixie' ("the land of the boll weevil / where the laws are medieval") and 'The Vatican Rag' ("Two, four, six, eight / time to transubstantiate").

He liked quoting Peter Cook about the efficacy of political satire, admiring the "Berlin cabarets of the thirties, which did so much to stop the rise of Hitler and prevent the Second World War."

The similarities between Lehrer and Newman – give or take an ability to come to grips with locally maximal elements in a random sample – do not need underlining, and 'Political Science' is without doubt Randy's most Lehrer-esque work. When he wrote it, as well as fearing it was "too obvious", Randy was worried that its shelf life was limited. He hoped that song would, before long, become a mysterious irrelevancy because, as he said at the time, "we're never going to have an administration this bad again [Richard Nixon was President]. We haven't in 200-some years. I believe in numbers and the odds are against it."

He was wrong, and later had cause to repeat himself, almost word for word, during the George W. Bush administration.

Randy wrote 'Burn On' after seeing footage of the Cuyahoga River in Ohio on fire in 1969. The river was heavily polluted. The pollution was flammable. The inevitable happened. "That's what gave me the idea," Randy told *Billboard*, "and I just wrote it. And the idea of saying 'Cleveland, City of Light' – I mean, I'd been to Cleveland, and I'd stayed in Swingos* and I heard eight car wrecks outside my door on a Saturday night. One guy got wrecked, his car was knocked over. He yelled, 'What happened?' and gets out of his car, and he chases after the car that just knocked him over. It was Cleveland, you know? What the hell!"

'Memo To My Son' is a compromised love song from a father to a son about the way in which men (and women) often struggle with a small child's habit of being a small child 24 hours a day with no let up, and how difficult it is to bond with a creature who's not yet smart enough to know how much smarter you are.

Amos, Randy's eldest, was a toddler when *Sail Away* was made and Eric a baby. The song provides more evidence to confound the notion that he's not an 'autobiographical songwriter'. He can be a lot of different people, but sometimes he's just him.

'Dayton, Ohio – 1903', previously heard on *Nilsson Sings Newman*, is a nostalgia-drenched pretty song, much more suited to Harry than Randy, but here treated with a precise and charming delicacy. The place and date are significant: the Wright brothers were from Dayton and their first ever heavier-than-air flight was in 1903. But suggesting that it's actually a song about the futility of hankering for an idyllic, pre-air-travel, prelapsarian time that almost certainly never existed is probably reading too much into it. It's delivered without a hint of a sneer. The veteran comedian George Burns, who was seven years old in 1903, sometimes featured the song in his live act, almost up to his 100th birthday.

'You Can Leave Your Hat On' is a song of distressed sexuality. The protagonist gives the soubrette precise instruction in how to remove her clothing, insisting that she must ignore the "suspicious minds" that "don't believe in this love of ours". "They don't know what love is / *I* know what love is." It's urged along by a thrusting bass riff with the right hand thumping eight to the bar. "We were really trying for a southern sound," Russ Titelman said, "for a Muscle Shoals feel. We even added horns, hoping to get the Memphis Horns thing going."

During a press conference in Sweden a reporter asked Randy what the song was about: "Fucking," he replied. "A lot of tunes in the guise of romanticism, have mainly fucking behind them."

---

* Swingos Celebrity Inn, Cleveland, Ohio was a must-do on any rock'n'roll tour of the US; described by Ian Hunter of Mott The Hoople as "a place you remember checking in and out of, but you can't remember anything in between."

Most people know the cover versions of the song better than Randy's original. There have been at least 15 altogether, the most famous being Joe Cocker's, used in the film *9½ Weeks*, and Tom Jones', used in *The Full Monty*. The difference is striking. In Randy's version you're fairly certain that the protagonist has either paid for or otherwise coerced the love in his life, and, like a fussy customer in a restaurant, expects his very precise requirement to be respected.

Joe Cocker and Tom Jones both do it as a barnstorming celebration of sexy sexy sex between sexy sexy people.

"You put it in a higher register, and it changes the whole song," Randy said – he does it in the key of E, Joe Cocker and Tom Jones in C. "I could have sung it like that, I can sing it up there. But I don't have the instinct. I meant it to be that. It's not a sexy song."

Etta James took a different approach again with a funked up version arranged by sax-player Trevor Lawrence. "I dug the tune, not just for the sneak-and-creep-around-the-corner groove," she said, "but for the story. The story's a mother! Randy's view of love... Randy's view of everything... is different. There's a hint of danger and intrigue. 'You Can Leave Your Hat On' ain't nothing but slow seduction, with me telling my man just how to undress. I like a song where the woman's telling the man what to do. She wants him to leave the lights on, to take off his shoes, to stand on a chair, raise his arms up and shake 'em high in the air; she wants him to strip, article by article, but, listen here, baby, you better leave your hat on! Randy Newman cracks me up, and today, 20 years later, I'm still singing his witty, wild-ass songs!"

'God's Song (That's Why I Love Mankind)' is a slow, minor drag. The lyric runs along the same sort of lines as 'He Gives Us All His Love' but proposes a less passive deity. This God burns cities, slays children, deliberately does nothing when the desperate and plague-ridden turn to him for help and guidance, principally because he's amused by their response: still they worship and adore him. And that's why he loves mankind.

"This is a song in which God is going to speak to you through me," Randy says, by way of introduction when he performs the song live. "I know. It's a surprise. You would have thought he would have chosen Paul McCartney or somebody." (Sometimes he says Dylan.)

Irving, Randy's dad, was an 'aggressive atheist'. In comparison, Randy's a model of tolerance. He told David Felton a story about a girl he used to

Maybe I'm Doing It Wrong

know calling him just before he went on stage to tell him that Jesus had come into her life and made her happy. "I said, 'Well, uh, I'm glad you're happy now, Libby.' She said, 'Yes, I'm happy now I've found Jesus.' And I said I didn't know he was lost.

"And she just kept going, you know, like I hadn't said anything. She was a different person. But she was happy. I believe in not hurting anybody, and not, uh, talking to 'em too long on the fucking phone. That kills me, it wears me out – long phone calls. I don't know what I believe in."

To celebrate the launch of *Sail Away* in May 1972, Pete Marino, a Warner's promo man, had 2,000 model aeroplanes launched from the roof of a San Francisco radio station. This was, perhaps, not the most appropriate or even interesting stunt, but all the same it was a vast improvement on his previous effort, which was to publicise White Witch's eponymous first album by launching 200 pigeons from the roof of a record store. Unfortunately, nobody spotted – or if they spotted, they failed to mention – that the birds' wings had been clipped. Thanks to the speedy intervention of the American Humane Association, emergency operations and patient nursing, many of the pigeons survived, but the vets' bills almost bankrupted Warners'.

The planes, luckily, brought no fatalities to beast nor human.

Stephen Holden in *Rolling Stone* called *Sail Away*, "Newman's most mature album, a work of genius, confirmation – as if any more were needed – of the fact that Newman is our most sophisticated art-song composer and also the most self-consciously American."

Mark Leviton in *Words And Music* said, "Randy's moaning voice is once again the perfect blend of pleading docility and off-the-cuff insanity" and "The Ace of Acuity Strikes Again!"

"God, Randy Newman can write a song," said *Playboy*.

"Incisive, pithy, satiric, nostalgic," said *Billboard*.

It was his best-selling album so far – 120,000 copies on its initial US release.

He played London again, this time, in stark contrast to his previous outing at The Revolution, in the salubrious surroundings of the Royal Festival Hall. He was a hit. Michael Wale in the *Times* described him as having "captured London… bringing a touch of satire into pop."

Brian Wilson of the Beach Boys acquired his copy of *Sail Away* a month or so after its release – around the time of his thirtieth birthday. He was in a bad mental state at the time. Though too bleary to fully participate in the Beach Boys' activities, he'd travelled to Amsterdam with the others in order to be around while they recorded their album *Holland*. He stayed in his hotel room most of the time and Randy's album became the soundtrack to his sombre mood, providing him with a strange and mystical inspiration.

"I just sat around and drank apple sap – that's like apple cider," he said. "And I just sat around and dreamed. And one night I was listening to that Randy Newman album called *Sail Away*. So I started playing the album and I was sitting there with a pencil and I started writing. And I found that if I kept playing the Randy Newman album, I could stay in that mood. It was the weirdest thing. I wrote the whole fairy tale while listening to that album."

The 'fairy tale' was a confection called 'Mount Vernon And Fairway (A Fairy Tale)'. It failed to engage the other Beach Boys, but it eventually got recorded and released as an EP to accompany the album.

It's a mostly spoken story of a Prince and a magic transistor radio that can fly into trees. The sound effects alone would get a BBC radio drama producer fired on the spot.

Chapter Eleven

In 1969, Merle Haggard released a song called 'Okie From Muskogee' which went, "We don't smoke marijuana in Muskogee / We don't take our trips on LSD / We don't burn our draft cards down on Main Street / We like livin' right and bein' free."

Hippies everywhere wondered whether it was real or a put on. The jury is still out. It was however, just one of an accumulating number of signs that a tectonic shift was taking place in the zeitgeist. The South, it seemed, was Rising Again.

The North had been sniggering about the South ever since Lee and Grant shook hands at Appomattox. Just as, to a certain kind of Englishmen, the French are beret-wearing garlic-stinkers who cannot be trusted with anything sharper than a croissant, to a certain kind of Northerner, 'down there' they kicked a lot of shit, played banjos all day, didn't have the sense of a fence-rail and saw lynching as a healthy multi-racial activity. At least the rural backwoods southerners did ("although wouldn't that be everybody? Did they actually *have* towns in the South? I mean, proper towns with paved streets and no spitting?").

Elvis was a worry to the civilised people of New York and Boston not primarily because he wiggled his hips in a way that intimated that he'd done it and liked it, nor because of the fear that his 'jungle music' might undo centuries of painstaking repression, but because he was a southerner. Enough said. He was a southern, rural primitive – the overt sexuality, the lack of moral intelligence, the strangely arousing backbeat were just part of the package. His truly unforgivable crime was being born in an unforgivable place – a shotgun shack a good few hundred yards on the wrong side of the tracks in Tupelo, Mississippi.

Common, as they say in Rochdale, as muck.

In 1956, *Life* magazine, being nice, called him a "Howling Hillbilly Success". *Time* magazine, in a piece published at around the same time, could not resist making some reference to his outlandish accent every couple of sentences, and captioned a photo "Hi luh-huh-huh-luv yew-hew". *Newsweek* described an early, unsuccessful show in Las Vegas as "a jug of corn liquor at a champagne party".

And the more the North ridiculed him, the more the South loved him. He was their boy.

Irish homes in the fifties and sixties often sported photos of the Pope and the Count (John McCormack, the Irish tenor) above the mantelpiece. White homes in Mississippi, Tennessee, Arkansas and Alabama had Elvis up there. He was conquering the world, staying true to his roots and he was one of their own.

By the early seventies, signs of a southern resurgence were everywhere.

Maybe Mr Dylan started it with his 1968 album, *John Wesley Harding*, recorded in Nashville with pedal steel guitar and his terrier bark coated in honey like a wayward baritone at a drunks' wedding trying to add a little gravity to the occasion by making up quasi-Southern Baptist holy-roller lyrics about St Augustine, the Judas Priest and the Watchtower.

That same year the Byrds, with new addition Gram Parsons (from Florida via Georgia), released *Sweetheart Of The Rodeo* which was pretty much uncluttered, straight down the line country music. After Parsons left to form the Flying Burrito Brothers, guitarist Clarence White (from Maine via California but marinated in Kentucky bluegrass and the sweet techniques of Nashville string-bending), joined the Byrds. Meanwhile they'd even had the nerve to play the Grand Ole Opry with their long hair and drug-related smiles – just the once.

The year after that, Mr Dylan tightened his embrace on all things southern with *Nashville Skyline*, on which he duetted with Johnny Cash and told us, just as he had once told us that he could see through the masks of the masters of war, that now, oh me, oh my, he loved that country pie.

Maybe I'm Doing It Wrong

And his friends, the Band – all Canadians except for drummer Levon Helm who was from Elaine, Arkansas – released an eponymous album in which, developing an idea they'd played with on *Music From Big Pink*, they invented the kind of music to which Confederate soldiers and their best girls might have danced if they'd had rock'n'roll back in 1865, and Telecasters and Hammond organs and reverb had been invented. "Virgil, quick, come see, there goes Robert E. Lee," they sang.

The floodgates opened. Laid back southern boogie with backbone-slipping guitar riffs, a moderate amount of chicken pickin' and the bracing smell of crowded barrooms and empty liquor bottles spread to places where the fulvous duck never whistled – like Boston dorm rooms, the Guildford branch of Dorothy Perkins and the developing consciousness of Jeremy Clarkson.

Even non-southerners, like George 'Commander Cody' Frayne from Boise, Idaho, and Lowell "Little Feat" George from Hollywood, California, felt obliged to role-play a Tennessee Lamb while another played Dixie Chicken. And if there were worries about the political implications or racial sensibilities of all this, the tripe-face boogie was always on hand to boogie your scruples away.

The battle lines were drawn when Neil Young, from Toronto, Canada, put a song called 'Southern Man' on his 1970 album, *After The Goldrush*, which, among other slights, suggested that the South was a semi-wasteland where he heard "screamin'and bullwhips cracking". He went one step further on his 1972 album, *Harvest*, when in 'Alabama' he says of the state: "You got the weight on your shoulders / That's breaking your back ... What's going wrong?" In reply to both songs Lynyrd Skynyrd, a band formed in Jacksonville, Florida who felt comfortable playing in front of a Confederate flag backdrop, released 'Sweet Home Alabama'. "Well I hope Neil Young will remember," they sang, "A Southern man don't need him around anyhow."

It was Fort Sumter all over again.

Randy, who considered himself half-southern and thus ideally positioned to be arbitrator and peacemaker, decided to pour a little oil on to the troubled waters, and then maybe set fire to it.

There was a two-year silence after *Sail Away*. Other acts felt pressure to strike while the iron was hot by releasing four singles and two albums a year and constantly touring. Luckily, Randy's iron had never been more than tepid.

"I've been doing a concert every once in a while, but mostly I've been doing nothing, just reading and playing with the kids."

"Actually, I could quit both writing and performing and just do nothing at all," he told Bruce Pollock. "I'm capable of doing absolutely nothing for long periods of time without much remorse. Recently I've overcome my guilt about it, which had always acted as a goad. But every once in a while I'll wake up and say, 'Jesus Christ, what a waste. What a big talent I used to be, like a meteor across the sky.'"

He wasn't entirely idle. One night he caught *The Dick Cavett Show* on ABC – a talk show, taped in New York. Cavett's guests that night included Jim Brown, the African-American fullback for the Cleveland Browns, the writer Truman Capote and the governor of Georgia, Lester Maddox.

Lester Maddox was a working class man-of-(some of)-the-people. He had chased black customers out of his fried chicken restaurant and then, when the Civil Rights Act was passed in 1964, preferred to sell the restaurant rather than serve them. In 1966, he was elected governor of Georgia, and in 1968 had caused a storm when he refused to close the state capitol for the funeral of Martin Luther King.

To Cavett, Maddox was a joke, a walking stereotype, a hick who had more in common with Deputy Dawg ("Dagnabbit") than a regular human being.

At one point during the interview, Cavett made a reference to the "bigots" who had elected Maddox. This provoked some argy-bargy. Maddox demanded an apology ("You apologize, sir, to the people of Georgia!"). After more argy-bargy, Cavett agreed to apologize to those Georgians who had supported Maddox who might not be bigots.

Not satisfied, Maddox left the studio. Truman Capote, a southerner himself by birth, but one who had lived in New York since childhood and thus passed muster, watched Maddox walk, then drawled, "I've been to his restaurant and his chicken isn't that finger lickin' good."

The show drew more hate mail than any other in Cavett's distinguished career.

Randy was among the horrified. "He (Maddox) wasn't even given a chance to prove what an idiot he was. [...] Now, I hate everything that he stands for, but they didn't give him a chance to be an idiot. And here he is, governor of a state – these people elected him in Georgia, however many million people voted for him – and I thought that if I were a

Georgian, I would be angry. I would be angry anyway, even if I were a nice, liberal, editor of the journal in Atlanta."

Randy put his anger into a song, 'Rednecks', in which he took the role of an outraged Georgian Maddox supporter. "Last night I saw Lester Maddox on a TV show / with some smart-ass New York Jew* / And the Jew laughed at Lester Maddox / And the audience laughed at Lester Maddox, too."

The song, though it states with vile pride, "We're rednecks, we're rednecks / we don't know our ass from a hole in the ground / we're rednecks, we're rednecks / and we're keeping the n*****s down", is at pains to point out that for all their holier-than-thou posturing, northern whites are no less bigoted than southerners; and though they talk of 'dignity' and 'freedom' what that means in practice is that the black-skinned man is, "free to be put in a cage in Harlem in New York City" and goes on to list all the other places in the North where he's "free to be put in a cage": the South and West side of Chicago, Hough in Cleveland, East St Louis, Fillmore San Francisco and Roxbury in Boston."

"There are some mistakes in [the song]," Randy said, later. "Like, that guy wouldn't know the names of all those ghettos, but, so what. But I wrote the song, and Northerners have recognized ever since that they are as guilty of prejudice as the people of the South."

The song's liberal use of the word n******** has, with the passage of time, become even more shocking.

"To me, the justification for a white person to use that word is a very narrow window," Randy said. "I thought I needed it for the song, but I was never that comfortable with it. I don't like writing it down, I don't like saying it and I hate hearing it, but not in the context of the song. It still isn't OK for any white person to say the word, almost never."

The Cavett show and the song led Randy to create a character – a blue collar white Southerner he called Johnny Cutler. Johnny, like Randy at the time, was coming up to his thirtieth birthday. He was a mill worker in Birmingham, Alabama with a drink problem and a wife called Marie.

---

* Later in an interview, Cavett, commenting on being called a "smart-ass New York Jew" said, "Yeah, I'm two out of three of those things" – his granddad was a Welsh Baptist minister.

**The authors feel almost as uncomfortable using weasely asterisks as they would spelling the word in full, but, having taken authoritative advice, have gone for weasely.

In February 1973, Randy went into the studio with Russ Titelman and started recording demos for an album – working title, *Johnny Cutler's Birthday*, a day in the life of a redneck. While the tape ran, Randy sketched out ideas, sitting at the piano, setting the scenes. "This begins with the sound of children playing... possibly some boys playing football... and, in the distance, a park band concert. Johnny Cutler and his daughter are at the park, presumably sitting on a bench or something. After he loses his temper, she goes off, and it quiets. He sings..."

Randy launches into 'Rednecks'.

"I don't want to preach" he told *Billboard*. "I want the person to make the best case he can make. In 'Rednecks,' the guy's making a case, a good case, and yet he's not... well, would you want to be his neighbour?"

There's a God song, 'If We Didn't Have Jesus (We Wouldn't Have No One At All)'.

Then the story moves to Johnny's birthday party, where the guys tell tales of the old days. They tell him about the Louisiana floods in 1927. Johnny gets drunk, rambles and tells them about his late father, a barber (like Randy's grandfather) who used to cut the hair of Dixie Howell, an Alabama-born sporting hero who played both professional football and baseball in the 1930s.

In 'My Daddy Knew Dixie Howell' Johnny addresses his dead dad. It's a song of crushed dreams and drunken pride set to a medium-tempo waltz, the kind of tune that will be familiar to British music fans from music-hall models of insensitivity like 'Don't Jump Off The Roof, Dad, You'll Make An 'Ole In The Yard' and 'A Muvver Was Barfing Her Baby One Night'.

When Johnny was born, his father put a football in his crib. When daddy died, Johnny put a razor in his coffin – the tools of his barber trade. Daddy didn't have much of a life, but he did once get to cut Dixie Howell's hair. And the smell of magnolias at his funeral was overpowering. "Tomorrow I will be sober, Daddy," Johnny sings, paraphrasing Winston Churchill, WC Fields or, possibly, someone much, much earlier than either, "And you will still be dead."

The party disintegrates into a drunken revel and Johnny, now very drunk, tells his wife, 'Marie', that he loves her – a sentiment that he is only capable of expressing when he is drunk.

Marie's position is made clear in the bitter complaint 'Shining'. She phones Johnny's mother and remembers "shining in the sun like gold";

but ending up with a "baby cryin'… laundry waitin' for me on the line."

In 'Good Morning', Marie wishes Johnny a Happy Birthday and encourages the children to do the same. Johnny's hungover reply is an unvarying 'Fuck Off'. "Now daddy may not spend much time with us (Fuck Off) / but I'm sure he loves you a lot."

In 'Doctor, Doctor' we hear that Johnny's brother (an individual even more screwed up than Johnny) has got himself locked up in an institution. Johnny goes to see his brother's doctor and explains something of the way his family and upbringing were to blame for the way in which he and his brother turned out. When Johnny gets home (presumably without securing his brother's release) he tells Marie how his brother came to be incarcerated: he had been caught wandering around the city naked after stealing an old lady's handbag.

Another song recorded on the demo was a rendition of the Albanian national anthem that was to be sung by the West Point Glee Club. There seemed to be some uncertainty as to how this would fit in with the rest of the project, but Randy thought maybe it would be on the TV in the background. "I haven't decided whether to include this," Randy tells the tape machine. "Who the fuck am I talking to anyway? Who's gonna hear this?"

Nobody. Not for a while, anyway. Although many of the songs from *Johnny Cutler* made it to Randy's next album, *Good Old Boys*, the demos remained the stuff of legend among hardcore Randy fans until their appearance as bonus tracks on the *Good Old Boys* 2002 CD re-release. "If I had a career to worry about destroying, I wouldn't let them put this out," Randy wrote in the liner notes. "It was never meant for anyone to hear. They should have waited until I was dead."

Some of the songs were previewed when Randy revisited the UK in the summer of 1974 to put in an appearance on BBC2's *Old Grey Whistle Test* and play the Theatre Royal, Drury Lane. He mentioned the new album he was working on. "It [the album] is constructed around the American South where Mr Newman spent much of his youth," Michael Wale announced in his *Times* review of the gig. "Judging by the briefest of previews he gave us on Sunday, the new work lives up to his driest reputation. It is in this dry sardonic approach to life, mirroring no doubt his own outwardly nonchalant approach to his career, that he is heard at his best. Often his asides tell you most about his attitudes.

'How can you applaud for this, you never heard it before' he growls mockingly.

"The manner of delivery is deferential, containing an honesty not often found in rock these days, as Mr Newman sits there at the piano peering up through pebble glasses at the shambles of the world around him."

Rob Partridge, in *Melody Maker*, was more grudging about the concert. "As a performer," he wrote, "Newman's hardly likely to qualify for the world's greatest talent. His voice strains too much for the high notes, his piano playing is, well, only adequate. But he has an ability to transform those limitations and turn them to his own advantage."

It took 18 months or so for *Johnny Cutler* fully to transmute into *Good Old Boys*. The story was abandoned along with Johnny Cutler – at least as a character with a name and a consistency – but the ideas, the themes and many of the songs remain.

Good Old Boys is about southern whites. It's about poverty and futility, alienation, racism, political corruption, stereotypes, madness and strong drink. It shows a region haunted by its past. Randy was taking his role of half-southern fair-minded arbiter seriously.

"If I had the civility of a Southerner that would be nice," he told Timothy White in *Billboard*. "It's a disappearing trait, but they do have that, you know: just for hellos and thank yous and how are you todays? They're better. They are ready to like you.

"There are a few subjects they're bad on: Jews and blacks and gun control. It's like getting all As and a couple of Fs. It's one of those ancient things, but they do go deeper with people than we do in the rest of the country: they always did. They just had it written down on walls: No Coloured. No Blacks, No Jews. Boston didn't have it written down, LA didn't have to write it down and LA is segregated – there's no doubt about it."

Lenny Waronker, in the sleeve notes for the 1998 box-set *Guilty: 30 Years Of Randy Newman*, said: "*Good Old Boys* is like a John Ford film, like *Grapes Of Wrath*. It created an environment. And it was small in a positive sense – it didn't veer off and try to be a lot of things. It was one powerful idea that resonated in many different ways – an acutely visual, cinematic moment in musical history. You actually see those characters, feel the dust."

Maybe I'm Doing It Wrong

As before, Lenny co-produced with Russ Titelman. Other musicians were the best that LA could offer, Jim Keltner and Andy Newmark on drums, Red Callendar and Willie Weeks (and sometimes Russ Titelman) on bass, Al Perkins on pedal steel and, for one track only, Ry Cooder on slide guitar. Don Henley and Glen Frey from the Eagles showed up, too, and sang backing vocals.

"We had a tremendous amount of fun doing that," Don Henley told *Billboard*. "When we were at the microphone singing, the comments that would come out of the booth were hilarious. Lenny Waronker would serve as the straight guy and Randy would be the funny guy. He's very self-effacing about his singing ability. When we sang background, he'd say we should sing like him – 'like a water buffalo'. But that crippled quality in his singing is what works really well for him."

The album opens with 'Rednecks', the Lester Maddox/Dick Cavett song. Its violence and anger infects everything that comes after – or at least it did in the days when sequencing mattered. Like the action sequence at the start of a Bond film, it establishes the mood of the piece, gives you a taste of what's to come. It's a nailing of colours, a threadbare, blood-stained Stars and Bars, that casts a sinister shadow over the blandest, most innocent sentiments in the rest of the album.

And then again, just like in an action movie, after the explosive opening comes the exposition.

In 'Birmingham', we learn something of our protagonist – previously known as Johnny Cutler, now nameless. He works in a steel mill and lives in a three room house with a wife and family and a big black dog called Dan. Without the first track, the song could easily be a song of civic pride, on a par with 'I Left My Heart In San Francisco' or 'I Belong To Glasgow': a hymn to modest decency and honest hard work.

But at the same time we know, or at least suspect, that the 'I' of the second song is also the 'I' of the first song – the man who saw Lester Maddox on TV and thought "he may be a fool but he's our fool"; in which context, the exhortation to the dog – "the meanest dog in Alabam'" – to "Get 'em Dan", an apparently everyday, affectionate thing to say to a pooch who likes chasing rabbits, takes on an uneasy ambiguity.

Bull Connor, the Birmingham Commissioner for Public Safety had, in 1963, authorised attack dogs to be loosed on Civil Rights activists. During the same demonstrations, Martin Luther King was arrested and spent eight days in Birmingham jail. Later that same year, the Ku Klux Klan bombed the 16th Street Baptist Church, killing four young girls – one was 11, the other three 14 – and injuring 22 other people. "Birmingham, Birmingham, the greatest city in Alabam'."

"Get 'em, Dan."

The third track, 'Marie', is a tale of damaged love, of failure, guilt and incompetence. The lyrics matched with one of the sweetest tunes Randy ever wrote. Russ Titelman cried when he first heard it sung by Randy "in his little workroom in his house in Pacific Palisades. [...] Randy wrote it about a girl named Marie he was once madly in love with; it's like a Stephen Foster song."

The track is blessed with a string arrangement by Liberty/Warner regular Nick De Caro in which any excess sentimentality is undermined by the occasional flattened seventh in the bass to let us know that all is not what it seems.

The protagonist sings to his wife. He's drunk, he confesses he's a hopeless husband, "weak" and "lazy", but insists, as only a drunk can, that he loves her: "You're a flower, you're a river, you're a rainbow." He could be any drunk man singing to his wife anywhere in the world at any time in history. And the tune helps us know that, right now, he means every word he says. But, to paraphrase Johnny Cutler's words to his dead dad, "Tomorrow I'll be sober, and your life will still be shitty."

'Mr. President (Have Pity On The Working Man)' brings some wider political context to the protagonist's life. It was recorded on the day that Nixon finally owned up, did the decent thing and resigned, the first US President ever to do so. It had taken the exposure of the Watergate scandal, two years of bitter public debate, deliberate obstruction of justice and sustained lying, but at last the mendacious bastard had gone.

"By taking this action," Nixon said in his address from the Oval Office, "I hope that I will have hastened the start of the process of healing which is so desperately needed in America," as if the cause of the illness lay elsewhere.

This, then, was the government that our protagonist was supposed to rely on for understanding and justice.

"It is cold and the wind is blowing / We need something to keep us going / Mr President have pity on the working man." As if.

'Guilty' is a companion piece to 'Marie', a drunk/stoned exercise in self-pity and self-justification.

Maybe I'm Doing It Wrong

Side two opens with 'Louisiana 1927', a song about the floods of that year. The strings play a theme that could be a banjo warming up or maybe a quote from 'Zip Coon', or Copland's *Corral Nocturne* or 'Ol' Man River', or the 1911 Arthur Collins song 'Steamboat Bill' – then goes into a variation on the nine note piano riff that underpinned 'Sail Away'.

"What has happened down here is the winds have changed," sings the narrator, like an on the spot weather reporter, "Clouds roll in from the north and it started to rain."

All bad things come from the north. In 1927 the Mississippi River overtopped the levees, flooding an area of 27,000 square miles up to a depth of 30 feet, leaving nearly 250 dead and many thousands homeless. It was the worst flooding the USA had ever known. Seven states were affected and there was a general feeling that the government and the rest of the US had abandoned the South. "They're trying to wash us away, they're trying to wash us away."

There is a theory that the wealthier parts of the city of New Orleans survived because the old elite French families ordered the strategic use of dynamite to ensure the water went elsewhere.

"The Bosses in New Orleans probably were behind the decision to let it flood there," Randy explained, "diverting the water away from the city. Anyway, the cotton fields were wiped out, changing America forever, disemploying hundreds of thousands of black field workers, most of whom held 'executive positions' in the cotton industry, meaning they were allowed to wear gloves while picking."

The next couple of songs are about the man who – possibly and in a roundabout way – helped Randy's dad find a place to study medicine, an event that led to Irving meeting Dixie and, ultimately, to Randy's birth.

Huey 'The Kingfish' Long was Governor of Louisiana from 1928-32 and a Senator for Louisiana from 1932-5. He was a Democrat who gained hero-status as saviour of the poor whites and blacks of Louisiana – increasing their voting rights by removing a poll tax that had served as a qualification. He built schools and gave them free text books, he instituted adult education, built hospitals and paved 13,000 miles of road. He also sold civic offices and jobs, and was never too meticulous about balancing the books.

Randy's aunt worked for Huey for a while and, presumably, like most state employees, was expected to pay a percentage of her wages into Huey's political fund. "If he was your friend, he'd help you," said a political rival. "If you were his enemy he'd stomp you down."

Huey went head to head with the oil companies when he tried to impose a 5c-a-barrel tax to pay for his programmes. There were moves to impeach him for misuse of state funds and use of "abusive language". Huey countered that the legislators had been offered as much as $25,000 for their votes to remove him from office – enough money, as he put it, "to burn a wet mule".

He was elected Senator and went to Washington. "I'm small fry here in Washington," he said. "But I'm the Kingfish to the folks down in Louisiana."

Gerald LK Smith, an ally of Huey's and head of the national "Share Our Wealth" organization, predicted that "the only way they will keep Huey Long from the White House is to kill him."

Huey Long was assassinated in Louisiana in 1935 outside the capitol building, allegedly by the son-in-law of a political rival, Judge Benjamin Pavy.

As a propagandist, Huey understood the power of music. One of his pals was Castro Carazo, the Costa Rican dance band leader at the Roosevelt Hotel in New Orleans. Huey gave Castro the job of running the University of Louisiana Tiger Marching Band and encouraged him to increase its strength from 28 to nearly 250.

Castro wrote songs and tunes for the band, often in collaboration with Huey. 'Touch Down LSU' was one of theirs. 'Miss Vandy: Dedicated To The Co-Eds Of Vanderbilt University' was another. ("The campus lights are gleaming bright at dear old Vanderbilt tonight and as the twinkling starlight gleams, I see the co-ed of my dreams".)

Not long before Huey was cut down, he and Castro had put together a stirring campaign song for his re-election, 'Every Man A King', which set out his 'Share Our Wealth' manifesto: "With castles and clothing and food for all / All belongs to you / Every man a king."

Randy and Lenny searched high and low to find an original recording of Huey Long singing it, without success. In the end Randy, Lenny and Russ Titelman with Don Henley and Glen Frey formed an impromptu chorus. "Randy was sort of conducting us while we were singing," said Lenny. "We must have done it 15 or 18 times on different tracks, and built up a men's choir that sounded like an LSU fraternity. Here we were singing these lyrics and we've just watched this guy [Richard

Nixon] resign as president, first time it ever happened. I can remember laughing real hard. Randy was looking at us with raised eyebrows, and at the same time we were singing 'Every Man A King'. It was an odd thing."

'Kingfish' is Randy's troubled tribute to the man who, had he become president, might indeed have had pity on the working men of the South. It trumpets the triumphs of Huey Long, pours scorn on the "Frenchmen in New Orleans" who wouldn't care if your baby drowned, reminds everybody how he 'whipped the asses' of "Standard Oil men" to ensure that the state would be run by "little folks like me and you".

"The Kingfish gonna save this land."

The idea for the next song came from a story told to Randy by Alan Adashek, a childhood friend to whom Randy dedicated his 2008 album *Harps And Angels*.

A certain individual, went the story, was accused of stealing a woman's purse while naked. The man came up with the most implausible defence in legal history. At the time of the robbery, he said, he was naked in the bedroom of a woman who wasn't his wife. The woman's husband came home unexpectedly, so he jumped out of the window and ran down the street, still naked. On the street, he encountered *another* naked man, also running, who handed him a purse and ran off into the night.

'Naked Man' was released as a single – a B-side anyway – and shows evidence of monkeying about with cutting edge production techniques, an attempt, perhaps, to make it conform to the perceived requirements of a mid-seventies 'hit'.

It was a time when great strides were being made in the whizz-bang recording technology business. No studio could be considered well-equipped unless it could handle 24-tracks of overdubs and took delivery, almost every week, of some new bit of kit that did something – flanging, phasing, automatic double tracking, 'enhancing'. Sometimes nobody knew what the black boxes did, but all the same they sat there in the racks, their knobs tempting, their lights blinking.

Randy's records tended to avoid fancy effects. To their credit, they usually sounded like a man singing in a room accompanied by some musicians. Impeccably recorded, but never fancy. "I know a lot more about how to handle an orchestra than I do about guitar sounds," Randy said. "I know nothing about getting different sounds in a studio and I've never been interested either."

"There are times when I'm recording that I'll complain to Lenny that I just wanna make a regular record like everyone else you hear on the radio," he told *Melody Maker* in 1974. "But then I find that when I double my voice, or when I put a lot of echo on it, I just don't like the result. I can't live with it. So I just go back to the old way of doing it."

'Naked Man' is an exception. Listen carefully and there's a hint of delay on the voice – a little slapback echo. Listen more closely and you'll hear a whistling sound something that isn't quite flutes. Is it tin whistles or a wheezing organ?

What happened was this: after laying down the vocal and rhythm track, Randy, Russ and Lenny took the tapes to Malibu where at the time visionary British geniuses Malcolm Cecil and Robert Margouleff kept TONTO (The Original New Timbral Orchestra), a synthesizer – or rather a grafting of several synthesizers – which looked like a larger and more complicated version of the flight deck of the Starship Enterprise.

Stevie Wonder had used TONTO on his previous three albums, all of which went top five. If ever there was such a thing as a hit-making machine, it seemed, this was it.

As Malcolm Cecil told David Kastin in *Song of the South*, his book about the making of *Good Old Boys*: "Once he [Cecil] and Margouleff had adjusted various filters and circuits to come up with the sounds that conveyed the feel Randy was looking for, the songwriter sat down at the keyboard, and three or four hours later the track was in the can."

The "feel Randy was looking for", you'll notice, sounds uncannily like a primary school recorder lesson.

'A Wedding In Cherokee County' is a song of sexual and romantic wretchedness. It derived its inspiration, Randy said, from the 'Albanian Anthem' on the *Johnny Cutler's Birthday* project. Having eventually abandoned the Albanian Anthem because, "I didn't have enough information", he first turned it into an Albanian wedding song, then relocated it to Cherokee County, Georgia (the place "Where Metro Meets The Mountains").

It's about the daughter of a midget and a whore marrying a man who fears that when he carries his bride across the threshold "she will laugh at my mighty sword". ("Why must everyone laugh at my mighty sword?")

'Back On My Feet Again' grew out of 'Doctor Doctor', another of the *Johnny Cutler* songs. It's Johnny's crazy brother's plea to be released from the institution in which he's incarcerated. There's a whole world of excitement going on out there that he wants to be a part of. His sister married a black man who subsequently revealed he was in fact a rich white millionaire who disguised his race and financial standing to test that her love was true. He's now teaching her how to play polo and how to water ski. So, please, "Open the door and set me free / Get me back on my feet again."

The album ends with 'Rollin'', an easy loping tune about the virtues of kicking back with a glass or two and leaving your worries behind. British listeners who, in 1974, returned from HMV and played the record through for the first time were glad of this last track. Having been through laughter, tears, shock, confusion, heartache and outrage, they were probably a bit overwrought and needed calming down. All the same, it was the best £2.45 they'd ever spent.

Russ Titelman approached the art director and photographer Mike Salisbury to design the sleeve. Mike had just designed the cover for Ry Cooder's album (Ry was married to Russ' sister Susan, but that's neither here or there).

The original submission was a shot of Randy at the piano – all curls and aviator specs. It failed to spark much enthusiasm, but Mike had another shot better suited to the album's themes: a picture he'd taken in the bar at Atlanta International Airport on his way home to LA. It was an out-of-focus shot of a middle-aged white man in a crumpled suit and dark sunglasses, his arm draped around a tired-looking blonde. They look as if they've been in the bar since opening time. Between the fingers of one hand, the man holds a cigarette burned down to its filter. In the other is a glass. His shirt has a sheen to it, as does his necktie.

On the back of the sleeve, you get the lyrics, and two small black and white pictures: one of Randy, the other of Huey P. 'The Kingfish' Long.

Good Old Boys was released in 1974 to the, by now customary, rave reviews.

Billboard went with, "A coherent, well done, most definitely deserving of exposure album." *Rolling Stone* with, "It mystifies, it confuses, it entertains, it swings. You don't know whether to laugh or cry, and that is Randy Newman's rare and bizarre skill." Clive James in *Creem* wrote: "There is nothing consoling about Newman's work except its quality. But that, needless to say, is all the consolation art need ever offer. Every year *Rolling Stone* expresses the commercially devout hope that Randy

Newman will make it. The wish is an irrelevance. Newman has already made it, and the real question is whether anybody else will."

It even got reviewed in *Country Music* magazine by Dave Hickey – who, as well as being a country music fan and critic, held an MA in Linguistics, had been a gallery owner, was for a while executive editor of *Art In America*, and later became Professor of Art Criticism and Theory at the University of Nevada, so stick that up your stereotype and toke it. "I'm writing about it in this magazine because there is a chance that the people who can feel and probably understand this record won't ever hear it," Hickey wrote. "There is a record called *Good Old Boys* written and performed by Randy Newman, a Los Angeles songwriter, which is the best record about the South I have ever heard. It ain't country music, it's a record about people who listen to country music."

The same week as *Good Old Boys* was released, riots broke out over the bussing of white kids to schools in black areas and black kids to schools in white areas, not in Birmingham or Little Rock but in Boston, Massachusetts. Proof of the 'Rednecks' line, "free to be put in a cage in Roxbury, Boston," was there to be seen every night on TV.

Some radio stations refused to play the album, afraid that the sentiments and the 'racist' language could incite further trouble. In an interview with *Playboy* that year, Randy expressed his fear that people might misunderstand the album and accuse him of 'closet' racism.

All the same, the record sold. It went top 40 and hung around the album chart for the best part of a year.

A month or so after the release, Randy was featured on British TV in BBC2's arts programme *Second House*. The listings page in the *Daily Express* told us that the programme would feature an item about the artist Paul Klee's later work, Isaac Bashevis Singer talking about the Polish-Jewish community in which he was brought up, and "Randy Newman talks, and sings from his album *The Good Old Days*".

Chapter Twelve

Randy was becoming quite the celebrity.
On October 5 he appeared at the Atlanta Symphony Hall for the world live premiere of his new album. He was accompanied by the 87-piece Atlanta Symphony Orchestra conducted by his uncle Emil. "I'd like to introduce my uncle," Randy said, "who's come all the way from LA to embarrass me in front of you."

Ry Cooder, whose fourth album, *Paradise And Lunch*, was released earlier in the year, opened the show. Then Randy did some of the 'hits', just him and piano. The orchestral section opened with 'Rednecks'.

Though the Symphony Hall was a high-tone, black-tie venue, Atlanta was still an edgy place for a Californian Jew to come and start shooting his mouth off about southern ways. A hundred and ten years earlier, General Sherman and the Union Army had bombarded the city with 3,000 artillery shells a day for a month, and then burned it to the ground. Sixteen years before Randy's concert, 'The Confederate Underground', believing that Jews were the real instigators of the Civil Rights movement, bombed a Reform Jewish Temple on Peachtree Street.

Besides which, it was election year and Lester Maddox was running for governor again.

Warners had put Lester Maddox on the guest list; although when Art Harris, from *Rolling Stone*, subsequently asked Maddox's reaction to this, he denied all knowledge of the invitation, the concert, the song or

Randy Newman, but, being a southern gentleman, sent Randy his best anyway.

"Here's a song," Randy said by way of introduction, "that's guaranteed to be offensive to black and white, Jew *and* gentile."

Nobody shot him.

It was the start of a 20-city tour. At most of the gigs he'd look around and shout, "I want Shea Stadium." It was a gag. He knew the audience knew he wasn't a Shea Stadium sell-out kind of guy, but on the other hand the venues were getting bigger, and... why not?

He was doing more TV, too. He was booked to do *Saturday Night Live*, Season 1, Episode 2, in the days when it was more a music show than comedy. Paul Simon essentially hosted the show and got to sing five or six songs, including Randy's own 'Marie'. Phoebe Snow got a couple of songs. Randy got one. Not that big a celebrity, then.

He went to Europe again and played the Concertgebouw in Amsterdam, an event celebrated in the 1975 song 'Amsterdam' by the Belgian singer-songwriter Kris De Bruyne ("In het Concertgebouw / Is het zeer dikwijls feest / Je weet toch nog / Dat zelfs Randy Newman daar ooit is geweest."). The song is now used in a Dutch TV ad for Old Amsterdam cheese.

Randy did an ad himself. The *Dr Pepper* people wanted a jingle for their new campaign. What do they want it to say? They want it to say that it's "the most original soft drink in the world." Randy obliged.

Later, when the ad was being aired, he phoned his then manager Elliot Albert and complained that he wasn't getting any royalty cheques. Elliot explained that it didn't work like that. You had to sing the jingle yourself to attract those kind of royalties and Randy had refused to sing it.

"Can we call them back?" Randy whined.

Critically he was up there with the gods. In 1975, Greil Marcus, the critic/political scientist/commentator wrote *Mystery Train: Images Of America In Rock'n'Roll Music*, widely regarded as key work in our understanding of pop music and its place in the culture. It consists of a series of essays, each concentrating on one artist. Robert Johnson's in there, Elvis Presley, The Band – and Randy Newman.

Marcus takes a scalpel to Randy, his career, his audience and his methods. He comments on the way in which his songs acknowledge the co-existence of great evil and great joy, how he "takes the moral shapelessness of his hometown as a given" and recognises that, "there's no way to separate The Beach Boys' smiling freedom from Manson's knife. Because this new world is a rich one, Randy Newman, as an artist, can work on it – he can laugh well and realise his fantasies of violence and death."

The essay draws attention to the cinematic nature of much of Randy's music and orchestration: "Listening to the music, irrespective of the lyric of any particular song, you might see John Wayne in Monument Valley, Charles Boyer in a final clinch. Chances are it won't be anything so specific: you will hear 100 movies whose titles you cannot just recall… His music is from a movie no-one ever made."

And it tries to pin down Randy's position in the public consciousness – and his own. "Newman works against the limits of privacy, domesticity and solipsism with his fantasies and the role playing of his songs, and yet he lacks the obsessive pop ambition to do more than that… the deepest thing keeping Randy Newman from the American audience is his own sensibility."

But 1975, the year Marcus's book was published, was also the year in which things began to change for Randy Newman. His album was top 40. At the end of the previous year, he'd played to black-tie crowds with an 87-piece orchestra. Maybe he could get to Shea Stadium without the "obsessive pop ambition". Maybe the "sensibility" that had been "keeping Randy Newman from the American audience" was vanishing, or changing, or less significant than it had been.

"Maybe in a way what I wanted, more than money or sales or fame, was praise, and now that I've got it, it seems I'm worried that I won't get it again," he told Bruce Pollock. "But it probably isn't as important to me as it was. Writing, although I know it's more important, is rough. Performing is so easy, so immediately rewarding. I had a talk with Nilsson once and I thought he was crazy. He said he didn't want to perform because he thought the audience would sway him unduly about songs. Now I'm not convinced that he was totally crazy. Or it might be that performing is so easy and lucrative that I'm getting the gratification that I used to get from writing, without all the grief."

Performing – the way he was performing now, anyway – also changed the meaning of the songs themselves. Played on a record in a patchouli apartment with John Berger on the bookshelf and Che on the wall, or in a club where men in intellectual glasses exchanged knowing laughs with amber-beaded women, the songs meant one thing: in a 2,000-seat concert hall filled with folk who've come from dinner and thought it might be an interesting change from last week's Mahler, or Jack Jones, they surely meant another. How is irony supposed to work, exactly, if everybody is in on the joke? And if they're not in on the joke, why are they buying tickets? And what, exactly, do they think these songs are about?

After the tour and the album and the hype and the bother, there was another fallow period that Randy later referred to as "the big freeze".

"For almost three years I did nothing all day. I'd get up in the morning and the kids would go off to school. And I'd say, 'By-bye, work hard, have a nice day' and I'd lie down and have a nice sleep or go sit in the sun. And I didn't feel bad about it for a couple of years. A lot of people aren't capable of doing nothing. It's not easy. I don't think I could do it again. I was idle, real idle."

There are times when 'generally taking it easy' rides so close to 'symptoms of chronic depression' that the distinction's barely worth making. The signs were there. "I was afraid I'd never write again," he said. "I came to dread the thought of returning."

Finally, in April 1976, Elliot Albert booked him an August 1977 date at the Universal Amphitheatre in LA. "I knew it would scare the shit out of him," Elliot said. "We deliberately put the tickets on sale early so when he said, 'I can't write any more,' I said 'But we can't refund 3,300 tickets.'"

Then he said, "But you know I was lying when I said I could do this."

To try and instil a proper work ethic, Randy eventually rented an office, "just a room next to an air-conditioning factory", installed a piano and a desk and started clocking on for work every day. Some days anyway.

One way or another, by the time he'd got enough material together to start work on a new album, according to Lenny, he was almost glad to be back in the studio. His friends were there. Lenny and Russ were producing. There was the usual crew of trusted musicians. Ry Cooder showed up to play some mandola. A good percentage of the Eagles – including people who weren't actually in the Eagles yet but would be later – helped out on one track or another. And a new addition to the team, Klaus Voormann, who'd known the Beatles in Hamburg, had drawn the sleeve of *Revolver* and played bass on John and Ringo's post-

Beatles albums, brought along his Fender Precision and came up with a line or two (cocaine reference not intended).

Little Criminals is not an attempt to build on the scope and conviction of *Good Old Boys* or to attempt anything like it. It's an album of stories: of outcasts, grifters, junkies, cowboys, fat boys, white trash and child murderers. In their mood and their economy, the songs are like the fragmented episodes of Raymond Carver stories, the photographs of Diane Arbus or the stark paintings of Edward Hopper.

Not forgetting that, in the most profound, most satisfying way, the songs are also funny; touching areas of feeling and experience that no mere tragedy or romance could ever visit.

The first track is Randy's only entry into the top five of the singles chart, of which more in a moment.

'You Can't Fool The Fatman' is a piano riff with bunched up chords, lazy drums, lots of syncopation, woodwind and horns making sunshine noises and a fragment of a story, a moment out of a Jim Thompson novel. The narrator and the Fatman are "spitting on the sidewalk / squinting at the sun." The narrator tries to chisel $50 out of the Fatman with a hard luck story: but 'You Can't Fool The Fatman'. That's it.

'Little Criminals', the title track, is more urgent. Glen Frey plays dirty slide guitar and the whole thing is pitched a tone or so higher than Randy can comfortably manage, making him strain for some of the notes – not painfully, but enough to get him sounding pissed off. The narrator and his associates have been planning a job. They've "got a gun from Uncle Freddy / got a station all picked out". But now Chuck, a "two-bit junkie", has showed up with his "junkie business" and it looks like he's going to ruin everything just when they "almost made it to the top".

'Texas Girl At The Funeral Of Her Father' is a song in which Randy sings the part of a female narrator. She stands alone, singing to her dead dad, a "sailor, a thousand miles from the sea". Three short verses finishing with, "Papa, we'll go sailing". There's no need to be ashamed if you well up. Most people do.

He almost whispers it into the mic, proving that, whatever people say about his singing, his ability to nail a mood, his taste and his intonation are impeccable.

"It has nice *Song of Bernadette*-like music in it," Randy told Timothy White. *Song Of Bernadette* was one of Uncle Alfred's Oscar-winning scores, one he was particularly proud of.

Then Randy changes his mind. "Actually, *How Green Was My Valley* I think it was" – another of Alfred's favourites, but one that only got nominated.

"You wouldn't know what 'Texas Girl' was about without the title. I wanted to write a song about being a sailor, with dust all around. There was a longer version of it. Linda Ronstadt and the Eagles heard it and they all liked the shorter one but I still have my doubts. I think it's all right. It will probably get me more ass in Texas ... now why did I say that? I write a nice song and then come out with a terrible line about it."

Even the title doesn't provide much indication of what 'Jolly Coppers On Parade' is *really* about. Or rather it does. It's about jolly coppers on parade. Keen listeners, when they first brought the album home, listened to it three or four times trying to find a double meaning. There isn't one. It's a song about a police parade, with a marching band and a procession of cars and motorcycles. The motorcycles do tricks. All the kids watching want to be police when they grow up and who can blame them?

"I really can't tell you why I wrote it at all," Randy told the *Chicago Tribune*. "My kids have been fascinated with uniforms lately and I wanted to do a song with uniforms in it."

After he'd written the song, he half remembered reading a reference to a song with the same title in an English detective novel. There is indeed another 'Jolly Coppers On Parade' by Charles Penrose, the British music-hall entertainer who also had a hit with 'The Laughing Policeman'.

The fifth time around, the keen listener begins to notice the overdone cheerfulness of Randy's performance and the overegging of "like angels come down from Paradise", and decides it's definitely a savage indictment of police brutality. Then you realise that exposure to Randy Newman has made you the sort of cynical, suspicious person who thinks that 'The Lonely Goatherd' from *The Sound Of Music* is a filthy song advocating bestiality.

'In Germany Before The War' came from a story that Roswitha told him about a famous child killer, Peter Kurten 'The Vampire Of Dusseldorf', who was guillotined for his crimes in 1931. Roswitha, also from Dusseldorf, told him that parents would invoke Kurten's name to scare their kids. He was a bogeyman. Fritz Lang, the film director, interviewed Kurten when his working on *M*, his film loosely based on the same story.

The story's told functionally, bare bones exposition and a cinematic montage of non-explicit images. At one point the lyric practically gives camera directions: in homage to Hitchcock's *Strangers On A Train*, the killer's victim is "Reflected in his glasses / As he watches her."

Randy doesn't usually bother much with harmonic complexities, not in his songs anyway. If three or four chords were good enough for Fats Domino and Ray Charles, they're good enough for him. A lot of the time he's happy letting V follow II and I follow V. 'In Germany Before The War' is an exception. The intro has a dying fall. The verse follows a descending pattern of sixths against a pedal bass, the movement away from stability made more uncomfortable by the introduction of a flattened fifth in the third bar, to make what, in Nashville, would be called an 'out of town chord'. After the chorus it shifts from the minor key to the major and then back again. The tempi shift and stutter. Frequently the expectation of line or a repeated phrase is denied: the voice peters out, as if the narrator is momentarily distracted or lost in thought. It's unsettling, haunting and haunted.

"Newman gropes down into diseased souls," the British critic Richard Williams said in the London *Times*. "I do not know if his discoveries frighten him, but they terrify me."

"We lie beneath the autumn sky / My little golden girl and I / And she lies very still …"

'Sigmund Freud's Impersonation Of Albert Einstein In America', as the title suggests, is a complex tale.

Freud visited the USA once, in 1909, to give a series of lectures at Clark University in Worcester, Massachusetts, for which he got $714.60 and an honorary degree. He travelled with fellow analysts, Carl Jung and Sándor Ferenczi. They did the sights in New York. They went to Coney Island. Possibly they went on some of the rides. The Teaser was popular and the Tickler. Time was limited so they probably didn't get to see the Lilliput Village, staffed by 300 midgets, or the exhibition of premature babies in incubators. A photograph of Freud, Jung and Ferenczi on the Bridge of Laughs would be a great addition to our understanding of psychoanalytic history.

What we do know is that Freud didn't like Americans much. He thought their 'obsession' with money was suspect. He called them 'savages'. In 1924, he was offered $25,000 to go to Chicago and psychoanalyse the celebrity killers Nathan Leopold and Richard Loeb for a piece in the *Chicago Tribune*. Sam Goldwyn, the movie mogul, offered him $100,000 to come and work in Hollywood. He turned both offers down. Meanwhile, America had taken Freud's theories to its heart. Freudianism, it was believed, could explain literature, sell car spares and above all, in theory but almost never in practice, make you happy. By the sixties, if you didn't have an analyst you were no better than an animal.

Einstein, on the other hand, loved America. He saw there a "joyous, positive attitude to life". During lengthy visits he went to the White House, was awarded the keys of the city by the Mayor of New York, befriended Chaplin. When the Nazis started burning his books in Germany, he moved over, worked at Princeton, and, in 1940, became a US citizen. Americans took Einstein's theories to heart, too. They built a bomb.

So, 'Sigmund Freud's Impersonation Of Albert Einstein In America' is a song about an ill-informed Jewish visitor to the US, impersonating another, better informed, Jewish immigrant.

How the song relates to any of the above is anybody's guess.

"When I start writing," Randy said, "lines just come into my head. It's like when you're almost asleep and you have disjointed thoughts going through your head, then you get one that wakes you up all of a sudden."

Freud's disjointed thoughts in the song are mostly filled racist misconceptions about the American Dream in which, in his interpretation, scary gypsies play a huge part, as does penis size.

"Freud in the song, because of his lack of knowledge of America, gets the dream mostly wrong," Randy said. "My first wife was German and to scare her, her father would tell her that the gypsies would get her (this, presumably, was when he wasn't telling her about Peter Kurten). It scared her. It's a European thing. You couldn't scare an American with that."

It's a catchy tune that liberally quotes the German national anthem and closes with "And may all your Christmases be white." Go figure.

'Baltimore' is a song about a city that's dying. There are hookers on the corner and drunks on the street. The narrator, with his sister Sandy and his brother Ray, are packing up and leaving for good.

Randy had never visited Baltimore when he wrote the song. He was inspired by an article in *National Geographic* which showed a prosperous and happy place with fine buildings: a stark contrast to the impression he'd garnered from news reports. The problems and desolation of Baltimore have since been paraded on the TV screens of the world in the critically acclaimed TV drama *The Wire*, but at the time they were less celebrated. The people of Baltimore took exception to Randy badmouthing their city.

A local, who later became Governor of Maryland, wrote a short poem: "Randy Newman / Is not human / For / He doesn't love our Baltimore."

When Randy played the town, Miss Baltimore came on stage to deliver letters. It's a tribute to the honesty of Baltimoreans that "half were in favour and half were opposed".

'I'll be Home' is one of Randy's many 'home' songs.

'Home' is one of the most powerful words in the lyrical lexicon and particularly the American lyrical lexicon – maybe because it's a big country filled with bears and snow, and beyond its borders are dangers you don't even want to think about. In song after song – not just Randy's – 'home' is a trigger word for fuzzy feelings of unconditional love and absolute safety: 'Sweet Home Alabama', 'You'd Be So Nice To Come Home To', 'Ain't Got No Home', 'Home Sweet Home', 'Home On The Range', 'I Can Never Go Home Any More'.

Randy's song 'I'll Be Home' was originally written for the Welsh singer Mary Hopkin at the behest of Paul McCartney, but never released. It had already been used on *Nilsson Sings Newman* and on *Randy Newman: Live*. Randy drops the key a tone or two for the *Little Criminals* studio version, to good effect.

'Rider In The Rain' is a half-parody of a cowboy song with an arrangement that pulls up just short of coconut-shell hoof beats. In fact, it's hardly a parody at all. It could pass as a fine example of the genre. Change the line about rape and pillage to something more wholesome, and Roy Rogers could have recorded it, with Trigger on whinnies and Gabby Hayes on spittoon. If you're the sort of person who regularly forgets his mother's birthday but can still retain every word of the sig tune from *Bronco* ("Next to a four square Texas twister / You'd call a cyclone meek and mild / You've never seen a twister, mister / Till someone gets him riled."), you might even consider it the best track on the album. Randy would disagree.

"I think it's ridiculous," he told *NME*. "The Eagles are on there. That's what's good about it."

"He's a rider in the rain," the Eagles sing in campfire harmony, and Randy hollers back, "You know I'm a rider". Then, after a false fade, he comes back with, "Take it boys," and the Eagles throw back some "Oohs" as only they can.

"You remember the fat kid at the pool when you were little whose mother made him wear nose plugs and earplugs and goggles and he'd have to hold them all when he jumped in?" Randy told Charles M. Young. "I felt like him when the Eagles sang."

'Kathleen (Catholicism Made Easier)' is a slow and funky minor key story in which the narrator, who is crazy about Irish girls, marries one in Chicago. The ceremony is conducted by a Spanish priest who recites the (Italian) lyrics from the song 'Volare'.

'Old Man On The Farm' is another song of loneliness. The old man waits for the rain, drinks whisky in the barn, slops his pigs. "Goodnight ladies," he sings, maybe to some imaginary women who once was there, maybe to a dead wife. And then, bleakest of all, "I love the way I sing this song," because there's nobody else to do so. If it was taken any slower there'd be time for a contemplative cigarette between the two and the four.

Early in the sessions, Lenny, faced with the slow severity of 'Old Man On The Farm', 'Texas Girl At The Funeral Of Her Father', 'In Germany Before The War' and 'I'll Be Home', decided that what the album needed was an 'up' song. The front-runner for a while was a tune called 'Hard Hat Blues' but it didn't work out. Something else would have to be found.

"One night Randy called me up and said, 'I've got this song,'" Lenny said, in the sleeve notes for *Guilty: 30 Years Of Randy Newman*, "and he played 'Short People' over the phone. My initial response was, 'Shit, there's goes our up song'. Randy called Russ after he called me. Then Russ called me and said, 'It's the funniest song I've ever heard'. And I said, 'Yeah, but it's not our up song'. To his credit, Russ was so taken by how good it was that he got me to think, 'Screw it – it is great – Let's use it.'"

It's a song about the stupidity of prejudice. When Randy had done songs about racists, people had, for the most part, understood that he wasn't advocating racism, merely adopting a persona for the purposes of comment and criticism. Prejudice against short people – and their "little cars that go beep, beep, beep" – is so obviously stupid that nobody could possibly misunderstand. Could they?

Maybe I'm Doing It Wrong

Lenny tried it out on a convention of Warner Bros sales and marketing people in Miami, showing them a little film he'd had made of Randy singing a demo of the song. They loved it.

Accordingly, Randy went into the studio and recorded it properly, with Glen Frey (of the Eagles), Tim Schmit (soon to join the Eagles) and JD Souther (who wrote songs for the Eagles) on backing vocals, Klaus Voormann on bass, Jim Keltner on drums, Milt Holland on congas and, at a later session, Waddy Wachtel on guitar.

There was a nice bridge, too, with Glen, Tim and JD representing the voice of decency in Four Freshmen harmony: "Short people are just the same as you and I / All men are brothers until the day they die."

'Short People', Lenny's near-as-dammit 'up' song, went in as Track 1, Side 1 of the new album.

Little Criminals was released in September 1977 on Warner Bros., the Reprise label having been put into cold storage. The sleeve was a black and white shot of Randy taken on the overpass facing south, where 7th Street crosses the 110 Freeway in downtown Los Angeles. Many people, including Randy himself, have pointed out that he looks as if he has either two penises or deformed testicles.

The reviews were less adulatory than usual.

"Here comes the sad man," it said in *Melody Maker*, "his unkind and indecisive mouth pursed against the camera's gaze, with another bunch of third person songs grudgingly released on a largely indifferent public."

It went on to say that many of the songs, "exist solely on their musical merits, which is far from easy in the light of Newman's limited melodic imagination," and called the irony in 'Sigmund Freud' "tritely obvious".

The general consensus was that the album was slick – maybe too slick – but didn't have the grit of *Good Old Boys* and *Sail Away*. Greil Marcus, looking back from 1997, summed up the mood: "It offers all the minor charms of Randy Newman's music and none of the major ones."

A couple of months after the release of the album, Warners released 'Short People' as a single.

Melody Maker's brief review was favourable, but ended, "Sadly, it'll sell about 14 copies or less."

By Christmas it had gone top 20. At the end of January, it went to number two on the *Billboard* Hot 100 and stayed there for three weeks, slugging it out for the top spot with the Bee Gees' 'Stayin' Alive'. On the *Cashbox* 100, for one glorious week, it went all the way to number one. In the end, the single sold 1.5m copies. Off the back of it, the album made number nine in the album chart and sold 750,000.

A radio station in Buffalo played the single continuously for an hour. America's sweetheart, Goldie Hawn, used it in a sketch for one of her TV specials in which she tried to join the Harlem Globetrotters basketball team, who sing the song to her with dance steps and actions. She ends the routine upside down in a hoop. America laughed.

People sang it in the street. If butchers' boys had existed, they would have whistled it.

On *Saturday Banana*, a UK Saturday morning kid's TV show with a talent contest section, a gangly, shy youth said he sang and played the piano.

"And what are you going to sing for us?" asked Bill Oddie, the host.

"'Short People'," said the lad, towering over Bill, with no hint of awareness that his choice might seem pointed. And he proceeded to do so, making a terrific job of it.

It was never going to end well. People sent letters to their local DJs saying that they found the suggestion that short people were liars and had "no reason to live" offensive. Radio stations in Boston, New York and Philadelphia banned it. Maryland's House of Delegates proposed a statewide ban: it didn't make the statute books because, as Attorney General Francis Birch noted: "The long and short of it is that we feel that the bill cannot measure up to Constitutional scrutiny. We hope that we have correctly sized up the situation."

An act calling itself 'Wee Willie Small And The Little Band' released a rebuttal called 'Tall People' (written by Wee Willie Small and Tiny Stump). "They got giant heads / And billboard faces / Elephant teeth / With great big spaces."

A couple of years later, Chevy Chase made another rebuttal, this time extolling the virtues of smallness. "They eat much less food / They breathe much less air / They're much smarter with their money / And only pay half-fare."

Diminutive protestors picketed Randy's shows. An old newsreel on YouTube, made at the time, shows self-proclaimed short people at an anti-Newman rally, angrily throwing eggs at a poster of his face.

When journalists asked for comment, Randy tried to clarify the exact parameters of his alleged prejudice. "A short person? Let's say three feet seven inches," he said. "No, that's too timid. Anybody under five feet six inches. No. That means some little karate guy is likely to kick the shit out of me. Actually I don't expect this record to be a big commercial success in Japan."

"I got a death threat, too, in Memphis," Randy told Kirsty Young on *Desert Island Discs*, "And my manager said, 'You know, I used to be on the road with The Carpenters and this used to happen all the time.' And I said 'Really?' And he said, "Yeah, about once out of every three concerts they would get a death threat.' And so I said, 'OK,' and went out and did it. When I was done I came back and said to him, 'It was pretty good that I did that. Actually, I was pretty brave because all the time I was thinking about getting shot.' And he said, 'Well, you had your head behind the mike half the show, but, yeah.' And I said, 'Did The Carpenters really get that many death threats?' 'No, I just told you that to make you go on.'"

On *Second City Television*, a Canadian comedy show, comedian Dave Thomas dressed up as Randy and some short people blew him up. "He blowed up real good," they said.

The controversy still rages. As recently as 2013, the journalist Rod Liddle published in *The Spectator* a selection of comments he'd found posted online underneath the lyric of 'Short People': "because of that one song... it made my life and a lot of others harder than it should have been. it should have not been released... i am 4 foot 9 inches and proud of it... i've been waiting for years to say this to him... bullying is not right in any form or fashion for anyone in this world."

"WTF? So crappy song that's full with hate... Well, I'm a short person (1.67 cm) tall and to be honest, it annoys me like hell but, what can I do about it? NOTHING alright I gotta live with it... but people like that retard really make me want to puke... Get a life you f**kin idiot... hope you lose a leg or hand someday then you will realize which one is better: being with little feet, or having no feet at all !!!"

"Are you f***ing retarded. There is no underlining meaning here. People try and find some gay ass reasoning behind every song. Randy Newman pleaded in court that this song was written by a narrator who hates short people. Where does it once say in the song that people find ways to hate on others. God you are f***ing stupid and you are what is wrong with America."

On the *Support For The Short* website, the two people listed as responsible for more prejudice against short people than any other are Alfred Adler (the psychotherapist who coined the term "Napoleon complex") and Randy Newman.

"You thought the whole thing was weird," Randy said. "Jeez, how do you think I felt about it."

He tried to spell it out. "I would never," he told the *Chicago Tribune*, "write a song just to make fun of someone or something. At least I hope I wouldn't. Even the songs I've written that some people might see as making fun, I've never considered nasty. What I'm making fun of is people's callousness and insensitivity, and often that callousness is exaggerated to the point where it's funny. I mean, as in 'Yellow Man' – that guy is an idiotic bigot. A pinhead. See, that's one thing that makes me a little different from a lot of other singers – I'm willing to act the part of an idiot in my songs."

Nevertheless, nearly 40 years later, it's still an issue that crops up in interviews, and still he feels obliged to explain himself.

"I had no idea that there was any sensitivity," he told Lydia Hutchinson in 2014. "I mean, that anyone could believe that anyone was as crazy as that character. To have that kind of animus against short people, and then to sing it and put it all in song and have a philosophy on it (laughs). And yet, there were people who took a genuine beating.

"I almost regret nothing that I've written… but you could make a case for that one. Of course I didn't mean it, but it doesn't do any good if someone is going into an office every day and gets ribbed about being short, or, 'Mom, I don't want to go to school today… this damn song.'"

"Ohh, fuck," he told Barney Hoskyns. "Why don't they leave me alone! Maybe I was right about the little pukes all along."

Chapter Thirteen

By the end of 1978, the worst of the 'Short People' kerfuffle had died down and Randy could walk through airports and so on without people pointing at him or shooting him.

He came over to the UK, this time for something more like a proper tour, with gigs at the Manchester Apollo, the Liverpool Philharmonic and the Birmingham Town Hall as well as Drury Lane in London.

"He was of course addressing the converted," said Ray Coleman in *Melody Maker*. "The audience at the Theatre Royal Drury Lane, hung on to his every word and knew the songs from the opening bars.

"Watching him on Sunday, I was suddenly aware of the musician of whom he reminds me. The arrogant way he sits at the piano, his brittle posture, his oblique flurries against aspects of society and situations, his controlled passion, his 'take-it-or-leave-it' attitude to his followers. There's a parallel it seems to me with John Lennon. […] Randy Newman's jaw juts in the same way too."

He played 'Short People' on *The Old Grey Whistle Test*. Neither the single nor the album had charted in the UK. Perhaps long-term exposure to Jimmy Clitheroe, Charlie Drake and the Krankies had left us feeling that the song did no more than state the bleeding obvious.

Chris Welch, of *Melody Maker*, asked him whether the success of the single had affected him.

"I turned into an asshole."

"Completely?"

"Uh-huh. I don't know... it was a funny kind of success because of the notoriety the single got in the States."

"I feel a responsibility to say something. I hear a lot of songs and to me the words are superfluous and it doesn't matter what they are saying. So I feel a responsibility to say something although I don't always do it."

Chris also asked him which British acts he admired.

"I like Ray Davies and Queen," he said. I like 'We Are The Champions' very much. It's such a pretty song."

Back in the USA, the *Chicago Tribune* asked the same "Will success change Randy Newman" question.

"Time will tell," Randy said. "Maybe the theory that success will spoil me is right." There was also the worry that his hard-core fans would drift away. "You mean they might feel I've sold out; that they've been betrayed? Well I can't help my success. But yes, I think there will be some backlash. Maybe with the next record. It wouldn't surprise me. But hell, I might change. I might write differently."

He was certainly unsettled. But a new album was a contractual obligation. Songs had to be written.

"It's my second record in a coupla years," he said. "I've got better work habits now. I work in a rented room in an industrial district... but I was just evicted. I always dreaded making records so much that I avoided it before or I was too lazy. I owe the company four more records over seven years; I just signed a new contract. They've been pretty easy on me, for a corporate giant. I can't even work up a good hatred for them, you know, but just out of principle, I'd like to."

Life in the Newman household got rough when Dad had songs to write. "I haven't been easy to get along with lately," he said. "I've been really irritable, rotten to the kids."

Roswitha did her best to placate the troubled genius.

"She's real good to me," he told Christopher Connelly. "I need someone to take care of me. [...] When she goes away to visit her family in Germany, the ship begins to sink. We don't get along, the boys and I. We mess things up in our own particular way. We need her."

Amos, the eldest boy, was coming up to the awkward age – the age at which Randy had been stalled all his life.

Maybe I'm Doing It Wrong

"I was at a beach where I haven't been since I was 15 years old," Randy said, "the same one I used to go to every day. I had my two sons with me. And these beautiful little girls recognized me. Randy Newman, famous songwriter. So I talked to them.

"Later, one of my boys said that I really embarrassed him when I talked to those girls. My heart sank. I said, 'What do you mean?' 'Cause I thought that, 20 years later, I'd handled this beach situation fairly well. And he did this vicious imitation of me just fumbling around.'"

Amos's musical tastes were diverging wildly from Randy's. Like most American teenagers at the time, he was a Kiss fan.

Randy had, for some time, been observing the Kiss phenomenon with a mixture of horror tinged with envy.

In February 1977, Kiss members Gene Simmons, Ace Frehley, Paul Stanley and Peter Criss gave blood samples to a registered nurse at Nassau Coliseum, in Uniondale, New York. The blood was stored in refrigerated containers kept under close guard. Some time later, Simmons, Frehley, Stanley and Criss were flown to the Borden Ink Plant in Depew, New York, where they poured their blood into vats of red printing ink – the ink that was subsequently used to print Marvel Comics' *Kiss Super Special*.*

That same year, as well as having their own comic book in which they battled evil in the way superheroes have to, Kiss played a 30-date sell-out arena tour and released two albums, one of which went platinum and the other double platinum. Over the next two years they sold an estimated $100m worth of merchandise – key rings, dolls, masks, lunch boxes, T-shirts, clocks, pinball machines, anything that could be printed with a name or an image.

In 1978, they figured out a way of quadrupling their income by releasing not one Kiss album but four solo albums – one by each member of the band – on the same day. All four went platinum on advance orders, though the stunt backfired when thousands were returned a few weeks later. Nevertheless, Paul Stanley proudly proclaimed, "We're the McDonalds of rock."

It had been ten years since Brian Epstein and the Beatles consistently missed chances and fumbled deals, making a fraction of the money they

---

* Rumours that a mix up resulted in the blood being used to print the next issue of *Sports Illustrated* have been hotly denied.

should have, but at last somebody had figured out how to turn the pop business into a slick, well-managed, money-making machine.

In the Marvel Comics version of the story, Kiss had sprung from the mind of Winda, an unfortunate young woman in the care of top psychiatrist Dr Morton Avery who had "studied the Freudians, the Behaviourists and the so called 'Third Force' in depth", but "nothing in his reading has prepared him to deal with the swirling seething savage nightmare rising in billows from Winda's skull". The swirling seething savage nightmare was, of course, Gene 'The Demon', Ace 'The Space Ace', Paul 'The Starchild' and Peter 'The Catman'.

The real version of how they were born and came together as a band is too prosaic to dwell on, but in essence they were four lads from New York who formed a band, got some terrific management and soon had more money than anybody ever had sense. The image was grown out of glam and metal with a bit of prog thrown in. They wore heavy black and white make-up designed in accordance with their 'Starchild'/'Catman' personae, and the kind of costumes that David St Hubbins' girlfriend Jeanine might have designed for Spinal Tap if she'd been given the budget.

They spat blood, breathed fire, detonated fireworks on stage and sometimes the drums elevated and floated around for a bit – anything to draw attention away from the music. They put it about that they were evil and maybe they were. They certainly put their tongues out a lot more than is acceptable anywhere except a doctor's surgery. The suggestion, however, that Kiss was an acronym for 'Knights In Satan's Service' has been rebutted, and anyway, these days 'Knees In Surgical Stockings' might be more appropriate, or 'Kindly Inform Social Services'.

For his new album, Randy, his whiskers a-twitch to every shift of the zeitgeist, saw strange parallels between the Kiss phenomenon and two other worrying societal trends.

In 1975, Chuck Colson, one of the Watergate conspirators, who served seven months for his crimes, wrote that while he was in prison, "words I had not been certain I could understand or say fell from my lips: 'Lord Jesus, I believe in You. I accept You. Please come into my life. I commit it to You.'"

The book in which he described his experiences, *Born Again*, helped many through those uncertain times.

In 1976, President Jimmy Carter declared himself to have been 'born again'. So did his opponent in the 1980 presidential election campaign,

Maybe I'm Doing It Wrong

Ronald Reagan. So did, then or since, Bob Dylan, Roger McGuinn, Alice Cooper, Steve Tyler, Randy Travis, Johnny Cash, Cliff Richard and millions more.

Randy didn't.

It would be a year or two before the word 'yuppie' passed into common usage, and eight years before Michael Douglas, as Gordon Gekko, told the world in *Wall Street* that, "greed is good", but the signs were all there.

In 1976, Tom Wolfe published an essay called *The Me Decade And The Third Great Awakening* which traced the way in which the caring, sharing ethos that had characterised the New Deal thirties and the hippie sixties had crumbled. The new focus was on 'realising your potential as a human being'. "The old alchemical dream was changing base metals into gold. The new alchemical dream is changing one's personality – remaking, remodelling, elevating, and polishing one's very *self...* and observing, studying, and doting on it." And making it rich.

This seventies combination of self-obsession, self-improvement and label-fetishism was impeccably captured in Cyr McFadden's novel of life and times in Marin County, *The Serial*, in which characters live in houses that are 'simply screaming with tranquillity', filled with Klip speakers, top-of-the-line Pioneer receivers, Brown-Jordan patio furniture and Rosenthal china, have children who drop out of some fancy foreign exchange programme because the Sorbonne 'didn't have a crisis centre', call their cats Kat Vonnegut Junior, write epic poems called 'Labia', and are into primal therapy: "It's really getting my head together. Like, it took me weeks of screaming myself hoarse, but I'm finally learning to reach through my defences."

Randy saw a way he could combine all three trends.

"I just thought it was funny to be Born Again," he said, "not as a Christian but as a money-grubbing Kiss kind of guy. It just came to me like a bad dream."

He announced that for his next album he was preparing a "larger insult" even than *Little Criminals* and 'Short People'.

Born Again is a set of songs about money and the power it buys, about bullies and about the decent, modest people who get crushed.

The opening track, 'It's Money That I Love', sets out the stall with face-slapping swagger. Randy spits the lyric proud and defiant: "Don't love the mountains / don't love the sea / I don't love Jesus / He ain't never done a thing for me." And then, "It's money that I love / It's money that I love."

Randy's proto-yuppie used to worry about the black man, the poor and the starving in India. "You know what I say now about the starving children of India? / I say, 'Oh, mama!' / It's money that I love."

"I think that money is tremendously important in the world," Randy told *New Musical Express*. "And more so than ever, money is making people mean. That's what I was writing about. I wasn't writing about myself per se. But I have played a few dates just for money, and they always turned out badly for some reason. But I am not... indifferent to its charms, though I don't think it's of overriding importance to me. A lot of people say that, and you don't know whether to believe them or not... and I don't know whether to believe myself."

'The Story Of A Rock And Roll Band' is a tribute to the majesty of ELO, the Electric Light Orchestra, the British band who, in the mid to late seventies, under the baton of leader-singer-guitarist-producer-composer-genius Jeff Lynne, enjoyed an unbroken run of five top ten albums in the US, and 27 top 40 singles. The records were lushly orchestrated and elaborately produced.

In 1979, the year that Randy released *Born Again*, ELO were the best-selling act in the UK and their album *Discovery* went double platinum in the US.

Randy gives a brief history of the band – their genesis in Birmingham, England and so on, their adoption of the violin and "the big violin / the one that stands on the floor", then presents a selection of their trademark sounds, or at least his impression of them. He does the piano stabs, he does the huge choir, he does the swooping strings, he does the monsta synth.

Is it a tribute, a parody, an affectionate parody, a condemnation or what? Does Randy Newman *like* ELO? And if he *doesn't* like them, what point is he trying to make by writing a song about them? Come to that, if he *does* like them, what point is he trying to make by writing a song about them? Is he saying, like a middle-aged man in a pub, "look how trite pop has become these days"? Is he saying "look how *commercial* pop has become these days" like some slightly younger but no less irritating man in a pub? Or has he plucked a name out of a hat to make a meta-observation about the nature of perception, celebrity and the marketplace – like Half Man Half Biscuit did in their seminal 'I Hate Nerys Hughes'.

The most accurate answer to all these questions is probably, 'yes'.

"What I like about it is that I got everything so wrong," Randy told Mark Leviton. "Mispronounced the name of the town [he sings 'Birmin-g-Ham' rather than the usual English pronunciation 'Birmiyem' or the Birmingham pronunciation 'Birmin-g-em']. And they do have these idiosyncrasies about their music that are funny. It's maybe a kind of a joke, but I wouldn't have done it if I really hated them like I hate some people."

Jeff Lynne later worked Randy on his 1988 album *Land Of Dreams*.

"Of course the press as usual said, 'Oh, it's him slagging off ELO'," Lynne said, "but I got to know Randy very well, and I said, 'What was that about?' He goes, 'Oh, I had terrible trouble with that. I was going to send you a copy and see what you thought.' I said, 'Was it a nice song or what? Was it a tribute?' He says, 'Yeah, absolutely, I really loved them records.' So there was no other side to it – he really liked it and I think he was just being silly."

Jeff Lynne has a longstanding and almost undisputed reputation for being one of the nicest men in rock'n'roll.

The next track, 'Pretty Boy', opens menacingly, with Spartan piano and grumbling synth, and gets more menacing as it goes on. The narrator's a member of a street gang. A kid from New Jersey and his girlfriend have encroached on their turf. "And he looks just like that dancing wop / in those movies that we've seen."

The 'dancing wop' is Tony Manero, the part that John Travolta played in *Saturday Night Fever*, with his "cute little chicken-shit boots on". 'Stayin' Alive', the big hit from the film, had kept 'Short People' from the number one spot in the *Billboard* chart, so maybe Randy was still harbouring some festering resentment against Travolta, white suits, the New York Hustle and falsetto harmony in general.

Randy's bullies are among his most accomplished roles. He taunts like a pro. "Have we got a tough guy here? / Have we got a tough guy from the street?" "Talk tough to me."

Seeing John Travolta as a tough guy was a stretch for anybody. You could tell by the way he used his walk he was a woman's man.

'Mr Sheep' is another bouncy little number with nasty lyrics. The conceit in 'Small People' – that it's a song about prejudice not height – was misunderstood by many, even though it wasn't particularly subtle. 'Mr Sheep' is quite possibly too subtle for its own good. Play it to people in the street and nine out of ten will say it's a critique of dull suburban conformism.

"People say, 'How can you take such an easy shot at a businessman with a briefcase?'" Randy said. "The clue was those haunting, terrible rock'n'roll, Nazi voices taunting the guy. Maybe I didn't do it well. But I thought it was so obvious."

The target then is not dull suburban conformism. The target, like the one in 'Pretty Boy', is the bully: in this case the sneering, cooler than thou, rock'n'roll bully. Stephen Holden, who reviewed the album for *Rolling Stone* thought that either way it was "appallingly smug". "We're supposed to frown on the hippie and pity the square, but we don't, since both characters are such ciphers that they're impossible to care about."

'Ghosts' is a song about a lonely old man, perhaps a victim of the Nazi taunter on 'Mr Sheep'. Somebody – maybe a daughter – has come to visit him and he begs her to stay for a while and talk. He's always tried to do the decent thing but now discovers "you end up with nothing / Live in one room like a bum".

The kick in the teeth is in the last lines. He apologises for his existence: "I just want to know / What was it all about / I'm sorry."

Musically, it could have been written in the thirties or forties. It has an introductory verse just like the "As Dorothy Parker once said" on 'Just One Of Those Things', or the "After one whole quart of brandy / Like a daisy I'm awake" from 'Bewitched, Bothered And Bewildered'. The melody could lend itself to cocktail piano and fine crooning. Instead, Randy deconstructs it, deliberately avoiding its inherent sentimentality by playing the chords almost ham-fistedly – left hand, right hand – and barely grunting the tune.

'Spies' is a song straight out of the newspapers. "The Russians are coming," said the *Chicago Tribune* on February 7, 1978. "So are the Czechs, Poles, Yugoslavs, East Germans, Chinese, Indonesians and Vietnamese and many of them are spies – so many, says FBI Director Clarence Kelly, that the bureau doesn't have enough agents to watch them all."

Spy paranoia had been a feature of American life since the forties, but a seventies escalation of the Cold War put a spike in the number of accusations, arrests and exchanges. More prescient was the uncovering of *Stasi*-like internal spy networks – Americans spying on Americans. The Chicago Police Department, it had been revealed, had been conducting covert surveillance and infiltration operations on 'dangerous' organisations such as the Parent Teacher Association, the League of Women Voters and the Catholic Interracial Council. Tendencies that operatives were advised to look out for that could suggest an affiliation or sympathy with the 'International Communist Conspiracy' included an interest in modern art and advocacy of racial integration.

On the back of which Randy put together a jazzy, sneaking-round-the-corner, Fender Rhodes TV spy theme, and some paranoid lyrics: "… they might look just like me / But they're… spies." And just so you know what the song's really about, the song ends with, "They've even got 'em in Chicago."

'The Girls in My Life, Part 1' is a short list, but the "Part 1" makes it a hopeful one. It's spoken against a sleepy shuffle. The narrator is no Don Juan. He's a middle-aged married man, lost in a pleasant reverie about his romantic encounters. They have been few and unexceptional. He says he has seven on his mind, but mentions just five, including his wife. There's the one with small feet and a pleasant disposition. There's the French girl he met when he was on holiday with his parents in Las Vegas. They had a "real nice conversation". Sadly for the lad, and maybe for the French girl, too, there is no salacious stress before "conversation". There is the girl he loaned his car to who mowed down a Mexican called Juan. There's a college girl – this one gave him a "real fine education". And there is his "very lovely wife". But that, he concludes, is only half the story.

'They Just Got Married' is what used to be called a 'sick joke' put to music. A sort of shaggy dog story with a horrible twist at the end.

'Half A Man' was possibly inspired by one of Randy's Dad's stories.

Dr Newman once came home from work and told Lenny and Randy that he'd been treating a middle-aged respectable gent who had just been beaten up at his sports club. Dr Newman asked him what happened. "Well, there I was standing in the shower," the gent said, "and I saw this guy and I thought 'What the hell'. So I started to go down on him. I don't know what the hell came over me, but he beat the shit out of me."

Irving then warned Randy and Lenny always to beware of men like that who, without warning or encouragement, will try to go down on you. The possibility haunted them for ever afterwards.

"One night back when we were doing *Little Criminals*," Lenny told Timothy White, "we were driving home, acting real dopey and laughing and Randy brought the story up. I said, 'Jesus Christ! Do you still think about that?!' He said, 'Remember it? How could I forget it?'"

The song is the tale of a homophobic truck driver who, spotting a "big old queen" on the pavement, decides to park and beat him up. But the gay guy stops him in his tracks with an appeal for his sympathy and to the truck driver's surprise: "Oh, the strangest feelings sweeping over me / Both my speech and manner have become much more refined." "I am half a man, Jesus, what a drag."

"I'm not very careful," Randy said. "I've written things that I didn't think were all right, and I let them go. I wrote a song, 'Half a Man', about homosexuality as a contagious disease. I got some letters and some calls on it, but I thought it was funny. It was a song about the lack of understanding of homosexuality, but it hurt some people. Some gay people said my doing the song wasn't worth it, but it was to me."

The 'contagious disease' suggestion is not explicit in the song's lyric. Indeed, another interpretation would be the far more likely scenario that a brief conversation was enough to make the truck driver acknowledge his true identity. And what a drag that's going to be when the guys at the depot find out.

'William Brown' is a song in praise of the unexceptional: the story of a man who moves from Virginia to Omaha and finds contentment wherever he goes – a companion perhaps to 'Ghosts' and 'Mr Sheep'. The question, "if this character is so uncomplaining, why is the music so unsettling?" should not be asked.

The original plan was to finish the album with a cover of a Kiss song, a song called 'Great Expectations' from their *Destroyer* album. Randy liked 'Great Expectations'. "I was talking to [Don] Henley and [Glenn] Frey about it, telling them the Eagles should record 'Great Expectations', and they looked at me like I was nuts, like when you tell someone you like Andy Gibb's stuff."

So instead, Randy wrote 'Pants' in which the singer, to a steady rock grind, threatens, or perhaps promises, to take off his pants. "It's about these big heavy pretentious rock'n'roll acts like Kansas or Styx. I saw some big rock shows, in a baseball arena, which I'd never seen before, and I couldn't believe what an impersonal thing it was," he told Mark Leviton. "This kind of false sexual innuendo, you know, 'I'm gonna take off my pants!'... the whole thing was a drag, and really demeaning to the audience. Who wants to put these... these... anybody on a pedestal like that?"

"It's artifice," he said. "It's like when you meet an actor, it's always a disappointment. This little guy is Tom Cruise?! There haven't been five tough musicians in history, and they're doing all this posturing and sneering and snarling. And that's fine, that's what you do. 'Street Fighting Man', 'Under My Thumb'. I mean, how long would it take you to get out from under Mick Jagger's thumb?"

The sleeve is a shot of Randy sitting behind a corporate desk, in a corporate office, with a corporate lamp, wearing a corporate suit, in every respect the model of a go-getting junior exec moving up the ladder — except that he's wearing Kiss-style make-up with dollar signs on his eyes. Mike Salisbury, the art director they'd worked with for the *Good Old Boys* packaging, put it together.

It "was Randy's idea to paint his face like Kiss, but with dollar signs," he said. "The set, wardrobe and props were a mutual decorative effort to support the gag, which Marty Evans shot.

"I do remember that to do the Kiss make-up concept right, it needed to be supported by the totally non sequitur cheap suit, the cheap desk, the photos of his kids under the obviously faux antique desk lamp, and staged in a black tableau to emphasize the face, the suit and the nerdy glasses over the surreal dollar signs.'

"The final effect looks so simple, but it did take work to get it reduced to a straightforward communication. *Born Again* was produced to be pedestrian-looking except for the face... a visual metaphor for Randy's music and his satiric style."

Randy's only criticism of the finished product was of the photo on the desk. "My family is even squarer looking than that one," he said. "I wish that family wasn't smiling."

The music industry was booming and marketing budgets keeping pace. The campaign for the four Kiss solo albums, released in the previous year, had cost $2.5m.

Since 1967, when Elektra Records bought hoarding space for a new Doors album, the billboards of Sunset Strip had been the place to be seen: The Rolling Stones had been seen on the billboards of Sunset, David Bowie had been seen on the billboards of Sunset, ELO had been seen on the billboards of Sunset, Mr Bruce Springsteen had been seen on the billboards of Sunset and now it was Randy Newman's turn to be up there, walking with the gods in the holy land.

The image they used for the poster was a huge head shot of Randy – so big that it stuck out beyond the edges of the poster – wearing the Kiss dollar-sign make-up with his pink tongue stuck out to its full extent and his eyes popping.

His dad was unimpressed. "I said to him, 'Randy, how can I say to my friends, with that billboard on Sunset, 'That's my son?' He said, 'Well, dad I'm an unhappy man.' And I said 'What are you unhappy about?' He said, 'I wish I knew. I'm not unhappy enough to have a shrink, but I know I'm a down sort of guy and I don't ever know what's going to come out when I sit down and play.'"

How his attested unhappiness related to a billboard on Sunset with his tongue sticking out is hard to say, but that's often how it is with family dynamics.

The album was released in August 1979.

"Everyone was so confident about it," Randy said, "about how well it would do. It was like the Titanic. They paid me lots of money like it was going to be big. And it was the first album I myself thought was going to be a success, believe it or not."

The reviews weren't good.

Billboard said it was a fine example of "his cutting, dirty, nasty, sick, sarcastic look at life through twisted imagery that overpowers the listener", and warned dealers to be careful which track they played in their stores because "several have 'problem words'."

Stephen Holden, in *Rolling Stone*, described Randy's voice as "unremittingly snide". He called 'The Story Of A Rock And Roll Band' "galumphing", 'Half A Man' a "bad surrealist joke", and the whole "less like a coherent song cycle than a sloppy nightclub act whipped up at the last minute in a fit of pique and 'produced' in a studio."

By the beginning of October, the album had hauled itself up to number 41 in the *Billboard* chart. It hung on for a couple of weeks, then slipped away.

"I really concentrated on that album, *Born Again*, on acting with my voice," Randy said. "It was a really difficult record. People who love *Sail*

Away, those more comfortable liberal attitudes, found *Born Again* tough to deal with. It's the same, but harder to get at.

"It's a strange album: it sounded very good but presumed people knew who I was, a presumption I'd never made before and have never made since.

"I sort of wrote myself into a dead end by taking nothing seriously."

Chapter Fourteen

EL Doctorow's novel *Ragtime* was the literary sensation of 1975. As well as earning critical plaudits and a couple of awards, it sold a quarter of a million copies in hardback.

Set in the years before US engagement in the First World War and steeped in American history and identity, the plot tells tales of three families and involves an abandoned baby, a successful African-American musician who has an altercation with a group of firemen, an attack on a library, a socialist who cuts paper silhouettes for a living, a strike and use of aeronautics in the early years of cinema.

It's a jazz structure – old New Orleans jazz with themes and plotlines weaving around each other like melody and counterpoint.

EL Doctorow knew music. His dad ran a music store in New York and, growing up, he'd had access to a huge record collection. His mother played classical piano; his brother played jazz piano.

The book incorporates real events – an expedition to the North Pole, the sinking of the *Lusitania* – and a sprinkling of real people – Harry Houdini, Sigmund Freud, JP Morgan, Henry Ford, Booker T. Washington and the notorious Evelyn Nesbit. "I was a big fan of the way the book took those historical characters and treated them so shabbily," Randy said. "And the period interested me historically."

Dino De Laurentiis, the movie producer who brought us Fellini's *La Strada*, Roger Vadim's *Barbarella*, Ingmar Bergman's *The Serpent's*

Egg and Michael Winner's *Death Wish*, had acquired the rights to *Ragtime*.

"Dino De Laurentiis hired me to do the score," Randy said. "I remember he had the best suit I'd ever seen anyone in. I'm talking about a $1,000 suit at a time when a good suit cost $60. He was on the phone, complaining about the casting. He didn't want Patti LuPone because he thought she was too short, which I thought was funny, because she was maybe 5-1 and Dino was what… maybe 4-11?"

De Laurentiis, with his baby legs that stood so low you had to pick him up just to say hello, also hired Robert Altman to direct. If Doctorow wrote jazz novels, Altman made jazz films. He was from Kansas City – a town that produced an unrepresentative number of jazz greats including Lester Young, Count Basie, Charlie Parker and Pat Metheny. He made films like a saxophonist approaches a jam session, not worrying too much about overall structure, letting accidents happen and working with them, encouraging actors to improvise. When they were good – *M.A.S.H.*, *Short Cuts*, *Nashville* – they were magnificent. When they were bad – *Popeye* – they were awful.

When it came to narrative, Altman didn't always see eye to eye with the Hollywood ideal. "Happy endings are absolutely ludicrous, they're not true at all," he said. "We see the guy carry the girl across the threshold and everybody lives happily ever after… that's bullshit. Three weeks later he's beating her up and she's suing for divorce and he's got cancer."

Altman usually had an agenda – nothing overtly political, just an attitude that informs the work. *M.A.S.H.* is an anti-war film. *Nashville* peeps into the soul of America on the eve of the 1976 bi-centennial. He did not suffer fools, or indeed most other people, gladly and was especially tough on producers.

The Player – one of his masterpieces – is about greed, megalomania and philistinism in the movie business. But it's "not a truthful indictment of Hollywood," he said. "It's much uglier than I portrayed it, but nobody would've been interested if I'd shown just how sadistic, cruel and self-orientated it is."

Doctorow, Altman and Newman: the dream team, all slightly strange, all with similar agendas, all big music fans, all more interested in proper story than structured narrative.

Ragtime was a big project. In effect it was Randy's first movie score – the bits and bobs he'd provided for *Cold Turkey* being no more challenging than the bits and bobs he'd provided for *Peyton Place* or *Voyage To The Bottom Of The Sea*.

Uncle Alfred had died in 1970. Uncle Emil and Uncle Lionel were both of an age to retire. It was time for junior to step up to the plate. "There was a little extra pressure," Randy admitted to *People Magazine*. "Standards are high in the family."

There was no shortage of other Newmans eager to live up to those standards: Alfred's sons, David and Thomas, both destined for distinguished careers in the family business, were coming on fast; Lionel's grandson Joey was still a toddler, so it would be a good few years before he'd be big enough to reach the conductor's desk; but Randy, 11 years older than David, 33 years older than Joey, was first to rise to the challenge.

Things had changed since Alfred's time. "He said never be afraid of melody," Randy said, "but nowadays, I think you do have to be wary of it because directors might not want it. He said not to worry about things going too slow musically, but I do. He said, 'Don't work at night.' But mainly that was because he was loaded every night."

Inevitably, Altman and De Laurentiis had a fight.

In 1976, Altman made a film, produced by De Laurentiis, called *Buffalo Bill And The Indians, Or Sitting Bull's History Lesson* starring Paul Newman. Like *Nashville* it was a sprawling ensemble piece, which dissected some of the key myths that propped up the American psyche. Unlike *Nashville*, it wasn't very good. De Laurentiis, who'd been anticipating a proper Western more along the lines of *The Searchers* or at least Altman's own *McCabe And Mrs Miller*, didn't like it at all but all the same submitted it to the Berlin Film Festival, where it won the Grand Prix.

Altman wanted nothing to do with the award, claiming that De Laurentiis had submitted a heavily re-edited version of his film, that it did not represent his work and thus to accept the prize would be an act of fraud.

Things got worse when Altman presented his intentions for *Ragtime*. He and Doctorow, brought in to write the screenplay, had devised an ambitious adaption of the novel which they reckoned would have a running time of about six hours. De Laurentiis suggested that a few trims might help the movie's box-office potential. Altman put his foot down. De Laurentiis fired him.

Instead he hired Miloš Forman, the Czech director whose *One Flew Over The Cuckoo's Nest* had just won Best Picture, Best Director,

Best Actor, Best Actress and Best Adaptation at the Oscars. It also got nominated for five other awards including one for Jack Nitzsche's score.

"I had read the book [*Ragtime*], so I knew it was beautifully written," Forman said. "The novel was crawling with characters whose stories Doctorow sketched in and quickly moved on. There could have been several completely different movies made of the book, which was a challenge that excited me, so I took Dino up on his offer."

Years went by before Forman was free of other commitments, the right cast was available and the movie could go into production.

By 1979 there was still no script. Doctorow was no longer interested. Forman approached Michael Weller, a playwright who he'd recently worked with on the movie adaptation of the musical *Hair!*

Weller's script defines a single current in the novel's turbulence of characters and themes: the story of Coalhouse Walker Jr, the black piano player with the Model T-Ford who runs into trouble with the racist firemen. Howard E. Rollins Jr played Coalhouse Walker in a cast that also included Elizabeth McGovern, James Cagney (brought out of retirement at the age of 81) and, in one of his rare acting roles, Norman Mailer, who was hired to play the architect Stanford White (one of the real-life characters in the book and the film) simply because he looked like him.

Randy recorded his score at Evergreen Studios in the summer of 1981. Three years earlier, he'd been sanguine about the art of conducting. "You go like his – and they get louder," he told *Melody Maker*. "And then you go like that and they get softer. That's all there is to it."

But, perhaps because of the pressure added by schedules, deadlines and timings, this time he found it "the scariest thing in the world".

Before one session: "Roswitha woke me up in the middle of the night – I was trying to crawl under her back to hide."

The stress was not helped by the independence he was given. 'Spotting' music – deciding where it should go, what kind it should be, how it should relate to the action on screen and so on – is an art that can make or break a movie. Miloš pretty much left it to Randy. It was a big responsibility. "It's a very arcane business," Randy told Paul Zollo. "I'm not saying that it's exalted. It's not like small particle physics, but it's odd."

Music can entirely change the audience's perception of plot and character. "You can give someone more intelligence that they might be indicating they've got. And you can do lots of stuff for action."

Most of the *Ragtime* score is made up of authentic-sounding period styles – ragtime, early jazz, minstrel songs and parlour piano music – the meat and drink styles that inhabit a lot of Randy's songs.

The main theme is a waltz – piano-led, lilting and melancholy. It's a simple, catchy tune – a natural ear-worm. Apart from a couple of tricky intervals, you could whistle it after one or two hearings. It provides a counter melody for 'One More Hour', a fragile number Randy wrote for the end credits, sung by Jennifer Warnes.

Another song, 'Change Your Way' – a shuffle, would you believe it – didn't make the cut but turned up, sung by Randy, on the soundtrack album.

There is a third, authentic period song: 'I Could Love A Million Girls' was written in 1906 by Cassius Freeborn* and Edgar Allen Woolf for a show called 'Mamzelle Champagne'. Randy did the arrangement. The song was chosen for purposes of historical verisimilitude (not elsewhere a preoccupation of novel or movie) because it was during 'Mamzelle Champagne' that Evelyn Nesbit's husband murdered Stanford White. In the movie, it's sung by Donald O'Connor – the 'Make 'Em Laugh' running-up-the-walls dancer from *Singin' In The Rain* – who'd been away from feature films for 16 years, busy with heart attacks and alcoholism.

The score was nominated for an Academy Award and 'One More Hour' for Best Song – the first of Randy's many, many nominations. This time, Vangelis walked off with the Best Score Oscar for *Chariots Of Fire* and Burt Bacharach and others with Best Song for 'The Best The You Can Do' from *Arthur*.

"When they had the Oscars," Randy said, "they did a medley of the nominated songs, performed by Liberace. My song was sung by John Schneider from *The Dukes Of Hazzard*, which I guess is what I mean when I say the whole experience is pretty strange."

On its release in November 1981, opinions about *Ragtime* were split to extremes. On the one hand, the *Toronto Globe & Mail* said it "twinkles with delight", and *Variety* called it "a superbly crafted screen adaptation." On the other, David Denby in the *New Yorker* called it: "a Keystone

---

* Cassius Freeborn was composer and musical director on a string of Broadway shows during the early part of the twentieth century. He would have almost certainly known the young Alfred Newman: more evidence that Randy has American music folded into his DNA.

Maybe I'm Doing It Wrong

Kops movie without laughs, a production of *Pirates of Penzance* without songs" and "a dud epic made by men who have lost their instincts as entertainers".

But even some of the bad reviews could find redeeming features: "*Ragtime* is better read than seen," said Michael Blowen in the *Boston Globe*, but he had the grace to prefix his remarks with: "Except for the evocative sets and Randy Newman's upbeat musical score."

In May 1976, a show called *Side By Side By Sondheim* had opened at the Mermaid Theatre in London. It was a revue consisting of 31 songs by Stephen Sondheim, organised into thematic groups and linked by a narrator. It was a huge success and transferred to Broadway where it ran for nearly 400 performances.

In March 1981, Randy was given the same accolade when director Joan Micklin Silver strung together 25 of his songs in a show called *Randy Newman's Maybe I'm Doing It Wrong*. It opened at the Production Company Theatre, an off-Broadway venue, and starred* Mark Linn-Baker (Peter O'Toole's minder in *My Favourite Year*), Deborah Rush (Piper's mum in *Orange Is The New Black*), Treat Williams (fresh from playing George in Miloš Forman's *Hair!*) and Patti Perkins. Randy himself had no involvement in the show, but his approval had been sought and given. Tickets were a steal at just $6.50, but it ran for just 17 performances.

A year later, an upgraded version of the show, now titled *Maybe I'm Doing It Wrong*, without the *Randy's Newman's*, ran for 33 performances at the Astor Theatre, just off-Broadway on Lafayette Street.

They say the neon lights are bright on Broadway. In 1982, Randy Newman wouldn't have known one way or the other.

Stephen Sondheim was elected to the American Academy of Arts and Letters in 1983. Two years later he got a Pulitzer Prize. But he's only ever won one Oscar. Randy has two.

He was doing okay. He and Roswitha and the three sons had moved into a sizeable house on Pacific Palisades, "an affluent neighbourhood" as the realtors called it, "on the Westside of Los Angeles offering an active outdoor lifestyle while still maintaining an easy drive to everything the City of Los Angeles has to offer." Take a left off Sunset and you're in the

---

* According to the ad in New York magazine – different sources vary.

Riviera Country Club, take a right, and you're in the Will Rogers Historic Park.

Roswitha had handled the purchase – "she did it all and showed me some pictures one time." Randy, in the words of one friend, "wouldn't know where the phone is".

Pacific Palisades was where he'd grown up. When he writes of 'home', as he often does, Pacific Palisades is the home he writes about. This is not to say he'd ever been overburdened with community spirit. "It's tough on Roswitha," he said. "She's friends with lots of people in the neighbourhood. They must think I'm a little strange. It's like Boo Radley in *To Kill A Mockingbird*. There's a presence in the house."

"I worry about the kids," he told *People* magazine. "People are really complicated. And if someone's got time to worry about nukes and all that stuff, I'm grateful, but I've got enough trouble figuring out the boys and Roswitha."

Schools had provided a couple of headaches, particularly when the boys were small. "The first kid we had," he told audiences when the kids were too old even to be embarrassed about it any more, "my wife was German, and expected them to eat with a fork and unreasonable things like that. And it was in the days of progressive schools, so we first tried a progressive school, and they sat around on little cots and got lice every couple of weeks, and you'd go and say he's got lice *again*, this is the third time. And some pothead would say, [calmly] 'Yes, we know, we know.' And it didn't work out so we sent him to a stricter school and he came home from one wearing these short kind of brown pants and my wife's eyes lit up a little bit and that worried me. But he went to one school which is distinctive only because it graded so comprehensively: every 20 weeks we'd get a report card that was 20 or 30 pages long – really it was. They'd break reading down ten ways, and writing and everything – he was six years old. And he got Ds and Fs in every subject but one in which he got an A with an exclamation point and it was 'Meets new situations with confidence'."

Paternal discipline was never Randy's forte. Amos, by this time, had grown way beyond the progressive schools and the little brown pants but was still 'meeting new situations with confidence'. He was a punk, with a spiky crew-cut and a single earring. When he came home from school with bad grades, Randy told him he definitely was not allowed to get his hair cut. The injunction shocked them both.

"I couldn't believe it came out of me. It took me a couple of hours. I had to walk around and think about what had happened, how I'd got to this position."

Amos played in a band. Peter Burg, who was at the time working at a Palisades music store, remembers them coming in to make a record in the little four-track studio there. At the time, Ted Knight, the actor who played the newscaster in *The Mary Tyler Moore Show*, was generally considered to be the Honorary Mayor of Pacific Palisades. Amos' band didn't think he was all that. Their song, though more direct than most of Randy's work, contained something of the same satirical intent.

"As I remember," says Peter Burg in his blog, "it was called '#*!% You Ted Knight'."

Randy was still trying to be a regular working man, renting a room with a piano and no phone to distract him, putting in the hours every day till lunchtime.

"I never write 24 hours a day," he told *Mix* magazine. "I can't do that. I never get an idea when I'm not sitting down to work… never. I'm so doctrinaire about it that I probably exclude them. I don't like thinking about it when I'm not working. I work from 9.00 in the morning until about 1.00, tops, and I try not to think about it the rest of the day. It doesn't do me any good.

"I think that's why so many writers and composers are drunks: to turn it off. I don't keep a pad by my bed the way Paul Simon and Stevie Nicks do. I work at the piano, and that's it."

He's often said that his dream has always been to look forward to going to work every day, but he's never achieved it – he's never looked forward to writing, only having written.

And having written, he had to go back into the studio and endure the torment of making another album.

Chapter Fifteen

Rock royalty turned out to sing and play on the new album: Paul Simon, Don Henley, Linda Ronstadt, Bob Seger, Rickie Lee Jones, three members of Toto, and Lindsey Buckingham and Christine McVie of Fleetwood Mac. "His peers have such a high regard for him," said Lenny Waronker. "They wanted to be a part of it and help get Randy's stuff out to a lot of people."

The album, *Trouble In Paradise*, is as near to straight pop as Randy Newman ever came. As with most of his albums, it has an approximate overarching theme. "It came to be about places and situations that could be ideal," he said, "but are somehow messed up."

He started with his home town.

"Don Henley said, 'Everybody's writing these LA breakdown songs, and we're writing about 'Hotel California'," Randy said. "You're *from* here [Henley was from Texas, Glen Frey from Michigan and Don Felder from Florida], so why don't *you* write one?' So I did."

"This town makes no demands on you and offers you everything good," said one-time Beatles press-officer Derek Taylor, describing LA in 1968. "Everyone you know or like wants to come here. Even The Beatles, who never go anywhere."

Later, in 2001, Randy fronted a TV documentary for PBS about LA, or at least about the 27 miles of Sunset Boulevard, for a series called *Great*

Streets. He plays a genial, shambling tour guide, presenting a generally rosy view of his home town.

Others, people who had neglected to tick the 'rose tint' box at the opticians, have called LA "70 suburbs in search of city", "a three-ring circus in search of a tent", "uptight plastic America crawling with buyers and sellers of flesh and the masters of artificiality", "like the scuzzier bits round the back of New Street Station, Birmingham, England, only hotter".

The first track of the album warms to its theme gradually.

Like 'Ghosts, it begins with the kind of introductory verse you get in proper thirties songs by the Gershwins or Cole Porter, and a nod to Rodgers and Hart's 'The Lady Is A Tramp'. "Hate New York City / It's cold and it's damp."

As soon as the rhythm kicks in with a heavy synth line that could come from a Michael Jackson track, you think, "Hullo, this sounds quite anthemic."

'I Love LA' is a wind-in-your-hair, sun-in-your face hunk of West Coast pop that, over the years since it was first recorded, has come close to supplanting 'I Love You California' ("I love you, land of sunshine, half your beauties are untold / I loved you in my childhood and I'll love you when I'm old") as the state's anthem. But …

"It's ambiguous, as all my best songs are, in that the driving around with the redhead listening to The Beach Boys is great. And you can do it all year round too – unless you can't find the redhead. [But] "Sixth Street! We love it!" There's nothing distinguished on any of those streets. No, nothing. They're all east-west and Imperial Highway's got nothing taller on it than I am. It's the kind of thing I find funny."

The streets get more than a name check. They are acclaimed as great wonders of the world with Lindsey Buckingham and Christine McVie on hand to endorse the message.

"Century Boulevard – we love it!
"Victory Boulevard – we love it!
"Santa Monica Boulevard – we love it!
"Sixth Street – we love it!"

The narrator finds delight in everything. "Look at that mountain / look at those trees / look at that bum over there / he's down on his knees."

The city itself, however, seems immune to Randy's ambiguity. 'I Love LA' was used as one of the theme songs for the 1984 Summer Olympics, held in the city. It's played at the LA Dodgers' baseball games, and at the LA Lakers' basketball games and it's played every time the LA Kings hockey team scores a goal. "Look at that bum over there, he's down on his knees."

"There's some kind of ignorance LA has that I'm proud of," Randy said. It's a place, in other words "that could be ideal", but is "somehow messed up."

The song was released as a single and a video was made – a marketing necessity now that MTV was here – in which the bum appears, just as he does in the song, except that he, too, is accompanied by a redhead in a bikini.

In the list of "Songs With Christmas In The Title That Were Never In With The Slimmest Chance Of Being A Festive Hit", Randy's 'Christmas In Capetown' would shame the competition. It's a vicious tale of a white South African, who, challenged on apartheid by a visiting British girl says, "Darling, don't talk about something you don't know anything about."

His anger is driven by fear. He snarls about lines of workers at the diamond mines who stare at him "real hard with their big yellow eyes". And he feels the winds of change. "The beer don't taste the way it ought to taste somehow."

Randy's talent is best deployed when he can put a bit of distance, a bit of objectivity between himself and his subject matter. *Good Old Boys* was as much about the hypocrisy of the North as it was about the iniquities of the South. In 1983, it was impossible to be objective about South African apartheid. There is no secondary target in 'Christmas In Cape Town'.

'The Blues', a duet with Paul Simon, is about as bluesy as 'Christmas In Capetown' is Christmassy. It's a medium-tempo, chirpy number with a jolly I, iii, vi, IV chord structure that, shorn of its lyric, could do sterling service as a sitcom sig. It's the story of a guy to whom all the worst things that can happen to a human being have happened. But he "ran to the room where his piano lay in wait for him. He played and he played."

Randy has often said he regrets the song: "I kind of made fun of people who are hurt or sensitive and found solace in music, because I never found solace (in it)."

It was the first single to be released from the album and almost made the top 50.

'Same Girl' is a love song with a simple arrangement of piano and synth strings and a vicious sting – "few more nights on the street, that's all / A few more holes in your arm." The arresting lyric, as is so often the case with Randy's songs, can distract the attention from the extraordinary melody, showcased more overtly in a lush cover version recorded by the sax player David Sandborn on his 1988 album *Close Up*.

In 'Mikey's' a customer wanders into a bar looking for his Marie. He grumbles about the way North Beach is going with the "spades" and the "Mexicans" and "Chinamen". He complains about the "ugly" music that plays all the time. Then he utters what, for many, is the best couple of lines in the entire Randy Newman canon, lines which old people use as a way of reminding themselves and each other how their attitudes and sense of adventure are hardening faster than their arteries. "Whatever happened to the old songs, Mikey? / Like the Duke Of Earl / Mikey, whatever happened to the fucking Duke Of Earl?"

'Duke Of Earl' was a 1962 doo-wop hit by Gene Chandler. The music and vocal performance lift the spirits wonderfully. The lyric – which alternates repetition of the phrase 'Duke Of Earl' with claims by the alleged Duke that his aristocratic status will enable him to protect and cherish the soon-to-be Duchess of Earl – should never be discussed with members of the House of Lords lest it exacerbate their confusion to fatal extremes. All the same, those who remember 'Duke Of Earl' when it was number one, who outlived that day and saw old age, will strip their sleeves and show their scars then turn one to another and say, with the chap in Mikey's, "Whatever happened to the fucking Duke Of Earl?"

The actor/comedian Steve Coogan once described his creation Alan Partridge as "sort of a dysfunctional alter ego". The character, he said, "becomes like a trash can for everything that's wrong with you."

The character that Randy plays in 'My Life Is Good' is, similarly, a paranoid vision of himself – an amalgam of many of his own characteristics remodelled into something that, in his worst nightmares, he could become – or worse, he already is. Psychologically it's probably very healthy to get all these things out. A form of role playing.

Like 'The Girls In My Life – Part 1', it's mostly spoken. In his sneeriest voice. The narrator of the song (who, we discover, is also called Randy) is a rich Hollywood bigshot, swollen with self-importance, who browbeats his son's teacher when she dares to tell him that his son is the school bully ("you old bag!"), boasts how he works his poor Mexican maid into the ground and speculates about giving his friend's pretty little wife "a poke or two".

In the final verse, he goes up to the Bel Air Hotel to see "a very good friend of ours" whose name is Mr Bruce Springsteen. They talk for a while about music, about "some kind of woodblock" and "this new guitar we like". Then Mr Springsteen gets down to the nitty gritty. He says, "Rand, I'm tired. How would you like to be the Boss for awhile?"

This is the cue for Ernie Watts, the tenor player, to pay homage to Mr Springsteen's sax player Clarence Clemmons with some choice honking while 'Rand' shouts, "Blow, big man, blow".

"It might be funnier just with piano," Randy said, looking back, never satisfied.

Joe Queenan, the journalist and critic, said about the track in the *New York Times*: "This is one of the few instances in pop-cultural history where anyone dared to poke fun at the sanctified Mr Springsteen, where anyone had the nerve to take the mickey out of the Boss and his studiously manicured image as the poet of the proles.

"Recording 'My Life Is Good' was the kind of jaundiced, disrespectful gesture that has long made Mr Newman an outcast at life's rich feast. Making fun of the Boss was like snickering during a Holy Communion service, like plopping down on a whoopee cushion during a State of the Union address. Was Mr Newman not aware that ridiculing Bruce Almighty, at least in the minds of white baby boomers, was like sneering at Mom, apple pie and the American flag?"

Yes.

'Miami' is another one "about places and situations that could be ideal, but are somehow messed up": except that, apart from one or two shady characters, it's hard to spot where the mess is. It starts with a little urgent chromaticism that suggests it's auditioning for the next Bond film, quotes Gershwin's 'Rhapsody In Blue', finishes with insane Kurt Weillisms played on what sounds like a barrel-organ, mentions that the dope is free and invites you to say hello to a double-jointed guy who works in the circus in St Pete. Does that sound messed up to you?

'Real Emotional Girl' is another of his love songs with a twist. A guy is telling his buddy about his new girlfriend. She "wears her heart on her sleeve", she "cries in her sleep", she was a daddy's girl. She's unconditionally trusting and loving.

"I don't really think that it's okay for the guy to tell his friend something so private and personal about the girl," Randy said. "I know some of you prefer to think of it as a straight love song. That's all right. I see it otherwise."

"'Real Emotional Girl' moved around on me a bit," he told *Mix* magazine. "I had written, 'she comes real quick, it's like a hurricane'; but I didn't want to hear that over and over. I sanitized it ['she turns on easy, it's like a hurricane']; it sounds better, more literate."

'Take Me Back' has autobiographical elements – a fairly faithful recreation of Randy's High School hi-jinks, his brushes with teenage gangs and even his night in the cells. The narrator is plainly a spoiled suburban fuck-up. But this fuck-up ends up living in a shack by the airport and not in that big house in Pacific Palisades. The parallels between the arrangement of 'Take Me Back' and that of 'I Love LA' might tempt a musicologist to trace thematic and structural links between the two but luckily there aren't any musicologists handy.

'There's A Party At My House' is a rolling, backbone-slipping boogie with some fine saxophone playing from either Jim Horn or Jon Smith or possibly both. Lyrically it's another visit to the 'Mamma Told Me Not To Come' territory, but much, much nastier. Everybody's dancing and having a good time. The narrator is watching the "little red-haired girl" "jumpin' up and down". He admires her blotchy face, her pink nipples. Then the chiller – "Hey Bobby, get the rope."

'I'm Different' is about a happy-go-lucky and insufferably smug individualist. He sings in a kinda folksy Deputy Dawg sort of a way. Linda Ronstadt, Wendy Waldman and Jennifer Warnes support his assertions in the sweet voices of the Caravelles. The treatment is pure Disney and thus foreshadows – although it is but a pale shadow of – his later work with Pixar.

'Song For The Dead' is a requiem with distant drums. Randy writes in the notes accompanying the compilation album, *Guilty: 30 Years Of Randy Newman*: "I thought it was safe to come out against Vietnam ten years after the war was over. I've since come out against child abuse and AIDS."

Trouble In Paradise was released in January 1984.

Reviews included words like "stunning", "thrilling" and "demanding". Some even used the g-word: not, it has to be said '*a genius*' but '*his* genius' which is the next best thing as well as being etymologically more accurate.

It made 64 on *the Billboard* LP chart.

"This album has been reviewed like it was one of Beethoven's late quartets," he told *People* magazine, "but that does no good. I want something different. I'd like to be able to play Kansas City without having to sneak into town, apologize to the promoter and give money back. To sell a lot, you have to have a record that people can have in the background and eat potato chips to. You can't do that with mine."

"I'm dissatisfied with a million things. I just worked with Don Henley and Paul Simon separately. Simon was trying to get rid of his acoustic guitar, which was always beautiful to me, and Henley was trying to bury his voice, which is also fine. I'm beginning to think it's endemic to musicians to not like what you do best. Like me, I hate the way I play piano and sing."

Randy did interviews all over the place, promoted the 'I Love LA' video and even had a TV special devoted to him and his music, during the making of which he came close to getting shot.

He was in New York to make the show, walking along the street with Ry Cooder and Linda Ronstadt, who were also appearing, to get some lunch at the Café des Artistes. "While we were walking," Linda said in her autobiography, *Simple Dreams*, "a police officer ran past us at full speed, breathing hard and trying to catch up with someone we couldn't see. He pulled several yards ahead of us, and his gun slipped out of its holster, falling to the sidewalk. We called out to him, but he was already out of range. I reached down to pick up the gun.

"'No,' shouted Randy, 'leave it there.'

"'What if a child picks it up,' I asked him, 'someone could get hurt.'

"'Throw it in there,' he said, indicating a large trash can.

"'It might go off and kill the poor garbage collector,' I argued.

"I picked up the gun and immediately spotted two police officers driving along in a squad car. I raised my arm to hail them like a taxi and started to wave the gun in their direction. Randy, who lacked experience with firearms, but had a lot of awareness of what happens to people who point guns at NYPD officers, managed to hide the gun from sight while he explained to me as tactfully as possible that I was a reckless moron."

Everybody lived.

More danger loomed on his European tour. In the UK, the IRA were bombing, Mrs Thatcher's Conservatives had just redefined the word 'unemployment' in order to disguise figures of four million plus, while, cruelly it seemed, Men At Work were at number one with 'Down Under'.

"Conditions are too tough out there to be hip any more," Randy said.

His UK tour fell short of a sell-out and though the rock glitterati gathered at the Dominion Theatre in Tottenham Court Road to honour and adore the master, around them were patches of emptiness. Still, the reviews were terrific.

Richard Williams, in the *Times*, explained something of the problem: "It is daring and demanding stuff, never more so than when Newman performs 30 or so of his vignettes alone at the piano on a concert stage, switching angle and attitude with such bewildering rapidity. Over such a distance one comes to admire even more his great musical range, allowing each song a distinctive setting, and the way he manipulates his extremely limited vocal technique so cleverly, mashing his diction for the frustrated incomprehension of 'Christmas In Cape Town' and clarifying it for the unfathomably tragic 'Same Girl', thickening it for the eternally ambiguous 'I Think It's Going To Rain Today'."

Williams praised the "brilliant images like the *Star Wars* motif painted on the lunch-tins of glowering blacks at the diamond mine; the eerie sky above the Rhine, enveloping the paedophiliac murderer and his victim; the potent symbol of the big black dog in the steel-worker's yard. And the small, inarticulate explosions of impotence, 'I'm drunk right now baby / but I've got to be.' 'Whatever happened to the old songs, Mikey? / Like the Duke of Earl'."

Tune into BBC2, and you could have seen more of the "daring, demanding stuff" on the *Leo Sayer Show*, where Randy guested along with Suzi Quatro and Tony 'Tie A Yellow Ribbon Round The Old Oak Tree' Orlando.

"I'd like to play in a string quartet," he told *Rolling Stone* in March 1983. "Play a little chamber music, if I could hack it. I'd really have to sort of practice, but that's one of the things I'd like to do. I could probably go to UCLA and see if I could do it – find a couple of guys... or four girls with big tits."

"See, that's what's the matter with me. There's a very, very bad streak of vulgarity running through my work. I mean, I worry about that stuff more than most, believe me. And I don't think I've ever done anything that is vulgar. But something in me says something ridiculous like that. Like a conscious attempt not to be sensitive about anything. It's living in America that does it. Manly, at all times. Can't read poetry or play in a string quartet."

Chapter Sixteen

Though you'd barely have noticed against the din being made by *E.T.*, *Indiana Jones*, *Ghostbusters* and Marty McFly, the eighties saw some respectable sports films.

It's a neglected genre, and if you've seen *Blades Of Glory* you'll understand why. But, among others, *Chariots Of Fire*, *Hoosiers*, *Field Of Dreams* and *The Color Of Money* (if you count pool as a sport) turned a healthy profit and attracted three or four-star ratings.

The Natural was a baseball novel by Bernard Malamud published in 1952, based loosely on the story of Eddie Waitkus of the Chicago Cubs and Philadelphia Phillies. It tells the tale of Roy Hobbs, a baseball hero, shot by a stalker, making a slow recovery and rediscovering himself and his game.

Sport in film and fiction is usually either a metaphor for some spiritual quest far beyond the realms of stump and changing room — see *Chariots Of Fire* and *Field of Dreams* — or it's a vehicle for screwball comedy probably starring Goldie Hawn.

The Natural is shot through with mythic undertones. Roy's bat is hewn from a lightning tree. His team's manager is called Pops Fisher — carrying echoes of the Fisher King of Arthurian legend and of TS Eliot's *The Waste Land*.

In 1983, the newly amalgamated TriStar Pictures put an adaptation of the novel into production as their first venture, to be directed by Barry

Levinson. Robert Redford played the lead, ageing from 19 to 34 during the course of the movie, a feat which, even with the softest of lighting, was a stretch for the 46-year-old actor. The screenplay, by Roger Towne and Phil Dusenberry, played fast and loose with the novel, particularly when it came to the ending.

The book ends with Hobbs accepting a bribe to lose a game, then changing his mind mid-game, then splitting his magic bat and consequently losing anyway. Afterwards, his corruption is exposed and the story ends with a paperboy looking at the headlines and muttering, "Say it ain't true, Roy."

In the film, Hobbs refuses to throw the game and wins with a hit that hammers into the floodlights, showering the field in phosphorescent sparks as our hero rounds the bases, bleeding manfully through his shirt.

Robert Redford defended the decision: "We knew we'd take some serious heat, deservedly, for that, but you had to have that ending for Hollywood. You couldn't get that movie made with the book's ending."

"America loves a winner," said Glenn Close, who played one of the film's love interests. "They don't like a loser."

Randy was hired to write the score. He played it straight down the line. This was a movie about heroic baseball players, so he gave them heroic baseball player music – instantly memorable, evocative of sunny afternoons, youth, nostalgia and muscle rub. "It's not in my nature to write heroic music for Robert Redford to run around the bases, but I'm glad that I did it in *The Natural*," he said. "And I don't see that kind of assignment writing as a sell-out."

The slow motion run – a production decision that had nothing to do with Redford's age – gave Randy the chance to out-Vangelis Vangelis, whose *Chariots Of Fire Theme* had taken away his *Ragtime* Oscar.

Barry Levinson was delighted with the results. He told Bob Costas: "We were racing to try to get this movie out in time, and we were in one room and then there was a wall and Randy's in the other room. One of the great thrilling moments is when I heard him figuring out that theme [...] You could hear it through the wall as he was working out that theme and I'll never forget that."

Randy calls it "Heromuzik".

The influences are varied. Aaron Copland is in all of Randy's work, although since both composers draw inspiration from the same well it's hard to say what's Copland and what's source music – Stephen Foster, folk-song, medicine shows and so on. There's always a trace of Uncle Alfred in there, too. Some have spotted remnants of Mahler, Wagner, Mendelssohn. But, "The source music was Duke Ellington," Randy told Sean Daly in the *Tampa Times*. "I love that stuff; Barry Levinson did, too. There was heroic stuff, romantic stuff with a blues influence. Mysticism – there was magic with that bat. But mostly it was American, Midwestern. I was really playing America, you know? Baseball was the American game – well before football became the American game."

The orchestration sounds opulent, as if it was paying the grocery bills of 80 or 90 musicians, but Randy remembers cheeseparing.

"They were blowing up a big light standard in the film and I couldn't get a second flute player for the orchestra and I'm going, 'You're going to spend $1 million on a light standard and I can't get another flute player. What kind of world is this, anyway?'"

Rob Sheffield, in *The Rolling Stone Album Guide*, wrote that Randy too often composed "stomach-turning treacle". "Pick a Top 10 of the schlockiest movies you've ever seen and the odds are that Randy worked on at least three of them."

Sometimes, though, the only thing that can turn the sight of a 46-year-old man running slowly round a baseball pitch surrounded by inexplicable electrical faults into a-stand-up-and-clap finale is stomach-turning treacle, and that stuff doesn't write itself. And, as anyone who made contact with their emotions for the first time while listening to the Act I finale of Puccini's *La Bohéme* will tell you, there are circumstances in which the most noble thing music can do is turn your stomach with its impeccable treacle.

Anyway, Billy Joel was only too pleased to use the big, boastful hero tune as his entrance music for live shows. "I don't give Billy shit for using 'The Natural'," Randy says. "I give Billy shit for visiting me in a dressing room a few years ago, talking about himself for an hour, and then leaving."

The score earned Randy another Academy Award Nomination. John Williams got two nominations that year, but in the end the Oscar went to Maurice Jarre for *A Passage To India*.

Randy did, however, pick up a Grammy for Best Instrumental Composition.

In 1985, Randy and Roswitha separated.

"I don't know why we broke apart. Things like that happen," he told *People* magazine, "I will always be her friend and she will always be mine."

"We wanted different things," he told Chrissy Iley in the *Telegraph*. "She wanted to do things like go up the Nile with lots of other couples and I don't like going on trips with people. You find out more about them than you want to know."

Years later, when introducing the song 'I Miss You', the love song he wrote for Roswitha long after both of them had remarried, he said, "I left her for someone else, someone who tricked me with artificial lighting and other means."

Lorne Michaels is a TV producer, writer, comedian and actor probably best known for producing *Saturday Night Live*. As we've heard, Randy guested with Paul Simon and Phoebe Snow on the show's second episode ever, but since then *SNL* had evolved from a music show with comedy to a comedy show with music.

In 1980, Steve Martin, a frequent guest on *SNL*, had come up with an idea for a movie called *The Three Caballeros*. He mentioned it in a *Playboy* interview suggesting *SNL* regulars John Belushi and Dan Ackroyd as potential co-stars.

Steve, Lorne Michaels and their friend Randy Newman got together to work on a script.

"We did it at my house in Beverly Hills when I had a house in Beverly Hills," Steve Martin told Bruce Fretts. "Lorne would walk over from the Beverly Hills Hotel and wasn't quite ready to work… he had to read the trades first. It was a joyful time for the three of us because Randy was writing the songs, but he also pitched in on the script. I was at the word processor… it wasn't a computer then, it was a word processor. I'm not kidding. If I wanted to move a paragraph, we would walk away and go sit in the living room. It would take maybe five minutes. But anyway, that's not important. We would go to lunch at the Grill, and it was really nice. We had a good time."

What developed was a story, loosely inspired by *The Magnificent Seven*, about three silent movie stars who are mistaken for real heroes by the suffering people of a small Mexican village and asked to come and protect them from the local bandits. It was eventually retitled ¡*Three Amigos!*.

The death of John Belushi put the kybosh on Steve Martin's original casting idea. At one point, Steven Spielberg was a possible director with

Maybe I'm Doing It Wrong

Bill Murray and Robin Williams, along with Steve, as the Amigos. Eventually the dust settled leaving Steve Martin, Chevy Chase and Martin Short as the amigos, with John Landis, of *The Blues Brothers*, *Spies Like Us* and *Trading Places*, directing.

Elmer Bernstein, who eventually accumulated nearly as many movie credits as Uncle Alfred, including *The Magnificent Seven* and *The Great Escape*, scored the movie. Randy provided three songs: 'The Ballad Of The Three Amigos', 'My Little Buttercup' and 'Blue Shadows On The Trail'.

Randy also appeared, or at least was heard, his voice altered by some electronic witchcraft out of all recognition, as a bush. The idea was stolen from the Book of Deuteronomy – except whereas the Bible bush is merely burning, this one goes one better as a *singing* bush. The Amigos, following cryptic instructions that are supposed to lead them to the lair of the bad guy, El Guapo, are told they must find a singing bush. Understandably they are relieved when, on the long and lonesome trail they come upon a bush singing 'She'll Be Coming Round The Mountain'. But they need to be sure.

"Excuse me, are you the singing bush?" they ask. And all the bush does in reply is to sing 'Blow The Man Down'.

"Excuse me, are you the singing bush?" they ask again, requiring absolute confirmation.

"Goodnight Ladies, Goodnight Ladies," the bush sings.

And so on, through 'My Bonnie', 'The Erie Canal', 'Dixie', until the Amigos, red in the face with questions, reckon it's safe to assume that this is indeed the singing bush.

Newman gives good bush. Martin, Chase and Short turn in fine comic performances and the script is never too proud to include lines like: "I was thinking later, you could kiss me on the veranda." "Really, the lips would be fine."

"Probably the funniest moment for me when shooting," John Landis told *movies.com*, "was when I had the Three Amigos on horseback in the desert […] and I was shooting while they were wearing those ridiculous outfits [they dressed like a Mariachi band made up entirely of pimps] and, after having been shooting for three weeks, Chevy objected to a line of dialogue and he said, 'I don't think I should say this.'

"And, remember, Chevy plays a character named Dusty Bottoms. So I said, 'Well, why not?'

"He said, 'Because my character would have to be a moron to say this.'"

"All I could think was, 'What movie has Chevy been making?' So I said, 'OK, I'll give it to Marty because it's a laugh.'"

"Then Chevy said, 'I'll say it!'"

After John Landis had submitted his final cut, the studio re-edited the film, shortening it. Landis was otherwise engaged with an urgent appointment in court.

Some time before, Landis had directed a section of *Twilight Zone: The Movie*. During the shooting, the actor Vic Morrow and two children were killed and several people injured in a helicopter accident. Landis was facing manslaughter charges. The trial, which lasted nine months, resulted in Landis' acquittal.

¡Three Amigos!, released just in time for Christmas 1986, made a profit at the box office, but not enough to buy anybody an island or a trip to space. The reviews were so-so.

"Nobody should write, direct or play in a farce unless they are prepared to treat it with the utmost seriousness," said Roger Ebert in the *Chicago Sun-Times*. "Everybody in *¡Three Amigos!* seems to think it's some kind of a joke."

Then Randy got sick. He contracted Epstein-Barr, a little understood virus that leaves its victims depressed and chronically fatigued and can, in some cases, lead to other illnesses.

"I couldn't get up a couple of steps without getting out of breath," he told *People* magazine. "But the worst part is in your brain. You just can't think of anything that you look forward to doing. Nothing looks good."

He had separated from his wife of 18 years. He had moved house.

"It may have been precipitated by depression," he said. "But it'll pass whenever you lie down and do nothing. Probably a philosophy I was looking for – lie down and do nothing for three years."

Randy, the son of a Hollywood physician and the brother of an oncologist, finally became so disheartened that he rejected conventional treatments to try homeopathic medicine.

That didn't work either. Nothing worked. Then ...

"It went just like it came. It was such a sort of nebulous kind of thing. The worst part about it was that people said, 'Oh, yeah, you've got that yuppie disease.' It was real. I mean, jeez, I had the symptoms, and I was wiped out.

Maybe I'm Doing It Wrong

"They'll read this in five years and they'll say ho ho ho he thought he had that fake Epstein-Barr thing. It was just another excuse not to put an album out and do any work."

Chapter Seventeen

Illness and movies meant he hadn't release an album for five years and now he wasn't sure he could. He was a man in his forties with grown-up kids. At the time the jury was still out on whether the more mature gent should be making pop records at all.

Dylan, who'd hit forty in 1981, had showed he still had it in him with *Infidels* but then *Empire Burlesque* brought doubts and whispers. Paul Simon's *Hearts And Bones*, now considered by some to be one of his finest works, was, at the time, a critical and commercial disappointment that left him at a creative dead end (a happy impasse, as it turned out, that led him to get on a plane to Johannesburg and make *Graceland)*. Joni Mitchell (just two weeks older than Randy) had been experimenting with electro-pop but sadly nobody hailed *Dog Eat Dog*, her collaboration with Thomas Dolby, as her *Court And Spark* for the eighties.

Paul McCartney released *Give My Regards To Broad Street*, which still has the power to induce mild panic attacks. George hadn't released a studio album since *Gone Troppo* flew like a cast-iron kite. Ringo was narrating *Thomas The Tank Engine*. John was dead.

"I was sick and I didn't know if what I was doing was worth anything," Randy told the *Los Angeles Times*. "I kept asking Lenny if my writing was getting a lot worse because I wasn't getting anything out of it. Finally, Paul Simon heard the stuff and said, 'This is good, representative work for you,' and I guess that's all I wanted. I just don't want to get worse."

Maybe I'm Doing It Wrong

Another concern was that Lenny, who'd produced or co-produced every album Randy had made would no longer be doing so. He'd gone up in the world. As head of A&R and producer, Lenny had given Warners hits – or at least well-respected records – by Arlo Guthrie, Little Feat, The Doobie Brothers, Gordon Lightfoot, Ry Cooder, Maria Muldaur, James Taylor, Rickie Lee Jones, Randy Newman and many of the other acts that a certain kind of record buyer in the seventies (kicker boots and dungarees, bean bags instead of chairs, Hermann Hesse on the coffee table, herbal smell in the air) latched on to as a matter of course. But after 15 years in the job, Mo Ostin promoted him to company president.

So, Lenny would not be behind the glass – this is not to say he was no longer available as Randy's cheerleader, coax, goad and prod.

"I would kid Lenny," Randy told *Rolling Stone*. "I would do my potato thing. 'Lenny, if I became a potato, would you dig me up and put me in the studio and say, 'Sing, potato, sing! Do it. You can do it. You are great. Get in there. Come on potato. You can do it. Let's do an epic.'"

Russ Titelman had other fish to fry, too, crafting award-winners for Steve Winwood, Paul Simon and George Harrison.

New producers were recruited.

James Newton Howard, who produced four of the tracks on the new album, was a classically trained pianist who'd toured and recorded with Elton John, and provided orchestrations for some of Elton's records (including the strings for 'Don't Go Breaking My Heart'). He'd also worked with one of the many incarnations of Toto and with Crosby, Stills & Nash. Since then he's become a very respected film composer – *The Hunger Games* and *Maleficent* were both his – and has been nominated for eight Oscars.

Tommy LiPuma, who produced another four of the tracks, was a name from the old Liberty/Metric music days when he'd worked on demos for Randy and Jackie DeShannon. Since then he'd produced an extraordinary variety of artists – National Lampoon, Barbra Streisand, Hugh Masekela and George Benson's number one, multi-platinum, Grammy award-winning *Breezin'*.

Six of the tracks were produced by Mark Knopfler, the British guitar hero of Dire Straits. He and Randy were brought together by, "… our lawyers. I don't quite remember the details," said Knopfler, "I was just excited about working with one of the greats."

"I'm doing this for Randy," he said. "I don't need the cash."

Which was no less than true. Dire Straits' previous album, *Brothers In Arms*, had kept the pressing plants of the world working overtime to make enough shiny CDs to satisfy the insatiable needs of the newly converted Devotees of Digital. It had reached number one in the US, UK, Australia, had gone double-platinum in Finland and had done wonders for the sales of National Guitars, one of which graced the jewel-case, flying in the sky.

Everybody wanted to work with Mark. He'd guested on and written for a Tina Turner album, produced Dylan's *Infidels* and now he was helping Mr Newman play the honky tonk like anything.

The fourth producer, who worked on just one track, was Jeff Lynne of ELO.

In parts, *Land Of Dreams* was Randy's best work since *Good Old Boys*: in other parts it wasn't. The good parts are the work of a man in his forties who has put excessive snidery and half-hearted attempts at making 'down with the kids' hit records aside in favour of quiet, witty songs of amazement about the world and the way things turn out: songs that can even generate – a quality rarely heard before on a Randy Newman record – a sense of joy.

The opening tracks are straight autobiography, but not of a deeply personal, confessional nature. "Maybe people want personal confessions," he told *Playboy* magazine. "Maybe that's why I don't sell two million records. In fact, I always thought people could tell what I was like from my stuff more easily than they necessarily could tell about a confessional kind of songwriter... I don't know what [Dan] Fogelberg is like from his songs. You can tell what I'm like."

In another context, he said of the album, "I found a way to write about myself that I don't object to. I lied."

The opening of 'Dixie Flyer' is a piano riff of extraordinary grace – a Baroque melody accented in a New Orleans/Spanish rhythm, tweedling and rolling around. Mark Knopfler, who produced the track, supports it with an airy pedal-steel-like guitar line.

The lyric starts with a bald statement of Randy's date and place of birth and goes on to tell the story of his mother's flight from LA, when he was a babe in arms, on the "Dixie Flyer"* to the Land of Dreams. Uncles from

---

* The fact that no train of that name ever went from Los Angeles to New Orleans is noted elsewhere, so don't go on about it.

Jackson, Mississippi meet them at the station, drinking rye whisky and generally trying to blend in by acting like gentiles, "Who wouldn't down there, wouldn't you?"

"Jews seem pretty assimilated in New Orleans, don't you think?" Bunny Matthews, the New Orleans cartoonist, asked him.

"No, they're not assimilated in America," Randy replied, "not really. It's not our country."

It ends, like all train songs should, with the sound effect of a real one, steam up and bell clanging, rounding off one of the most pleasant ways of passing 4'10" ever devised.

'New Orleans Wins The War' continues the story of his childhood and is, of course, a shuffle. He remembers how his mamma used to take him to the park and introduce him to the rudiments of racism; the way in which the ice-cream wagon had "one side for white and one side for coloured". And then, later on, how his mother introduced some of the more advanced concepts; "here comes a white boy, there goes a black one, that one's an octoroon" and how easy it was to absorb this as an unimportant element in the great waves of information that wash into the child's understanding – "this little cookie here's a macaroon, that big round thing's a red balloon."

And as effortlessly as the racism is absorbed, the song breaks out into some gentle New Orleans jazz.

He tells of how his dad came to New Orleans and told everybody they'd won the war. The people were pleased, if confused: "I knew we'd whip the Yankees".

And then it floats into a complete new song that could have been sung by Fats Domino, or played by Sidney Bechet: "Blue, blue morning / blue blue day / all your bad dreams drift away."

'Four Eyes' is a traumatic tale dredged from the depths of Randy's psyche and sung to traumatic music. It's the story of a kid – could be Randy Newman, could be anybody. His dad wakes him, and tells him to put on his "cowboy pants" and his "cowboy shirt" then drives him a long time in the car to his first day of school. "You're not gonna leave me here are you?"

The poor kid wears glasses and gets taunted by the other kids.

Randy said that the song wasn't strictly autobiographical but "felt right": "School was painful. It was not the best time of my life, like they said it was going to be."

"I think we all construct pasts for ourselves out of pieces we pick up here and there, and how true that imagined past is doesn't matter. If you built it, that's what your past is."

The fourth track, 'Falling In Love', is a joyous overview of that ecstatic pastime. Jeff Lynne, from Shard End, Birmingham, formerly of the Nightriders, the Idle Race, the Move and ELO, then with the newly formed Traveling Wilburys, produced it.

They recorded at the garage of Mike Campbell, Tom Petty's guitar player. When the time came to record the backing vocals, Tom, Mike and Jeff assembled around the mic and left a place for Randy. Randy backed away.

"I said, 'I can't really do that,'" he told Scott Jordan of *Offbeat* magazine. Tom encouraged him. "No, you can do it – with Jeff. I didn't think I could do it either, but when I did it with Jeff, we could do it." So Randy stepped up. Tom, Mike and Jeff went "Ooh".

"So I put my hand over my ears like I'd seen people do, and the thing came up, and I went, 'Uungh'.

"And this went on for a while, and I saw Jeff Lynne shaking his head like he smelled something bad. And he looked over at me, and it was a look of, 'Are you putting us on? Are you kidding?' It had a little pity in it, but it was mainly like, 'You're joking, aren't you?' So we did it again, and I went 'Aaah'. And apparently he had never heard anyone that bad. So he just said, 'Maybe you better sit this one out.' So you can't help but getting smacked no matter how far you go."

"He wanted a different angle on one of his tracks," Jeff Lynne said. "He wanted some different guitar style. So I went round to his house, like this vacuum-cleaner salesman, with my guitar in my case: 'Hello? Mr Newman? I've come to do the drains.'"

The song is full of lazy, loping Caribbean sunshine, with some kind of steel-pan synth patch (the Yamaha DX7, popular at the time, had a lovely one) and a four-to-the-bar cowbell. Randy's backup vocals might not be much to write home about but his rhythm and phrasing are rarely less than impeccable. Here he bounces around the beat singing – a man in love: "Now you're walking in the holy land / Yeah, that's you there, walking with the king / You ask 'What have I done to deserve this?'" And, best of all – "Why, you haven't done a thing."

'Something Special' isn't very. It's a love song. Like 'Jolly Coppers', you can study the lyrics for a trapdoor or a twist, but if you find one it probably says more about you than the song. By the time the record was released, the track had already appeared at the end of *Overboard*, a romcom starring Goldie Hawn and Kurt Russell. Randy didn't think much of it, either.

"I like its lick and that arrangement," Randy told the *Los Angeles Times*, "but maybe I don't like it as much because it was in a movie with Goldie Hawn and Kurt Russell and Garry Marshall directed, where she was a very rich woman and he was a kind of workman."

'Bad News From Home' brings the album back to safer ground. If 'Falling In Love' and 'Something Special' are the beginning and middle of the love affair, 'Bad News From Home' is its sad, doom-laden ending.

The narrator, who works in a gas station, is abandoned by his wife. She runs off to Mexico with her lover. Like so many of Randy's songs, the lyric reads like a movie script with hints to the art director and lighting department: "I drove to the station in the pouring rain, sat all night behind my big iron desk, the oil on the water made a rainbow."

He drives down to Mexico, possibly with murderous intent. "You can run, but you can't hide / You said you loved me, but you know you lied."

Mark Knopfler produced the track. "That song is written from the heart," he said. "The song is so right that it couldn't be any other way."

"From the heart", it must be stressed, is not the same thing as "autobiographical". Mark Knopfler is not suggesting that Randy worked in a gas station or that he followed anybody to Mexico with murderous intent, just that genuine feelings and experiences have been melted down and recast.

When he introduces the brutal 'Roll With The Punches' on stage Randy sometimes says: "This is a song I wrote not meaning it, as usual – but it has now become public policy in America."

In it, the callous narrator hands out advice to the unemployed and disadvantaged of America. The advice is that, "They just gonna have to roll with the punches, yes they will. Gonna have to roll with them." The heartlessness is compounded by the inclusion of a tap dance in the middle performed, possibly, by some sort of beggar: "Look at those little shorts he's got on, ladies and gentlemen. You can see all the way to Argentina."

'Masterman And Baby J' is a rap about a boy living with his brother (J) hoping to escape their life of grinding poverty and become rap stars. It's hard to figure out quite what's going on here. Robert Christgau calls it "a compulsive ironist's parody of a parody". If you like compulsive ironist's parodies of parodies then it's catnip.

'Red Bandana' seems to be about a gang member living in LA who returns home to Buffalo to find his mother drunk or stoned and his old girlfriend hanging out in a bar with "Charley Hobbs and this ugly little dude whom I didn't know". They all want to know why the guy's wearing a red bandana and he tells them, "It's red just like your blood is."

A reporter once asked Randy whether audience reaction affected his opinion of his songs. "No, not my own opinion," he said, "but whether I play it or not, sometimes. I will play 'Red Bandana' for instance, whether an audience particularly likes it or not. But I like it."

It has to be said that audiences, though patient, often find themselves thinking, "Two or three minutes of this, then he'll do 'Simon Smith'."

'Follow The Flag' is a sort of patriotic anthem assembled from clichés. "Into every life a little rain must fall." "If you can believe in something bigger than yourself, you can follow the flag forever."

The ironies are so deeply buried that the song could happily be pressed into service as a replacement for 'The Star Spangled Banner'. The tune's more singable and any lyric would be an improvement on the clumsy inversion of, "O say can you see, by the dawn's early light / What so proudly we hailed at the twilight's last gleaming." In fact, since neither colour nor design is ever specified in 'Follow The Flag', it could replace any national anthem in the world. Or all of them.

"It's difficult," Randy said. "It's not meant to be patriotic, but it's a close call. It's obvious to me, but... maybe I didn't do it well enough."

'It's Money That Matters' is a revisiting of 'It's Money That I Love' with elements of Dire Strait's 'Money For Nothing' thrown in. Mark Knopfler has crafted some of the world's finest riffs, and here he's done Mr Newman proud. It's not quite got the iconic kick of the 'Money For Nothing' riff, but what has? The organ from 'Money For Nothing' has been imported, too.

The narrator talks of people he grew up with who now work in book shops and on public radio. He acknowledges that: "All of these people are much brighter than I / In any fair system they would flourish and thrive / But they barely survive." Because the only thing that matters is ...

"I like the stuff about public radio and bookstores," Randy said. "When I learned a couple of years ago that the world isn't fair, I fairly jumped for joy and revelled in my good fortune."

"The inequity of the rich and poor is a big deal," Randy told Mark Horowitz in 2013. "I mean a very big deal at the moment. [...] It interests me that even people who don't have money are not for raising taxes on the rich. And someone told me recently that's an aspirational thing; they think that someday maybe they'll be rich and they don't want their taxes up there. I don't understand that exactly, but it interests me."

'It's Money That Matters' was released as a single and got hugely promoted. For a short time, Randy was everywhere doing the song with Mark on guitar: on *Saturday Night Live*, on *The Tonight Show*, on *Late Night With David Letterman* – he even came over to the UK and did *Wogan*, with Mark, Lord Longford and Dame Edna Everage.

The single made number 60 in the *Billboard* Hot 100, but went all the way to the top in its subsidiary 'Mainstream Rock' chart.

A video was made featuring Randy driving a huge Buick convertible with yet another "nasty redhead" beside him. Mark sits on the trunk of the car playing a shiny Stratocaster. They visit a theme park called Counterculture Land. Then the young Randy (played by a child actor) learns some life lessons from the old Randy (played by a veteran actor) who's got "a great big pool" in his backyard "with another great big pool beside it".

One commentator described the last track on the album as "a well-observed impression of the way in which repressed depression can be expressed in aggression." It's called 'I Want You To Hurt Like I Do', and is a song of epic, self-justified selfishness in which the narrator tells his new girlfriend, the one he left his wife and family for, what her future holds. "I ran out on my children / And I ran out on my wife / Gonna run out on you too, baby / I've done it all my life." He tells of how, when he was leaving his family, he put his hand on the shoulder of his sad little son and said, "I want you to hurt like I do."

That last line – "Honest I do, honest I do, honest I do" – is stolen from Sam Cooke's hymn to the tender excitement of young love, 'You Send Me', which makes the song even more distressing.

The biographer's most sentimental error is to make convenient links between the work and the life, but in this case the temptation is strong.

"Once, we came out of a restaurant, and Roswitha was with us," Randy's dad told *People* magazine. "Two of the boys got into Randy's car and the little one looked up and said, 'Daddy, which house do I go to?' That broke Randy's heart."

"It's so easy for kids, since they're so egocentric, to blame themselves," Randy said in the same interview. "There's a goddam earthquake and they think it's their fault."

The kids were in fact doing okay. Amos, the eldest, was close to hand, working out a summer internship in the Warner Bros. publicity department.

Randy insists that 'I Want You To Hurt Like I Do' was written with a wider vision – one of a "rough, rough world." He sees it as an anthem in the manner of 'Do They Know It's Christmas?'.

"I wanted to put a bunch of voices on there and do a celeb video," he told Bunny Matthews, "but having them singing not 'We Are The World' or 'Save The Crippled Squirrels' but 'I Want You To Hurt Like I Do'. I still may do it. I like that song."

The album was released in September 1988 on Reprise – the label having been reactivated by Warners. Reviews were good. The consensus was that the autobiographical tracks put the others into the shade.

The review that everyone was waiting for was that of his ex-wife. "I think Randy had to prove to himself that he could make it on his own," Roswitha told *People* magazine. "I guess he did it. He is doing very well. This is one hell of an album."

As usual, Randy kvetched about the reviews and the sales: "What do you think they would say if Dylan made this record? They would think that it was the greatest thing since Beethoven. That's my opinion. I just wonder, I read a review of Brian Wilson or Dylan and think, 'I'd like a break like this. I'd like them to look at me through rose coloured glasses. I wonder why I'm so mad. What could it be?'"

The artwork features a shot of young Randy dressed in his cowboy outfit, squinting down his guns at the camera. Inside there's a black and white shot of him at the age, maybe, of ten, hitting a home run in the backyard. Both shots were taken by his mum, who's duly credited in the liner notes: "Photography: Adele Newman".

She died a month after the album was released. The Dixie Flyer.

Eighteen months later his dad died.

It was "tough, a big deal," Randy said. "We were close, but there was a contentiousness in our relationship."

"Won't be no God to comfort you," he'd sung, 18 years earlier. "You told me not to believe that lie."

Maybe I'm Doing It Wrong

'Old Man' turned out to be closer to reality than I thought," Randy told Barney Hoskyns. "I would have expected to summon up more warmth, though I did better than the guy in the song: I didn't tell him on his deathbed that this was the way you raised me so this is what you get. I saw him every day, but he took a while dying. I wanted to show more somehow and later I thought about that song. [...] I thought of him hearing 'Old Man', and wondered if he ever listened to it. I think he tended to personalise some of these things."

Chapter Eighteen

From the age of 19 to 26 (29 if you include guest-appearances), Ron Howard played Richie, the frighteningly wholesome teen lead in the TV show *Happy Days*. After that he became a movie director, making exactly the kind of movies that Richie would have made: the kind of movies that, if your heart isn't three or four degrees warmer when you come out than when you went in, you should seek medical advice.

Not all Ron Howard movies star Tom Hanks, but somehow Tom's always there in spirit making sure that, in the end, the Grinch will give Christmas back and even Russell Crowe's mind will be beautiful.

In 1985, Ron was making a film called *Gung-Ho* which involved some location shooting in Argentina. Ron had a young family at the time and liked to stay with his wife and kids as much as possible, so they all flew down to Argentina together – Ron, his wife (and High School sweetheart) Cheryl, four-year-old Bryce and the seven-month-old twins, Jocelyn and Paige. "What was intended as an opportunity for family togetherness quickly turned into a near catastrophe," Ron said.

Some 45 minutes into the flight, Bryce threw up all over Ron, and while the twins slept on and off, they alternated in a sleep-howl cycle that lasted the full 17 hours.

As a result of which, Ron conceived a movie, *Parenthood*, a catalogue of the withering traumas, the epic struggles, the psychological ticks and, yes, the heart-warming triumphs that afflict families. White, middle-class families anyway.

The movie starred Steve Martin, from *¡Three Amigos!*, then just on the cusp of following Robin William's lead in bringing disappointment to comedy fans by going mushy, Mary Steenburgen, who'd been the nameless 'Mother' in *Ragtime* and relative newcomers Joaquin Phoenix and Keanu Reeves.

Randy was offered the movie score.

His attitude to the subject matter of the movie was equivocal. "It's hard to say what's the most important thing," he told *People* magazine. "If it came down to a wish – I could either have my children be guaranteed they will live out their full span and be happy or guaranteed that I would continue to do quality work that I love for the rest of my life – I would take the kid thing. But it's close."

When all the razzmatazz of *Land Of Dreams* – the PAs and the talk shows – had died down, he started putting in the hours. "Starting can be difficult," he told Paul Zollo. "The real secret to that, like so much else, is stamina. Hanging in there. And showing up every day. With a movie deadline, you have no choice."

"I'd written a main title but Ron Howard wanted a song, so I wrote one," he said in the liner notes for *Guilty: 30 Years Of Randy Newman*. "A word here about the relationship between director and composer: it's like the relationship between a farmer and a mule, but with a tighter rein. Anyway, the song, 'I Love To See You Smile' [the hit from the movie], is the most lucrative song I ever wrote. I was able to hire four new stable boys and someone to play with my children for me. Ironic, isn't it? A movie about being a good parent allowed me to put even more distance between my children and myself."

'I Love to See You Smile' is what could be described as the "Randy Newman default Song #1", a style that became more common as the years went by but traces of which had already been frequently glimpsed. It consists of the shuffle rhythm, a tune and structure derived from the ragtime hits of the early twentieth century, a rolling piano style and maybe some Dixieland instrumentation – a clarinet or tuba.

'I Love To See You Smile' is a fine example, beaten only perhaps by the uncannily similar 'You've Got A Friend In Me' from *Toy Story*.

Lionel Bart, the British songwriter responsible for *Oliver!*, once said that the trick of writing a successful song is providing a melodic line, harmonic structure and lyric so predictable that listeners can accurately guess what comes next, then, just when they're feeling safe, you throw a spanner in the works – a weird note, an out-of-key chord, an unexpected rhyme. Randy recognised that, on the whole, people are happier without the spanner.

'I Love To Hear You Smile' is a Werther's Original of a song, comforting and familiar. 'Don't want to take a trip to China / Don't want to sail up the…" – which river is the singer unwilling to sail up (bearing in mind that the last line of every verse is the song's title)? Here's a slightly harder one: "Like a sink without a faucet / Like a watch without a …"

"I don't feel any sense of prostituting myself if I'm not always being this acerbic, ironic individual," Randy said. "I'd like to think, if somebody gave me the assignment to write a Moroccan Christmas song, I could write one. And it would still show musical talent. Even if you didn't know it was me."

The rest of the score is workmanlike and used sparingly – just 22 minutes of music in a 117-minute film. It's Ron Howard music, sentimental where it needs to be and undeniably wholesome. Maybe from time to time it crosses over into fluffy, but the line judges would have to be consulted for a more accurate ruling. There's even a hint of what might, at a push, be considered self-parody in the baseball sequence and the pompous waltz for the graduation scene.

The film took $10m on its opening weekend and nobody left the cinema saying they loved the movie but hated the score, so job done.

The song – 'I Just Want To see You Smile' – was nominated for an Oscar but beaten by Menken and Ashman's 'Under The Sea' from Disney's *The Little Mermaid*.

It was, as Randy said, a gift that kept on giving.

"I sold it to toothpaste companies, mule-packing teams, anywhere I could," he said. "I worked eight to ten months on *Faust* [his later musical – see below] but never made a dime on it."

Randy was still renting an office to work in. The receptionist at the building was a woman by the name of Gretchen Preece. Randy asked her out. She said no. He stuck at it.

"She treated me worse than anybody. I thought it might be aberrant behaviour – that I chased her because she ran away."

Eventually she stopped running.

Gretchen, like Randy, grew up around the entertainment business. Her grandmother, Thelma, was one of the first female business agents in Hollywood. Her dad, Michael, was a director who worked on shows like *The Streets Of San Francisco*, *Dallas* and *Knot's Landing*.

Gretchen and Randy were married in October 1990. Amos, Eric and John – Randy's sons – were best men.

During their honeymoon in Italy, Randy asked Gretchen if she would like to get to know his ex-wife.

"I heard what a wonderful woman she was, and I met her and [found that] everybody was right," Gretchen said. The two met at Michael's restaurant in Santa Monica. "Randy sent champagne, and we had a ball."

"It's very Hollywood, I guess," Randy said, "but everyone gets along great. I've been lucky. Life has improved... I'm used to being in a family, and that's what suits me."

Avalon was the third in a series of semi-autobiographical movies written and directed by Barry Levinson chronicling the life of a Jewish family living in Baltimore and their gradual assimilation into America. Eventually there would be four in the series – *Diner* (1982), *Tin Men* (1987), *Avalon* (1990) and *Liberty Heights* (1999).

Though the family happens to be Jewish, Levinson was keen to stress that their experience is not exclusive to or a product of their race or religion.

The big family reunion, for instance, takes place not on a Jewish holiday but on Thanksgiving. "I think certain things impact on the family structure," Levinson said. "In my lifetime, television was one, transportation and the growth of suburbia were others.

"I think some of these things are responsible for many of the problems we have today because the idea of a family unit goes back thousands and thousands of years and it's really only since the late forties that it started to come apart."

Sam, the head of the family, becomes furious when he learns that his son and his nephew have changed their names from Krichinsky to the easier-to-pronounce Kaye and Kirk. Sam thunders: "What makes them think a person's name should be easy to pronounce? A person is not a candy bar".

Randy faked surprise at getting the gig in the first place, having already given Levinson his heromuzic for *The Natural:* "Hardly anyone works with me twice."

"I just wrote from what I saw in the movie," he said. "Directors were a little more hesitant to be specific about what they wanted then. It was clearly a Jewish family, based on Barry Levinson's family. After the movie came out, I remember *Saturday Night Live*'s Lorne Michaels saying to me, "Do you realize that not one of those actors is Jewish?" I mean, Aidan Quinn as a Jewish dad? That's really wishful thinking."

At the beginning of *Avalon,* an old man in voice-over tells us he came to America in 1914, landed in Philadelphia and arrived in Baltimore on July 4. In Baltimore there are fireworks, and bright lights and kids everywhere with sparklers and excited people filling the streets. But there are no bands playing 'The Stars And Stripes Forever', barely any explosions or even any shouting. Just the old man talking, and a plaintive piano tune, a minor waltz which develops – 'builds' would be the wrong word – into an orchestral theme, a little bit Jewish maybe, but not overtly so: no klezmer clarinets or *krekhtsn*.

The music, if anything, detracts from the obvious dramatic impact of the scene, which, with the fireworks and crowds could be considerable. Instead it redirects the focus. This isn't a scene about the fourth of July. It is about the young man's wonder and it is about the sadness of the old man, the voice-over, looking back, envying his younger self, wishing he still had that ability to be surprised and excited.

The temptation to put just a little acknowledgement of the fireworks in there – nothing as crude as cymbals or raspy trombones, but maybe a couple of trumpets fanfaring the main theme – is rightly resisted.

The whole score derives its strength from a similar simplicity – delicate orchestration and lots of solo passages for piano, violin and flute. Randy Newman understands the value of sparse. If he was British, he would by now possess a Royal Warrant – 'Supplier of Exquisite Poignancy to Her Majesty The Queen'.

He also freely acknowledged the contribution of Jack Hayes, the veteran orchestrator he used on most of these earlier films. "I've learnt more from him than from anyone else."

Hans Zimmer, who scored, among others, *12 Years A Slave, Interstellar* and *The Dark Knight Rises,* described Randy's work on *Avalon* as the "most beautiful American score ever written."

Randy wasn't so enthusiastic, particularly about the way in which the music was mixed. "What happened was that he [Levinson] heard it in the theatre and it was too loud so he took it down," Randy said. "You know, people tell me, 'I loved your score for *Avalon*,' and I say, 'Well, how can you hear it?' I mean it's down so far."

After the film was released, Levinson agreed. He'd overcompensated.

It got an Oscar nomination anyway. The winner was John Barry's much louder score for *Dances With Wolves*.

In February 1992, Randy and Gretchen had a son, Patrick, and a year later a daughter, Alice. He'd never had a girl before.

In concert, he often quotes Lorne Michael, who told him that if he'd had a girl first he would have thought the boys were retarded.

"And there's a great deal of truth in that," Randy says, "inasmuch as girls don't eat so much mud or bump into trees."

Film composers tend to specialise. John Barry did sweeping like no other. He did other things as well, but if you wanted big canvas, Barry was your man. Similarly, John Williams does stirring, Ennio Morricone does pistols at dawn, Dmitri Tiomkin did men doing what men have to do, and Uncle Alfred and Miklós Rózsat divided up the Bible between them. Randy was staking himself a strong claim deep in the heart of Sensitivity, just on the outskirts of Americana, at the confluence of the Smarty and the Arty.

Oliver Sacks, the neurologist and author, had a kindness in his eyes that was crying out for a Randy Newman score. In 1973, he wrote a book called *Awakenings*, based on 20 case studies of survivors of the *encephalitis lethargica* epidemic that had raged during and just after the First World War. The symptoms ranged from sore throat to psychosis. Most of those who contracted the illness died. Some survivors lapsed, apparently irrecoverably, into strange mental states: some into patterns of obsessive, repetitive behaviour, others into catatonia, unable to move or speak. When Oliver Sacks came on the case, many of them had been unchanged, 'locked in' for 40 years and more.

In the late sixties, a new drug, L-DOPA, initially developed for the treatment of Parkinson's Disease, was discovered also to have remarkable effects on the *encephalitis* patients. They woke up, they walked, they spoke and, like Rip Van Winkle, they found themselves in a strange and alien world.

"The book is an extraordinary compound of clinical observation and, one feels, deep understanding of the plight of these people," Richard Gregory wrote in *The Listener*. "One senses in the author a passion to communicate his discoveries with all the power of his intellect, knowledge and deep compassion – so that we may 'awake.'"

Penny Marshall, like Ron Howard, was an actor turned director. She'd played Laverne in the TV sitcom *Laverne And Shirley*. Then she'd had a huge hit and won three Academy nominations as director of the Tom Hanks film *Big*. Her next project was an adaptation of Sacks' *Awakenings*, scripted by Steven Zallion, with Robin Williams playing the Oliver Sacks part (rechristened Malcolm Sayer for the movie) and Robert De Niro as the patient who wakes up and learns slowly to engage with his new world.

The movie deals with huge, stirring themes of life, death, rebirth, hope, despair and madness – themes for which a couple of hours of Wagner might seem too flippant.

The script and production, however, are admirably lightfooted and Randy's score is made to match. There are moments of lush, there are moments of darkness, there are 'inoffensively atmospheric' moments, there are moments that sound suspiciously 'new agey', and there are moments that have the emotional impact of a ringtone, but nothing's ever weighty. No one could accuse the score of overegging. Even when the orchestration gets a little dense, it's usually supporting a nursery tune.

One critic called it "perfect music for a person seeking a self-induced catatonic state". But that's how it is with movie music. There are times when a 90-piece orchestra is a waste of time, money and dramatic tension, but a well spotted triangle can bring an audience to orgasm. Randy is on record as saying that he reckons *Awakenings* is one of his best scores. A strong case could be made.

On January 15, 1991, the night that bombing started in the First Gulf War, Randy went into a Los Angeles recording studio and made a protest record. It was called 'Lines In The Sand': "The blood of these children / A stain on the land / If they die to defend some / Lines in the sand."

It wasn't released on record for another seven years, but Randy passed it to various radio stations. He declined to be interviewed, suggesting through a Warner Bros. representative that 'the song spoke for itself'.

work at the piano, and that's it." RICHARD E. AARON/REDFERNS

Lou Reed, Bob Dylan and Tom Petty admire Randy's dazzling white shirt backstage at Farm Aid, 1985. DEBORAH FEINGOLD/CORBIS

"I'm doing this for Randy," Mark Knopler said. "I don't need the cash." MICHAEL PUTLAND/GETTY IMAGES

"There isn't anything more important than being able to write well." STEVE STARR/CORBIS

Randy enjoying the respect of his peers – with Jools Holland, Neil & Tim Finn, Candida Doyle, Jarvis Cooker and Morrissey.
ANDRE CSILLAG/REX/SHUTTERSTOCK

Randy and Gretchen at the Oscars in 1997.
RUSSELL EINHORN/LIAISON

"I recently stumbled into a new family with two little children in school." RON GALELLA, LTD./WIREIMAGE

Randy, with his first Oscar and an arm around Jennifer Lopez: "This is as close as I'll ever get to heaven." DAVID LEFRANC/GAMMA

nny Waronker and Randy: "Sing, little potato, sing!" L. COHEN/WIREIMAGE FOR NARAS

ndy as the Devil in Faust: 'You Can't Keep A Good Man Down.' WALTER MCBRIDE/GETTY IMAGES

Russ Titelman: producer of choice to Rock Royalty.
BRUCE GLIKAS/FILMMAGIC

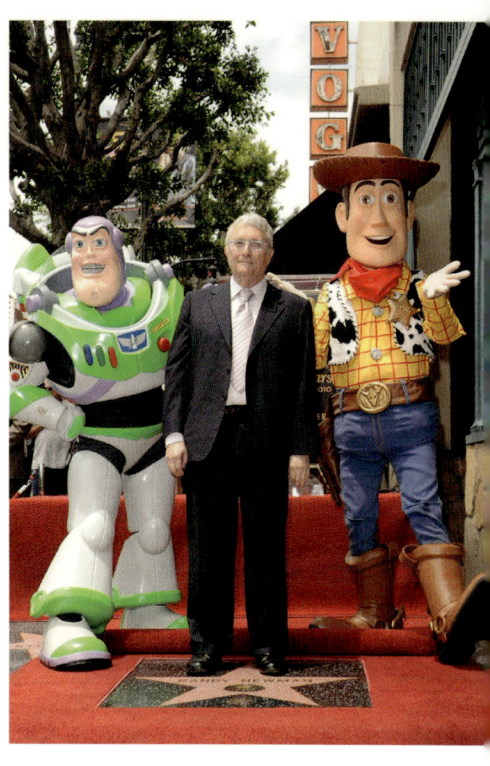

Randy having the time of his life with Buzz and Woody.
JASON MERRITT/GETTY IMAGES

Randy and Amos: "Your children are your children even when they're grown." DIMITRIOS KAMBOURIS/GETTY IMAGES

ndy inducted into the Hall of Fame in 2013: "Why do I go on and on and on…" KEVIN WINTER/GETTY IMAGES

her Newmans are also available: David Newman….. …and Thomas Newman. KEVORK DJANSEZIAN/GETTY IMAGES
STER COHEN/WIREIMAGE

Randy Newman: "The Hoarse Foreman of the Apocalypse." KEVORK DJANSEZIAN/GETTY IMAGES

Maybe I'm Doing It Wrong

A couple of months later a Band Aid/'We Are The World' assembly of musicians, sportspeople and celebs including Celine Dion, Luther Vandross, Garth Brooks, Michael Bolton, Little Richard and Mark Knopfler, calling themselves 'Voices That Care', put out a morale boosting EP and video for our boys over there – proceeds to the International Red Cross.

"You had to take a stand," Celine sang, "in someone else's land / life can be so strange." And, "I just can't let you feel alone / When there's so much love at home".

In his song Randy sang: "We old men will guide you / Though we won't be there beside you."

It didn't get much airplay.

Chapter Nineteen

The writer Richard Henderson, in his delightful 2010 monograph devoted to Van Dyke Parks' *Song Cycle*, tells of a visit to Van Dyke's music studio in the early nineties where he "noticed the framed photo of a racing greyhound; beneath the dog's image was a small plaque bearing the name 'Van Dyke Parks'.

"Of course, this piqued my curiosity. Van Dyke explained that a businessman who raised and raced greyhounds in Florida was a fan of Californian pop music. The guy owned three dogs that each made good showings at the track. He'd named them after his favourite recording artists: 'Van Dyke Parks', 'Randy Newman' and 'Harry Nilsson'. Parks had asked the breeder which dog was fastest. Turned out that Randy Newman was far and away the champion of the pack. Van Dyke mentioned this to Harry Nilsson who in turn demanded a canine urine test."

Randy again disproved the notion that "hardly anyone works with me twice" when he did another Ron Howard movie, *The Paper*, a newspaper romp set over a 24-hour time period in which Michael Keaton tries to nail a story and Glenn Close tries to stop him.

Randy's score did not redefine the use of music in cinema, but did its job – a little ragtime here, a few sweeping strings there. There was also a song, 'Make Up Your Mind', about the taxing nature of free will.

Maybe I'm Doing It Wrong

The lyric – "Comes a time in every man's life / When he must decide / Whether he wants to drive a bus / Or just go along for the ride" – isn't exactly Lorenz Hart, but the track is both down and relatively dirty: a slow soul rhythm with funky organ and quirky turnarounds. It's also sung as a duet with session singer Alex Brown (at the time, no dew-eyed teenager herself) with an excitingly smeary commitment. If 'it' was whatever the thing Randy Newman had had when he was 25, then there was no doubt that he still had 'it', and if 'some' was an additional command of rhythm and nuance (qualities that often diminish with age, as witnessed in the phenomenon known as 'Dad dancing') then one could even add 'and then some'.

The song earned him another Oscar nomination. Sir Tim Rice and Elton John – soon to become Sir Elton – won the statue for 'Can You Feel The Love Tonight' from *The Lion King:* 'Circle Of Life' or 'Hakuna Matata' you could just about understand, but 'Can You Feel The Love Tonight'? Really?

William Goldman is the finest screenwriter ever to have walked on earth. His CV is pretty much identical to a list of 'Best Movies of the Past Half Century': *Butch Cassidy And The Sundance Kid*, *The Stepford Wives*, *Marathon Man*, *All The President's Men*, *A Bridge Too Far*, *The Princess Bride*, *Misery*, *Chaplin*, and so on and so on. He's also found time in his busy schedule to write a shelf-full of novels, a few stage plays and a couple or three musicals – one of them with Stephen Sondheim.

In 1994 he revived *Maverick*, the TV Western about card sharps, rogues, ladies' men and dudes in the Old West that ran on ABC from 1957 to 1962 and starred James Garner as Bret Maverick and a pre-Bond Roger Moore as his cousin Beauregard (who had been away in England for a while and picked up the accent).

Richard Donner, who had just made the three hugely successful *Lethal Weapon* films, directed Goldman's script, with Mel Gibson in the Bret Maverick role and James Garner as a US Marshall who later reveals himself to be not quite what he seems.

The score makes no attempt to avoid the obvious clichés. It contains echoes, and sometimes straight quotes from Uncle Alfred's *How The West Was Won* as well as liberal borrowings from the works of Elmer Bernstein, Dmitri Tiomkin, Ennio Morricone and Aaron Copland – but why wouldn't it? If the director had had his way, the clichés would have been even thicker on the ground: Randy complained that he wanted banjos in nearly every sequence.

Randy got to sing and play a song, or rather a medley of songs segueing one into the other – the first a dance number, the second a lament about a dying virgin who will never know love and the third a yee-haw cowboy yikee about that old prairie moon. On the soundtrack album they're collectively given the title 'Tartine de Merde' which translates as 'Shit Pie'.

"I saw as it as source music in a saloon," Randy wrote in the liner notes for *Guilty*. "Some guy singing a medley of his hits. It's afternoon. I tried to get the director and his film editor to add applause as if each time he went into a new tune they recognized it. The music would be so far down you really wouldn't notice. It isn't important, but from a show business standpoint I love the idea of a guy doing an afternoon saloon tour."

Later, in 2011, Randy featured parts of the *Maverick* score in a concert performed by the Cleveland Orchestra. He advised the audience to avoid laughing at the deliberately quirky introductory music for the film's lead actors as it was definitely a rollicking, Western-themed score written about a "lost time when people still liked Mel Gibson."

At the beginning of 1995, Randy came over to the UK, his first visit for six years, and played the Theatre Royal Drury Lane.

Barney Hoskyns covered it for *Mojo* magazine. "He is ten seconds into his second song, 'Yellow Man', when a bank of spots from *Miss Saigon* bathes him in a hepatic yellow light. "What facilities!" he exclaims mid-verse, looking up. "This is like the Pink Floyd show… a very crappy, shitty Pink Floyd show."

"You didn't know that an evening with Randy Newman could be this painful," Randy said, after making a couple of mistakes in 'Marie'. And, in 'Lonely At The Top', "I look at my hands sometimes and I can't believe the stupidity of the shit that I'm playing."

He always maintains that in the UK his appeal is confined to London. He once played a concert in Slough for the BBC that was free and even that didn't sell it out.

"One time my promoters thought that I could play more than one town and booked me in Manchester and Liverpool," he told Jon Ronson in a BBC4 documentary. "So we were headed up to Manchester and the car throws a piston. Right through. Really wrecked it. We stopped and I said, 'I've got to get to the date'. So I hitched. And I got into a truck and they've been down on the docks and they've got all these ropes in the back – ropes with knots in them. We get to the show and I say, 'Here's a couple of tickets' – of which there were plenty.

"And so I play Manchester and when I'm done I see them after and it looks like they've been beaten with clubs. These guys have spent a day at the docks and then they've had to listen to the Dean of Satire here. Oh man, I just made them go through hell. I know they wished they hadn't picked me up. There was nothing in it for them – nothing."

For ten years he'd been talking about writing a musical based on the story of Doctor Faustus – the man who sold his soul to the devil and came to a terrible end. Shakespeare's contemporary Christopher Marlowe had already had a crack at it, as had the eighteenth century German poet/playwright Johann Wolfgang von Goethe, but a proper version – one with songs and jokes – was well overdue.

"Really what inspired me," Randy told Scott Jordan, "was that I've always been interested in depictions of heaven. In Goethe's version he's only there one time, and I go there more often. But I read it, part one of it at least, and it's great. It's an easy read, and you know you've bumped into some sort of giant mind. There are tremendously smart things on every page of it, and I felt it had to be destroyed."

Though Uncle Alfred had been conductor and music supervisor on most of the big Rodgers & Hammerstein movies including *South Pacific*, *Carousel*, *The King And I* and *The Sound Of* Music, Randy had never taken much interest in musicals. Nevertheless, writing musicals seemed a way in which a pop star could grow old gracefully, so in 1984, he'd had a tentative crack at making something out of the Faustus story.

"I wanted to try one, just to see if I could do it. I did a couple of songs and an embryonic version of the book and put it aside until 1993 to earn a living."

In 1994, he teamed up with James Lapine, who'd previously collaborated with Stephen Sondheim, directing and writing the books for *Sunday In The Park With George*, *Into The Woods* and *Passion*. By November, the show had backing in place from Warners and from Lorne Michaels of *Saturday Night Live* and *¡Three Amigos!*.

They started preliminary rehearsals at the Lincoln Center in New York. The project, still without a title, began to take shape.

The plot was "your basic Faust one", James Lapine told the *New York Times*, "sort of Goethe's version: a student sells his soul for money and women. Except that it's set at Notre Dame* and Lucifer is first mistaken for someone from the dean's office. And the student is a metalhead, sort of a child of Nirvana. [...] It's not Marlowe's intellectual quagmire.

"Randy's got three grown boys. He's really aware of the rudderless lives of young people today. The sense of morality being non-existent. So it's that much easier for the devil."

But ultimately, Randy and James Lapine did not share the same vision for the production. Randy felt that James wanted to take the whole thing in a more serious direction. Michael Greif, who had just become artistic director of the La Jolla Playhouse, was brought in to replace him.

La Jolla Playhouse is a 500-seat theatre on the San Diego campus of the University of California. A couple of years earlier it had staged the world premiere of *Tommy*, the Who's rock-opera, which subsequently transferred to Broadway and the West End. It was also just a two-hour drive from Pacific Palisades and the studios of Hollywood and Burbank. Ideal, then, for an opening.

Andrew Lloyd-Webber and Tim Rice had released 'concept albums' of *Jesus Christ Superstar* and *Evita* to drum up interest before opening the shows. It worked for both. Consequently, to coincide with the opening of *Faust*, Reprise released an all-star album with Don Henley as Faust, James Taylor as God, Elton John as the Angel of England, Linda Ronstadt as Margaret the ingénue and Bonnie Raitt as Martha the bad girl with the heart of gold. Randy played the Devil. Obviously.

Ry Cooder was in on the sessions, along with Waddy Watchel, Benmont Tench from the Heartbreakers, Bill Payne from Little Feat, Kenny Aronoff from John Mellencamp's band and the drummer's drummer's drummer, Jim Keltner.

Peter Asher and Don Was produced. Peter was an Englishman of good family. He'd been a child actor (*Outpost In Malaya* with Claudette Colbert at the age of eight), had a three or four hits in the early sixties

---

* Not the Parisian cathedral but the Catholic university in South Bend, Indiana, with a formidable football team known as "The Fighting Irish".

as half of Peter & Gordon, then, as Jane Asher's brother, had come *this* close to being a Beatle brother-in-law before relocating to LA and launching himself in a hugely successful career as producer, manager and executive.

Don Was, with David Was, was Was (Not Was). Then he went on to produce for people so famous they don't need second names (or even, in one case, any more than one letter), like Bob, Ringo, The Big O, Willie and the Stones.

The story of Randy Newman's *Faust* starts in 4004 BC, "when all those people in Samaria and Egypt were busy getting things done so all the carbon dating works out fine". God and his angels celebrate His creation of the universe with a rousing gospel number 'Glory Train' exhorting everyone to jump on the train and ride to salvation.

Everyone's having a fine old time until Lucifer, Randy, God's best looking angel, wades in to "inject a note of reality". "In all my life," he says, "I don't believe I've ever heard such bullshit / Even from you / A master of bullshit."

God doesn't take criticism well, so banishes Lucifer to hell where he whiles away the centuries distinguishing himself, as it says in the liner notes for the album, as "an effective administrator – harsh to be sure, vicious, even sadistic, ruthless when necessary but always fair. It's a harsh life for him, too, and he longs to return to heaven where they now have golf, roller coasters and Hawaiian music."

Optimistically, Lucifer sings 'You Can't Keep A Good Man Down', a rolling Dixieland number in which he complains that he's being treated like dirt by those "flyin' high up there".

Lucifer decides that he's being framed for everything that's wrong up on earth and pays God a visit to shake things up a little.

Up in heaven, the angels crowd round the Lord to sing 'How Great Our Lord', a ramped-up gospel shouter. Tetchy and smug, God sings of turning Buddhists away from the Pearly Gates and bats away any doubts about mankind's welfare by echoing some of the sentiments expressed by Randy all those years ago in 'God's Song'.

Lucifer goads God into making a bet. If he can corrupt a mutually agreeable human and win his immortal soul, God will let him back into heaven.

A deal is made. God and Lucifer cast around for a suitably representative specimen, rejecting a clean cut Canadian (in the duet 'Oh Northern Boy') on the grounds that he's "As thick as a tree, as dull as a butterknife", and instead lighting upon heavy metal fan, Henry Faust, a student from Notre Dame University.

On cue, Don Henley, playing Faust, blasts out 'Bless The Children Of The World', a song that starts out "Sometimes you know that I think that I will / Surely go insane / Got suicide and murder / Runnin' in and out my brain", then runs mostly with the murder theme conjuring Mansonesque images of slaughtered piggies – "one little piggy gets a bullet in the eye" – before segueing into a bland stadium anthem which asks for God's blessing on the children of the world – "We're the ones who'll have to carry on / Even though all hope is gone".

Lucifer makes his move and offers Faust a contract. In return for his soul, he gets the best seats in clubs, bodyguards to make him feel important and – not to put too fine a point on it – tits.

Faust signs without argument. This, thinks Lucifer, is shooting fish in a barrel.

Back in heaven, the plot's through-line gets a bit nebulous. For some reason an English Angel called Rick (Elton John) is introduced. He's pissed off because, ever since the war, God seems to have favoured the Germans and Japanese over the Brits. He sings an elegy to British greatness, 'Glory Lost In The Mists Of Time'.

Now that Lucifer's return to heaven is beginning to seem a real possibility, God has started to regret ever making the bet. But, never one to brood, he sings the Act I finale, 'Relax, Enjoy Yourself'.

In Act II, God has a plan. He sends Cupid down to earth (the notes for the CD point out that the Lord's personnel resources are "staggeringly comprehensive") with instructions to bring love into the life of Henry Faust.

During the big St Patrick Easter Bunny festival, Faust meets the winsome Margaret. Goethe called this character Gretchen. This was, of course, the name of Randy's wife. He probably thought advisable to change it because later things get sticky.

Margaret is lovely, virtuous, wholesome and played by Linda Ronstadt. In 'Gainesville' we learn: "I have tried all my life to be kind to others / Even when others were unkind to me."

She may be a sap but her friend, Martha (sung by Bonnie Raitt), is a lot more sophisticated – so sophisticated that Lucifer falls for her – "as only a middle-aged man can fall for a beautiful heartless young girl." Martha's song 'Life Has Been Good To Me' is a raucous bump and grind that Lucifer counters with the hyperactive 'I Gotta be Your Man'.

Martha, rather improbably, seems to be won over by Lucifer, and sings, in a simple and sweet way, the show-stopping, audience-on-their-feet-with-lighters-in-the-air ballad 'Feels Like Home'.

It's one of Randy's best known songs – a stalwart at weddings around the world and it obviously means a lot to a lot of people. Randy never liked it. But, as previously mentioned, that one word 'home' is a cruelly effective bell-ringer. And, as a thousand songwriters have repeatedly proved, personal pronouns – 'you', 'I', 'me' and so on – are also guaranteed button-pushers.

'Feels Like Home' has 14 instances of 'me' (including repeats), 15 of 'I', six of 'my', seven of 'you', four of 'your' and 10 of 'home'.

And the beat kicks in for the chorus (as in "I-I-I-I-will always love you").

And it's a repetitive chorus (as in "Let it be, let it be, let it be, let it be").

And it name-checks those other two quasi-Biblical string-pullers, 'dark' and 'light' (as in the complete works of Bruce Springsteen).

And it suggests that the singer has known loneliness, which is kind of uncanny, because you remember I told you about that time when I was *really* lonely after my cat died and it's, like, whoever wrote this song can actually, like, *see inside my head*.

Pavlov and Goebbels working as a team could not have written a more efficient song. If somebody sings 'Feels Like Home' to you and you don't subsequently marry them, you have a disease of the spirit. And if you don't like the Bonnie Raitt version, rest assured because it's been covered by Neil Diamond, Chantal Kreviazuk, Aled Jones, Edwina Hayes, Diana Krall and Bryan Adams, Katie Meula and a score of others.

When the ecstatic applause is over, when the tears have been wiped away and the spur-of-the-moment proposals in rows D through H have been happily concluded, the plot grinds on.

Margaret has fallen in love with Faust. He poisons her mother to get Margaret to himself, seduces her, impregnates her and, for good measure, murders her little brother because the lad happened to spot Faust leaving her bedroom.

Having had his fun, he then skips town with Lucifer (who has been dumped by Martha, probably because of his poor performance in the bedroom – who would have thought the devil would be a crap lay?) and they stay in Lucifer's holiday home on Lake Superior.

Back in South Bend, Indiana, things are not going well for the abandoned Margaret. In what Randy describes as "the comic high point of Goethe's original play, and one of the most delightfully urbane moments in all of German literature", she drowns her newborn baby.

Margaret is arrested and thrown into Indiana State Prison. In her cell, crazed by grief, she sings the lullaby 'Sandman's Coming' for her dead baby. "It's a great big dirty world / If they say it's not, they're lying / Sandman's coming soon / You know he's coming soon."

"Randy's songs can be bleak," Linda said. "Not to seem a hard man, he will insert a shard of comfort so meagre it seems Dickensian. His songs are superbly crafted with musical tension that results from this combination of hope and utter despair. In his orchestrations he might comment on the narrative being carried by the singer, using the instruments to deliver the jabs. Singing in the midst of one of his arrangement can feel like taking part in a boisterous discussion, with people of unevenly matched intelligence, sensibility and insights ranting and squabbling."

Randy's songs present technical difficulties, too, Linda said.

"He writes these things that are so outrageously challenging that you have to have 97 octaves to sing them. I think he holds us (singers) in the lowest esteem. I sometimes think it's because he puts so little value on his own vocal abilities."

Margaret is sentenced to death, but, because she is such a good egg, the angels whisk her spirit off to heaven anyway.

Faust witnesses this. Filled with remorse he takes some of the poison left over from the dose he used on Margaret's mother. He cries out for forgiveness. As Goethe put it: "Das Ewig-Weiblich / Zieht uns hinan" ("the eternal feminine draws us upward"). Don't worry, nobody else is entirely sure what it means, either.

God sees Faust's contrition as his chance to win his bet and keep Lucifer out of heaven. He nips in quick. Angels descend and snatch Faust up.

The game is over. Lucifer is outraged – he goes through the stages of grief – denial, rage, despair, depression and then – "the wind blows" read the liner notes "… his cape billows to the east. He wags his tail. He thinks of something that makes him very, very happy …"

Vegas.

Maybe I'm Doing It Wrong

Lucifer belts out 'Happy Ending': "... the little man is king, here in Las Vegas / Man, they got ev'rything, run with it / They got English girls with legs so long / You gotta use a stepladder to lick their love thing."

The *Faust* score has gospel, blues, soul, funk, heavy metal, New Orleans boogie – pretty much every musical style except show-tunes. Randy thought he'd done all right.

"I'm very satisfied with it," he said. "This subject was so big I could put everything I knew about music into it, too. It makes me want to do something like that again. Like Wagner's *The Ring*. That has great stuff on matrimony, work, big people pushing on little people, pretty girls making fun of an ugly guy... I could really butcher it..."

Rolling Stone liked it too: "*Faust* not only revives a great songwriter's career, it breathes new life into a musical-theatre tradition hijacked by the likes of Andrew Lloyd-Webber."

Robert Christgau in *Playboy* magazine said: "*Faust* ain't Goethe. It ain't Sondheim or Rodgers & Hammerstein either – too earthy and too cynical, respectively. Slightly Rodgers & Hart, maybe. Newman's musical-comedy rewrite of the soul-selling tale revels in the high-spirited cynicism that has been his specialty over nearly three decades as Hollywood rock's most respected songwriter. [...] Musical comedy is the perfect medium for his unique synthesis of soundtrack grandeur, blues-savvy studio rock, and general Americana. If he ever does reach Broadway with this thing, he'll put *Hair* and *Tommy* to shame – and maybe Sondheim, too."

Reprise Records followed up the release of the album with their first "enhanced CD" which could be played on ordinary CD players, but, when played on a computer, yielded a whole new layer of digital extras including exclusive interviews with Randy, Bonnie Raitt, James Taylor and Don Henley.

"You'll be able to listen to the original demos that Randy did and then click to the finished tracks," an excited creative at Warner Bros. told *Billboard*. "Or you can call up a page from *Faust* and see Randy's notations."

"We're expecting to reach a whole other group of people who maybe aren't Randy Newman fans right now, but should be. It will be a whole second wave campaign for the album."

Disappointingly, *Crash Randycoot*, a game for Xbox, PlayStation and Wii, in which the player drives in a Buick with a nasty redhead at his side and gets chased by Lester Maddox through the byways of LA, never happened.

Neither did the promotion do much for sales. Later, Randy said the album didn't earn enough to pay for his children's toothpaste (bearing in mind that he did have five children by now). He put it down to having all those famous people on the record: "They really slowed me down."

The album was released on Tuesday, September 19. On the following Sunday, the live show opened at the La Jolla Playhouse.

A week before, the *Los Angeles Times* sent a reporter to interview Randy at the rehearsals, which were taking place in a shiny office building.

"I've been around music since I was five years old but this is such a strange world to me," Randy said. "I used to hold actors in low regard, just like in the Middle Ages, because, you know, they don't write their own stuff. You meet 'em and they're disappointing often. But what these Broadway people can do… they dance, they sing in tune, they do back flips, they play instruments. There can't be a thousand of these people in the world. They're like NBA basketball players, except they don't get paid anything. They should get subsidized."

Randy had been dividing his time between fine tuning the musical at rehearsals and Hollywood, where he was working on a film score (a big one, more of which in a moment). "Coming down here is like leaving a coal mine and going to work in a jewellery store," he said. "The process… there's something nice about it. With movies, there's so much baggage: so many people, so much money. It isn't quite as human. I can see why people are in [theatre], because it isn't the money. I've never done anything that paid me less money than this. Up to now, like, nothing.

"I don't think of [Broadway] as a higher art form. Rock'n'roll is where the best songwriting's been done for 30 years, except for Sondheim. I've seen Broadway shows lately that I thought were from a different galaxy. Anyway, they'll all just be waiting for me to do worse."

On the stage God was played by Ken Page, a basso profundo. He'd played God before, or at least the God character, Old Deuteronomy, in *Cats* on Broadway. Randy's Devil role was taken by David Garrison and Kurt Deutsch played Faust.

Michelle Green described the atmosphere at the Playhouse for *People* magazine: "… the audience is murmuring expectantly. A pair of sixtyish theatergoers are surveying the program. [...] Turning to his guest, the man says, 'This looks like a good cast.' She frowns. 'Yes,' she replies, 'but it's written by Randy Newman, and you know how I feel about Randy Newman.'"*

"The show opens with a big gospel-infused number," said the *Variety* review, "and like Newman's best work, the songs segue effortlessly from blasting rockers to sentimental ballads, hard blues and even 'Lovetime', a tap number for chorus girls in underwear that prompts Henry to mutter, 'I hate that oldtime shit.'

"On the downside, Newman – who wrote the book as well as the score – doesn't really have a clue about writing a musical (and thank goodness that hasn't stopped him). There is a terrific show inside *Faust* that needs time and the laying on of more experienced hands to advance it. Now the songs, wonderful as they are, tend to come out of nowhere, and in several cases just stop the show dead in its tracks."

Laurie Winer, in the *Los Angeles Times*, praised the score, but plot, structure and dialogue came in for a caning. "A great team effort," the review concludes, "cannot hide the fact that Newman is playing with a form whose ground rules he has not mastered."

Randy told Chris Willman of *Entertainment Weekly* that Faust "might be offensive to fundamentalists and people of good taste," but he was confident it "doesn't state the atheistic case more effectively than the case for religion. I have enormous respect for the power of faith [...] As I would for anything that's that big a hit.

"This is a comedy, 100-percent. Outside of the ballads, there isn't any attempt to be anything but *A Funny Thing Happened On The Way To The Forum*. It's not as challenging as David Mamet. Maybe it's more challenging than Lloyd Webber."

Perhaps in an attempt to make it more challenging, Randy's next move was to approach David Mamet and suggest collaboration on a re-write.

---

* There have always been gender issues surrounding Randy's work. Harry Shearer, Derek Smalls – the bass player of Spinal Tap and the voice of nearly everybody in *The Simpsons* – with the collusion of Lenny Waronker and Russ Titelman, once made a mock promo which opened: 'Newman! Music *men* like.'

The La Jolla production closed on October 29, but, despite the bad reviews, Warners were still interested in taking it to the next stage. Broadway beckoned.

David Mamet had already won a Pulitzer Prize and a couple of Tony nominations for *Glengarry Glen Ross* (1984) and *Speed-The-Plow* (1988). He had a street smart, cynical way with dialogue that everybody hoped would lock right in with Randy's lyrics and music.

The rewrites and rehearsals took – with time out for movies and other commitments – a year. The pre-Broadway try-out for the new show opened at the Goodman Theatre in Chicago on September 30, 1996. Michael Greif, from the La Jolla production, was still directing.

Much had changed. The Devil was a corporate high flyer. We see him at his desk, stamping documents: "Burn" – Stamp; "Fry" – 'Stamp'; "Bake" – Stamp.

The Lord and Lucifer pick Faust with the aid of a computer database. Aphrodite and a tap dancing Don Juan help out.

Thomas Lynch's set consisted of brightly coloured sliding panels that sometimes had cartoon thought-bubbles projected on them. It looked, according to critic Robert Brustein, like "a cross between an industrial warehouse and a supermarket".

The score had new orchestrations by Michael Roth which, according to some, were brighter, brasher and louder than those heard at La Jolla.

The *New York Times*' Ben Brantley called the score, "a shimmering, multi-faceted gem", but found the production needed to be "refined and further thought through" if the show were to move to Broadway.

Richard Christian of the *Chicago Tribune* agreed: "The musical further suffers from presenting us with a slightly repellent hero. Henry Faust, played with jumping-jack energy by Kurt Deutsch, is such a total jerk that there's little saving grace or basic appeal about him. Indeed, when Margaret (the radiant Bellamy Young) appears, it's a relief to find that the musical at last has unearthed a character who commands sympathy and support.

"When it is right, however, this show, beginning with Newman's incredibly rich score, is gloriously right. Michael Greif's direction has the entire 23-person cast, including three terrific youngsters, jumping for joy, in a perfect collaboration with Lynn Taylor-Corbett's brilliant choreography."

Maybe I'm Doing It Wrong

Faust never made it to Broadway.

Years later, when he was asked by a reporter, "What did you discover about musical theatre?" Randy replied, "There's no money in it."

There is, however, a coda to this tale.

In 2014, Encores! Off-Center – an initiative devoted to glories of musical theatre – presented, at the New York City Center's Mainstage, a one night only production of Randy Newman's *Faust*.

It was a stripped-down concert version, heavily rewritten. Randy reprised his Lucifer role alongside a new cast that included Isiah Johnson, Vonda Shepherd, Laura Osnes and Tony Vincent.

Randy wore horns and a cape.

David Gordon, on the *Theatremania* website, said that the show "highlighted both the material's flaws and strengths: in the former column, an already hard-to-follow story made largely incoherent in its concert abridgement; in the latter, a smart, clever score that showcases Newman at his finest."

Predictably, Vonda Shepherd's 'Feels Like Home' "brought the house down".

Chapter Twenty

John Lasseter, a talented animator at Disney, while working on *Mickey's Christmas Carol*, came across videotapes showing strange floating blobs. They were the results of experiments the company had been conducting with a type of animation created not with paper and pencil, but inside a computer.

Lasseter was excited: even more so when he saw some of the early rushes for *Tron*, a movie made using this new miracle known as Computer Graphic Imagery, or CGI, in which Jeff Bridges gets beamed into a mainframe where he wears a shiny hat and encounters scarily glowing lines.

When he got fired from Disney, Lasseter started working with Dr Ed Catmull (pioneer of bicubic patches and spatial-antialiasing) at Industrial Light and Magic, the Computer Graphics Division of George Lucas' company Lucasfilm. Together they animated a knight composed of bits of stained-glass who could threaten a real-life vicar in *The Young Sherlock Holmes*.

Then George Lucas, largely to finance a divorce settlement, sold his graphics division. Steve Jobs of Apple Computers bought the biggest slice, and the new company was called the Pixar Graphics Group. Lasseter and Catmull went with the takeover.

Ten years and many exponential leaps in technology later, Pixar were making their first computer-animated full-length feature film. They hired

Randy Newman to write the music and were punishingly keen. "They have a November release date," Randy said, "and that's more important to them than my life is."

Animated movies, in Randy Newman's career, were like buses. After years of being the go-to guy for sensitive Americana with a healthy dose of comedy and not a Road Runner, Tweety-Pie or Wabbit in sight, now three 'toons came along at once: one called *Cat's Don't Dance*, one called *James And The Giant Peach* and one called *Toy Story*.

The last, the Pixar one, a co-production with Disney, had a plot based on the conceit that toys, though apparently mute and immobile when humans are around, spring into life as soon as backs are turned. The implausibility – CCTV for a start – was gloriously disregarded. The protagonists were Woody, a cowboy doll, voiced by Tom Hanks, and Buzz Lightyear, an astronaut action figure, voiced by Tim Allen. John Lasseter was directing.

John was a Randy fan. "He walked in and I'm, 'Oh my God, it's Randy Newman.'"

Randy thought John was okay, too.

"He's a tremendously charismatic fellow," Randy told Tommy Pearson on Classic FM. "An enthusiast. He has a childlike enthusiasm and an intellect for things. I saw a little bit of what it was going to look like – a storyboard and John Lasseter telling the story."

"I don't have much visual imagination," Randy told the *Los Angeles Times*, "so when I look at a storyboard, I can't interpolate the whole picture and figure out what it's gonna be. But I knew that the film would be funny, and they talked intelligently about what they wanted to do and what they wanted music to do."

It was a new challenge. "You have to, I think, in most cases catch the action. If Tom Hanks falls down in a movie you don't have to go 'balumph balumph', but if Woody does, you have to fall with him.

"Sometimes I ask the filmmakers for adjectives. You know, very basic things that they might be too embarrassed to say, like 'happy', 'warmth' or 'friendship'. Then I go to work."

Perhaps more in evidence here than in any previous score is the breadth of Randy's musical vocabulary and his surefooted confidence in leaping from one style to another. The cue identified on the soundtrack album as 'Andy's Birthday', for instance, starts with a couple of flourishes that live somewhere between Sousa and Tchaikovsky, segues into a grand symphonic theme from maybe 1850s Germany or 1950s Hollywood, and then slides effortlessly into an Elmer Bernstein western theme – we're still less than a minute into the cue – then into a few bars of Prokofiev, a few bars of Leonard Bernstein and a jazz walking bass takes us into a show-tune-overture variation of 'You've Got A Friend In Me'... and so on. And still it's good to listen to.

'You've Got A Friend In Me' is the big hit. It came about the easy way: "They told me they wanted to emphasize the friendship between Woody and the kid, so I just went, 'You've Got A Friend'."

It's a perky song, cheerful, open-hearted and folksy. As soon as the intro kicks in you get the impression that the clarinet player's embouchure is being compromised by his inability to stop smiling. The tuba's smiling. Randy Newman's smiling. In concert, where violent rebellion would result from any disinclination to include the song in the set list, he warns the audience not to be fooled by the sentiment.

"It's a fucking lie, of course. What do you expect? It's a cartoon."

Toy Story took $362m at the box office. The last time anybody counted, merchandise had made $2.4bn.

In the run-up to Christmas 1996, British toyshops ran out of Buzz Lightyear dolls. A black market developed. All the therapy in the world can never heal the psychological damage wrought on the thousands of children who woke up that Christmas morning, opened their presents and, cruelly disappointed, closed down their emotions, certain for ever after that their parents and Santa hated them.

Toy Story was the first animated film to win an Oscar nomination for Best Screenplay. It got Randy his 1996 nominations, too. Two of them – Best Score and Best Song.

He bought himself a new house. Gretchen found it. It was where he'd always liked to live, as close as possible to the house he grew up in Pacific Palisades.

He thought it was a good house, properly valued, and paid the asking price. Then Gretchen decided to remodel it, which essentially meant tearing it down and starting again. And in a set-up that could form the basis for a so-so sitcom, the architect that Randy's second wife used to remodel their new house was Randy's first wife's second husband, Don Boss.

It was Gretchen's idea to use Don. That was fine. The possibility of a revenge motive ("Oh, my God, why has he connected the pool

Maybe I'm Doing It Wrong

to the sewage outlet?") never entered anybody's head. It was all "very Hollywood," Randy told the *New York Times*. "He did a great job. I love the high ceilings. When we built the house, all I asked for were bookcases and high ceilings.'"

And no square rooms. "That was the main inspiration," Don Boss said. "All the rooms are either round or angled."

Randy ended up with a custom-built 6,500-square-foot house – "a beige stucco building with blue trim that has the feel of a golf clubhouse in Palm Desert." Inside, according to a wide-eyed *New York Times* reporter, "the look is part preschool (tiger-print rugs on the stairs), part hotel lobby (high-ceilinged living room overlooking patio and pool) and part pro-athlete's bachelor pad (black coffee table, white couch, giant brown velvet pillows)."

Randy had little time to appreciate the angular nature of his rooms or to lay back on his giant brown velvet pillows. The second half of the nineties was just one damn movie after another.

Cats Don't Dance spent a long, long time in preproduction hell.

It had started out – somewhere back in 1993 – as a vehicle for Michael Jackson. He would appear live in the film, acting and reacting with a parade of animated Looney Tunes characters.

Then Michael Jackson pulled out.

Then Warners went through corporate convulsions, the full story of which can make houseplants wilt with boredom, and the idea of reviving the Looney Tunes characters was used in the 1996 film *Space Jam* with Michael Jordan, so now the movie was being made by Turner Feature Animation and pretty much the only thing remaining of the original project was the title – *Cats Don't Dance*.

Every week or so, it seemed, there'd be another shake-up in management and a new posse of executives would descend on the creative team demanding changes. The usual sort of thing: "Those whiskers are too long. Shorten the goddam whiskers." "Why do they have to be cats? I'm allergic to cats. My kids are allergic to cats. Why can't they be prisoners of war? *The Great Escape*, now *that* was a movie."

In the end, no less than 11 writers shared a credit.

The production was, however, graced by the presence – often only in spirit – of the 83-year-old Gene Kelly, star of *Singin' In The Rain*, as 'choreography consultant'. Mr Kelly was uniquely qualified for the job having once, in *Anchors Away*, danced with both Tom and Jerry. Mercifully, he died not long before the film's release.

The plot concerns a cat who comes to Hollywood with high hopes of making it as a song and dance cat, and gets a small part in a movie with a vile child star and a piano playing elephant.

Randy provided six songs. The best is 'Tell Me Lies' ("And I'll come running"), a torch song sung by Natalie Cole against a film-noir arrangement featuring slimy sax. The most interesting is 'Little Boat On The Sea', which could have come straight out of *Faust* and tells of how the Lord saw the sinful work and made the rains come down: "And all the people drowned / With the animals it was different / Though some of them drowned too."

The box office returns were somewhere between disappointing and ruinous although the film did walk off with the Best Animated Feature award at the Annies (the Oscars of Animation) with Randy picking up the one for Best Individual Achievement: Music in a Feature/Home Video Production.

Roald Dahl's initial title for *James And The Giant Peach* was *James And The Giant Cherry* but then he decided a peach was "prettier, bigger and squishier than a cherry". Besides which, if at any point in the story James were to lose his cherry, the sniggers would have been deafening.

Dahl, unhappy with the movie adaptations of *Charlie And The Chocolate Factory* and *The Witches*, had resisted all offers to film the book, but after his death his widow, Felicity, accepted an offer (reported to have been in the region of $2m) from Disney.

Henry Selick, whose credits included Tim Burton's goth-classic *The Nightmare Before Christmas*, was given the job of directing.

Disney was preoccupied, financially and strategically, with their new big musical extravaganza *The Hunchback Of Notre Dame* and their experimental co-production with Pixar, *Toy Story*. There were management shake-ups here, too, and knives out in the boardroom. *James And The Giant Peach* found itself low on the pecking order and sometimes starved of funds. It was not a happy ship. For a time, the whole production was shut down.

Selick kept his head. "We've had some real rough spots," he said. "But I've never heard of great movies coming from Party Atmosphere Productions."

The first 20 minutes or so are live action. James' contented life is curtailed when his parents are eaten by an angry rhinoceros and he has to go and live with his beastly aunts. Only when, in their garden, he finds and enters a giant peach does the film flip into animation.

Randy wrote the score with five new songs, borrowing the lyric for one of them, 'Eating The Peach', from Dahl.

"I think what I did there was probably the most I've ever done to help a movie. The songs I wrote were really good for the characters. You know, you can't make a bad movie look good, but you can take a good movie and kick it up a notch."

Randy himself sings 'Good News', a rousing gospel tune and other songs are performed by cast members including Richard Dreyfuss and Susan Sarandon.

"*James And The Giant Peach* achieves a joyously unhinged, go-with-the-flow loopiness – the domesticated surrealism that gave Dahl's book its pungency," said Owen Gleiberman in *Entertainment Weekly*. But then he went on to complain that "the animation is framed by stridently crude live-action scenes that effectively douse the spell. In the opening section, James' crooked house is transparently a movie set, and the actresses playing the aunts, Joanna Lumley and Miriam Margolyes, overdo the shrieky, hothouse camp, as if they were wicked witches gone absolutely fabulous. The leap to animation, when it comes, is jarring, but also a relief."

Nevertheless, it got Randy his 1997 Oscar nomination for Music (Original Musical Or Comedy Score). Rachel Portman won with *Emma*. You have to roll with the punches.

Then he was hired to write an action movie. In *Air Force One* a group of terrorists hi-jack the President's plane. Harrison Ford plays the President, Gary Oldman the bad guy. The President wins. Bill Clinton loved it.

It was directed by Wolfgang Peterson, winner of two Academy Awards for *Das Boot*.

Randy wrote some stuff he hoped might suit.

Nobody liked it. They thought it too much of a parody. They suggested this. They suggested that. They drove him crazy. They suggested he do something a little more like Ennio Morricone (the Italian composer best known for his work on the Sergio Leone/Clint Eastwood spaghetti Westerns). At one point there was talk of hiring Morricone to collaborate with Randy. Then they fired Randy and hired Jerry Goldsmith instead. Jerry had the job done and dusted in 12 days.

Luckily, Randy was able to use some of the rejected music in his next project.

John Lasseter had started work on Pixar's second full-length feature.

A Bug's Life has a plot reminiscent of *¡Three Amigos!*. An ant by the name of Flik recruits a band of tough warriors to save his ant colony from some greedy grasshoppers. The "tough warriors" turn out to be not-so-tough performers in an inept circus troupe. As the mayfly comments as he watches their show, "I only have 24 hours to live and I'm not wasting it on this."

By cruel coincidence, Dreamworks, the company started by, among others, Steven Spielberg, was making its first computer-animated full-length feature *Antz*, a film about ants. They had an all-star cast voicing their movie – Woody Allen, Sharon Stone, Jennifer Lopez, Sylvester Stallone. *Bug's Life* had gone for critically acclaimed actors rather than mere marquee names – Kevin Spacey, Julia Louise-Dreyfus, David Hyde-Pierce.

Pixar was part funded by Apple. Dreamworks was part funded by Microsoft. It was pixels at dawn. Lasseter accused Dreamworks executive and co-founder Jeffrey Katzenberg of stealing his idea. Katzenberg denied it. Both decided to press on regardless. But *Bug's Life* had an ace up its sleeve: a score from multi-Oscar nominated composer, Randy Newman.

John got him involved early.

"We like to talk to Randy even in advance of having any finished film and start thinking in terms of themes. On *Bug's Life*, we just gave him boards with images on them, not necessarily even images from the film, to evoke what we're thinking of, along with single words that describe the emotion, and we just had him concentrate on themes."

"*Bug's Life*," Randy told Paul Zollo, "was like three times the size of an average score because the ants are really moving. And it doesn't look right if you don't move with them. There's a school of thought that says, no, you don't have to move with them. But in an animated picture, you do."

"I'll write on a synth and then put it down on paper," he said. "If it's an action scene, nothing's going to make enough noise for you usually but brass. [...] So you play a brass figure [on synth]. I come from a background and a family that would have hated that."

Maybe I'm Doing It Wrong

There are composers who feel it's 'cheating' to write at the piano, believing that the music should come straight from the imagination on to the page without being mediated by the clankings of a Steinway. Using a synthesiser, which can approximate the sounds of the various instruments, would be considered utterly *infra dig*. Whenever he worked with a synth, Randy would feel the ghost of his uncle over his shoulder shouting, "Evil! Evil!', in his ear.

There's some huge music in *Bugs Life*. The action sequences are scored with brass flourishes, rattling snares, banks of trombones. There are nods to Elmer Bernstein's *Magnificent Seven* – understandable given the plot – and one or two big band swing sections that sound as if Count Basie and Stan Kenton have combined forces for secret military purposes.

"For me," John Lasseter said, "probably the funniest part of making these movies is when we're at the scoring stage and Randy's up in front of the 105-piece orchestra [...] We go out and stand among the orchestra while he's performing, and it brings absolute chills every single time. He just gets it. He understood what we were trying to achieve. He's the modern-day Carl Stalling."

Carl Stalling was the genius who scored many of the Looney Tunes cartoons at Warner Bros. Management would let him have the Warner Bros orchestra for half an hour at the end of the day. The musicians, tired from a hard day slaving over a hot Dmitri Tiomkin, would be presented with their parts for the latest *Road Runner* short, black with 32nd notes, dynamic curve-balls, arrhythmic accents, unwieldy slides, toots, farts and glissandi. By all accounts, they loved it.

There was just one song in *Bug's Life*, a cheery slice of vaudeville with Andrews Sisters-like backing singers called 'The Time Of Your Life': "Was a bug, little bug, hardly there / How he felt, what he dreamed, who would care?"

Randy had difficulty finding enthusiasm for insect-based songs. "I remember writing a lot of non-specific songs, because let's face it, a song about a bug isn't going to travel well. You aren't gonna see that on Barbra Streisand's, *Greatest Hits From The Movies*.

A Bug's Life took nearly $163m in its US opening run. *Antz* took not quite $92m.

The score got him one of his three 1999 Oscar nominations, this one for Best Original Musical Or Comedy Score. Stephen Warbeck won for *Shakespeare In Love*.

"If I had won for that one," Randy said, "it wouldn't have been a mistake. I helped that picture. But it was a hard job. Think about it – a bug chasing a bug. For a composer, that's tough, just in terms of the amount of notes you need for the music. I mean, what John Williams did on *Hook* was even harder, in terms of technical facility, but I did my best."

His other two 1999 nominations were for different movies entirely. God he was busy.

Babe: Pig In The City was the sequel to *Babe*, the 1995 hit about the pig that becomes a sheep-dog.

Randy's contribution was a single song, sung by Peter Gabriel, accompanied by full orchestra supplemented by the Black Dyke Band (formerly the Black Dyke Mills Band) and, in the intro, Paddy Moloney of the Chieftains on uilleann pipes.

The Black Dyke Band are from Queensbury, on the outskirts of Bradford, West Yorkshire, but they're well-travelled. They toured the US 58 years before the Beatles, have played sell-out gigs in Russia and Sierra Leone and are very, very big in Japan. Back in 1968, Paul McCartney signed them to Apple and released a single which sadly failed to chart. And in 1993 they had the honour of being the first brass band ever to play Carnegie Hall, so a session with Randy Newman and Peter Gabriel didn't butter any parsnips or cause a mass exodus to the foot of our stairs.

They did themselves proud, though, and they did the song proud. Nearly as effective as the word 'home', the sound of a brass band is an instant trigger. It is the sound of peace, of comfort, of steadfast reliability and, most obviously, it is the sound of brown bread.

"Boy, that movie was a troubled production," said Randy, who had, by now, become something of a specialist in troubled productions. "They left [director] George Miller completely alone for two years somewhere in the outback in Australia to make it. And then, when they previewed the picture for the first time, it had these scenes where there's a lab where the bunnies have cigarettes taped to their mouths and a scene where a bullfrog is drowned and, well, the kids just ran out of there crying and stuff. There's also a scene where Mickey Rooney's walking around in his underwear, which might have raised a few eyebrows. My song is about how steadfast the pig was supposed to be and it's a good song, but at the end it still had to say 'pig' in it, which probably hurt my chances for a big hit."

Pleasantville is about two teenagers who are given a magic remote control that teleports them from their dysfunctional nineties family into a black and white fifties sitcom where everything is wholesome and neat. But, rather than the kids improving their nineties manners as a result of their transportation, they get the fifties to loosen up and in consequence the world gradually changes from black and white to colour.

Gary Ross, who had co-written *Big*, the Tom Hanks hit, was writing and directing. "What attracted me to the story," Randy said, "was that it was about television, which occupies about five hours a day of the average American's time."

"This is pretty damn close to the way I grew up," he later said. "The family time was consumed every night with watching television: my mother in a chair, dad on the sofa, me lying on the floor and my brother sitting behind me was our family unit, and it's something I was very comfortable with."

The score was restrained, more akin to *Avalon* than the stuff he'd been writing for the cartoons. Randy would have liked it to have been even more so. But all the same, he tried to please. "I remember there was one scene where Gary Ross, the director, wanted the music to be a much bigger deal. So I did my best to make it bigger. And when the film came out, one of the reviewers says, 'Randy Newman has to get less excited when he tries to put a little drama into a scene.' So I took the fall for that."

Still it got him his third 1999 Oscar nomination for Best Dramatic Score. Nicolai Piovani pipped him with *Life Is Beautiful*. Competing with a film about noble Italian Jews keeping their spirits up despite the Holocaust was never going to be easy.

Just in time for his fifty-fifth birthday, Rhino/Warners produced a boxed set, a retrospective of Randy's career so far, called *Guilty: 30 Years Of Randy Newman*.

It consisted of four CDs, 105 tracks and an excellent 80-page booklet, with an essay by Timothy White, editor-in-chief of *Billboard* and ex-senior editor of *Rolling Stone*, and interviews with Randy, Lenny Waronker and Russ Titelman – a bargain at $59.98.

Gary Norris, Randy's archivist, a snapper up of apparently unconsidered demos, made Randy's complete collection available. As well as the 'hits', there's a selection of movie cues, demos and previously unreleased songs like 'Jesus In The Summertime' ("Baby, I'll lay down my life for you / Just the way that Jesus died for me") and 'Beat Me Baby', a song for masochists.

It even has his first single, 'Golden Gridiron Boy'.

"That was one of the things I tried to negotiate out of," Randy said.

The praise was unstinting.

"… chockful of all the loneliness, godlessness, cruelty, misery, and misunderstanding the species can muster; wrapped in orchestrations so spectacularly beautiful they can only be described as transcendent…" said *Entertainment Weekly*.

"… King of Hollywood's hokum and still a cynical goat. Good ol' Randy," said *Mojo*.

Scott Jordan of *Offbeat* magazine asked Randy whether he enjoyed having his career laid out before his eyes and ears: "I dreaded looking back," Randy said. "I remembered horrors that weren't really so bad when I looked back.'

"One thing I was glad when I looked through it, I don't see any particular decline. There's stuff at the front that's okay, stuff at the front that isn't so good, and stuff at the end of the 30 years that's very good. So it isn't like I did good work and then I didn't. Like people will come up to me… and they do often… and say, 'Jeez, I just love…' some fucking thing I did in 1962. It's just what you want to hear: 'I loved 'Sail Away'. What have you been doing?' 'Uh, nothing.'"

The box-set was an apt underlining of Randy's time at Warner-Reprise as well as, perhaps, an acknowledgement that reissues were, from now on, their sole source of revenue from him.

There had been shake-ups in the upper echelons of Warners, or Time-Warner as it was by now. Mo Ostin had resigned. Lenny had been offered his job, but declined and also resigned. They both fetched up at DreamWorks Records, the music division of the *Antz* company set up by Steven Spielberg, David Geffen and Jeffrey Katzenberg.

"I followed Lenny to DreamWorks," Randy told Barney Hoskyns. "Well, I've sent Warners an amusing letter of resignation, having been there for more than 30 years, and I haven't heard back from them. It's like trying to find a general to surrender to. I think I've gone, y'know?

And I've signed with DreamWorks and haven't heard from them. So the people I'm leaving don't give a shit that I'm leaving and the people I'm going to don't give a shit that I'm coming.

"I'll be back with Mo and Lenny and we'll finish our twilight years together."

"It's very good for DreamWorks to have someone like Randy," Lenny told *Billboard*, "because our other artists look up to him and he affects the whole aesthetic of the company – as he did at Warners. Very few artists can offer what he gives: records that stand alone, that are special and very important – especially for a young company."

Or, to put it another way, he gave a shit.

Chapter Twenty-One

He'd moved to DreamWorks, now he had to supply them with some product.

Bad Love is an age-appropriate album, which is to say it steers a straight and certain course between, on the one hand, the Scylla of leather trousers, pony tails and sexual yelping and, on the other hand, the Charybdis of the old codger's resentful sneer at a world that has passed him by.

It's the honest work of a 55-year-old man exercising a skill he's always been pretty good at and applying it to matters of genuine and sometimes scholarly concern like sixteenth century ecological imperialism, Marxism today and the phenomenon of 55-year-old popsters still trying to get away with those leather trousers and that sexual yelping.

At 24, when he'd started out as a recording singer-songwriter, Randy had had the foresight to sing wherever possible like an ancient blues man with an hour or so left to live and, when performing live, to sit at a piano as if moving might expose him to gunfire. Even the bother of moving his hands around on the keyboard was a harsh imposition. He'd also had the good sense never to wear tight jeans, shirts open to the navel, fancy spectacles or anything else that might encourage young women to ask him to autograph their breasts. Consequently, when he turned 55, as he did in 1998, he looked and sounded pretty much the way he had when he'd started out – better, if anything – more rounded, more confident, more at peace with himself.

Maybe I'm Doing It Wrong

The voice had mellowed. The critic Richard von Busack described it as having reached the "point somewhere between the syrup of Hoagy Carmichael and the poison of Robert Mitchum in *The Night Of The Hunter*."

He had no shortage of blessings to count, professionally and personally. He'd had 12 Academy nominations, five Golden Globe nominations, and three Grammy nominations: he'd won three Annies, three ASCAPs, an Emmy and a BAFTA, become the first recipient of the ASCAP Henry Mancini Award for Outstanding Achievement In The World Of Film and Television, released a retrospective four-CD set of his work and had rock'n'roll royalty praying to get a shot at maybe some backing vocals on one of his records. He had a lot of money, a fine house, books to read, TVs to watch, two families and good friends who made him laugh. And yet still it didn't come easy.

"Music was always something I felt I was forced to do," he said in the press pack for the album. "I've done very little playing just for fun in my life."

And, "I think I don't like work, but I always feel better when I'm doing it. Which is not the same as finding comfort there. If you bury yourself in something, it's an excuse for not having a life. You can excuse anything: 'No, I can't come to your ball game today, Sonny, because I have to write two minutes of music.' Film composers, especially, are some of the worst fathers since Caligula."

And, "I will always write songs, and I hope I can always make albums. I'm not sure I will always make albums, though, because it requires self-discipline, and I don't have any."

Two hotshots were brought in to provide it: producer Mitchell Froom and engineer Tchad Blake had worked with Elvis Costello, Paul McCartney, Crowded House and Suzanne Vega. Like Randy, Mitchell studied music at the University of California (Randy in LA, Mitchell in Berkeley) so he knew about mixolydian modes and enharmonic spelling. Both he and Tchad are technically savvy: they can talk about EAB 3E1m full channel strips with dual parallel transformer-based outputs without feeling the least need to apologise.

Randy enjoyed working with them: "[Mitchell's] ideas almost always improved things," he said in the liner notes. "I don't necessarily know when a drum part really comes across, and I was able to trust him on that stuff. I did the arrangements and conducted the orchestra, and he trusted me to do that part. Plus, Mitchell made me feel comfortable about my singing and playing."

The admiration was mutual. "Randy's musical knowledge is on a different level," Mitchell told *Filter* magazine. "I'm not saying he's better than anyone, but, again, he's more of a Gershwin character than he is the Beatles or Bob Dylan. […] His skills are used in more of a fine-art way. My musical knowledge is usually greater than most of the people I work with. That's what I'm looked to; to provide musical understanding where people haven't thought it through. But in his case, it's far beyond me. I feel lucky to be in the room."

Most of the tracks are variations on the theme of bad love, the album's title. Indeed, the same could be said for much of Randy's work as a whole.

The first track is about the love of a man for his television. 'My Country' opens hard, no intro. Randy barks: "Let's go back to yesterday / When a phone call cost a dime / In New Orleans, just a nickel / Turn back the hands of time." The rhythm settles and the lyric paints a picture of an all-American family gathered to watch television together – "their faces glowing softly in the light."

"When I can get my wife and kids to watch television with me, I get a sense of comfort – it's like what I remember. As long as they're watching, I don't have to; I read or something. But at least we're all there together."

It's a patriotic song, with rolling snare drum and flutes playing like military fifes, about the glory of living in a country that mediates reality through the TV screen.

And when, later, the kids have left home and "have TVs of their own", they can be a distraction: "much as I love them / I'm always kind of glad when they go away."

"That's where this person lives – it's his country, televisionland," said Randy. When he used to visit his dad, often as not he'd feel he was interrupting the main business of the moment, which was *Matlock*. "But I've felt the same thing. I'm watching a ball game and one of my kids threatens to come over, and I say to myself, 'Shit'. Hopefully I'm not that bad, but I'm pretty close to it."

"Feelings might go unexpressed," he sings, "think that's probably for the best / Dig too deep who knows what you will find."

"People who know me personally are surprised as to how personal I've got on this record," Randy told Jon Ronson. "It's almost an exercise in

Maybe I'm Doing It Wrong

how far a writer will go in disrupting his private life. Maybe it's a little showy to do that to your kids. But part of the song is about being ruthless as a writer.

"I'm sorry they got raised that way. But I don't think they were too deprived being raised in front of the television every night. It's not the fireplace, but it's not nothing. At least we were all in the same room together."

'My Country' is about isolation and the all too human bond between a man and his TV. 'Shame' is about the loneliness and desperation of an older man discarding any semblance of dignity in his pursuit of a younger woman. "I love the idea of the power that young, beautiful people have, the power to crush and maim and destroy. People with all the money in the world, all the power in the world – and some 19 year old can rip 'em up."

The song is a lazy shuffle, and the lyrics half sung, half spoken as a dialogue with a chorus of censorious backing singers – harking back to 'Ask Him If He's Got A Friend For Me', the Fleetwoods track from nearly 40 years earlier – who wag their fingers and wail "Shame, shame, shame" until temper gets the better of him and he tells them to shut up. His mood ranges from egregious self-pity ("I don't get out much now") to rage ("God damn it you little bitch") to conciliation ("All right, let's talk a little business, you know what I'm saying?").

At the end he mentions he's recently bought a Lexus. It is not within the remit of the current work fully to address the question, "What does a Lexus signify?" but readers eager to learn more are referred to an excellent discussion of the matter in *Mass Communication Theory: Foundations, Ferment, And Future* by Stanley Baran and Dennis Davis.

The bad love theme extends, in the third track, to delusional self-regard and the phenomenon, mentioned at the beginning of this chapter, of male-menopausal leather trousers and sexual yelping.

That year had seen Bob Dylan start his "Never Ending Tour", Bruce Springsteen his "Reunion Tour" and the Rolling Stones their "No Security" Tour. Paul McCartney had just lost his wife, Linda, but he'd be back in 2003, embarking on a 23-gig tour of the USA. A couple of years earlier, Pat Boone, at the age of 63, had released an album of heavy metal covers and showed up at the *American Music Awards* dressed head to toe in black leather. In 2000, Jeff Lynne would revive ELO for a couple of gigs. No one, as Randy said, was leaving the stage.

"People who said at 20, 'I'm not doing this when I'm 30', they're out there on walkers. The stages are clogged with thick, grey-haired people."

'I'm Dead (But I Don't Know It)' addresses the problem. It's a rocker, with fuzz guitar, gated snare, organ stabs and raucous taunting backing vocals reminding the singer, "You're dead, you're dead." Nevertheless, the old guy persists with the stadium tours because no one in his management has the heart to tell him he's just embarrassing himself.

There was speculation on Randy's fansites that 'I'm Dead' could be seen as a clue that *Bad Love* would be his swansong. He made no efforts to deny the rumour. "There's a chance it's my last record," he said when challenged by uber-fan Jon Ronson, "I don't have any new ideas."

Just to dispel any tension – it wasn't and he did.

A few years earlier, Michael Jackson's management had asked Randy to write something for their poor mad boy. Randy obliged. Michael, or the management, or maybe Elizabeth Taylor or some critical chimpanzee, passed on it. So Randy recorded it himself.

'Every Time It Rains' is a slow, lonely weather song, tracing its lineage all the way back to 'I Think It's Going To Rain Today'. The 'pathetic fallacy" – Ruskin's phrase for the tendency, common in poetry, to "credit nature with human emotions" – runs deep in Randy's work, particularly the invocation of rain as a symbol of despair. See how many other instances you can spot.

"A lot of my tunes, if you write 'em down, are just three notes. But they serve what I'm trying to do."

When he writes for other people he allows himself to spread out a little more. It's a pity Michael Jackson didn't record 'Every Time It Rains'. It was built to suit his pure high-tenor. Joe Cocker did a terrific cover, but it's not the same.

'Great Nations Of Europe' is a song inspired by Alfred Crosby's seminal work of bio-history *European Ecological Imperialism: The Biological Expansion Of Europe 900–1900*. Crosby (no relation to Bing or David) traces the spread of plants, animals and pathogens that followed in the wake of European exploration, conquest and colonisation. As inspiration for a catchy tune goes, it might not have the same immediacy as meeting a gin-soaked bar-room queen in Memphis or taking a walk in the valley of the shadow of death, but Randy was prepared to put in the work to winkle out its potential.

Like, 'Follow The Flag', it sounds straightforwardly patriotic – fifes, drums and martial brass. But the lyric gleefully presents a catalogue of genocide. It traces the way in which the great nations of Europe brought "TB and typhoid and athlete's foot, diphtheria and the flu" to the rest of the world – though Randy is first to admit that the "athlete's foot" might be a slur. He mentions the benefits of European cultural values as well, and how Vasco Núñez de Balboa, encountering a group of gay Native Americans, had them "torn apart by dogs – on religious grounds, they say."

In the final verse, he mentions the spectre of AIDS: "But there on the horizon is a possibility / Some bug from out of Africa might come for you and me."

It's the kind of catchy tune you might find yourself absent-mindedly singing in a crowded supermarket, "'Scuse me, Great Nations, coming through."

'The One You Love' is another slow shuffle, a warning about the pitfalls of neglecting or misunderstanding the loved one, sung with a bemused resignation.

"This guy's going on about how women are so changeable, and he's frightened of some little girl. I can relate to it, though. My wife and I had a turbulent courtship, and she scared me half the time. I'd talk to her on the phone, and maybe when she hung up she'd say, 'Okay, bye.' And I'd think, 'Uh-oh.' It was a bad goodbye. I was like 48-years-old or something, and a bad goodbye would just kill me."

"If she's hungry, she won't say," he sings, "you'd better get a burger or something in her right away / if you don't you're gonna pay …"

The threat is underscored by a Mike Hammer sax and Bernard Hermann strings.

'The World Isn't Fair' is a consideration of the apparent failure of Marxism in the modern world.

Randy (and we are fairly certain that our narrator is actually Randy this time) tells Karl Marx that recently he has remarried and is raising his second family. When he goes along to a school orientation evening with his young children he is faced with the unedifying tableaux of beautiful women – "countesses, empresses, movie stars and queens" accompanied by "men much like me, froggish men, unpleasant to see."

The narrator cites this as evidence that Karl's aspirations for equality would never be realized and the world just isn't fair.

"You start out as a nice liberal and you think bad people will be punished for their misdeeds, or at least that undeserving people should not and will not profit," Randy told Paul Zollo. "But it just doesn't turn out that way. So I imagined explaining this to Karl Marx. The guy in the song is saying, 'Karl, take a look at this. How does this correlate with your plans, the way this beautiful young gene pool is being diluted by us old geezers?'"

"It's the kind of thing I find funny," he told *Billboard*. "Those little nonsense things, like in 'The World Isn't Fair' that's on *Bad Love* that goes, 'No one could rise too high/No one could sink too low/Or go under completely like some we know, 'cause I know people who never got off the beach – so they never laughed at it. But that's what I like. You know, in Sweden, you can't go under completely, and in Europe you can't go under completely. Here, you can go under completely, and I've seen it, and I've loaned money to help them avoid it."

Randy thought that 'The World Isn't Fair' was "about the best song I ever wrote", but he wasn't wholeheartedly pleased with its construction. "It's like one long verse. It doesn't get to a tonic, or something. It never stops."

He'd been doing a lot of reading. 'The World Isn't Fair' doesn't present a particularly incisive reading of the economic analysis expounded in *Das Kapital*, but it's certainly more cogent than, say, Eartha Kitt's 'Mink Schmink', or Woody Herman's 'Who Dat Up Dere Saying Who Down Dere While I'm Down Here Saying Who Dat Up Dere?'.

'Big Hat, No Cattle', however, is based on a somewhat closer reading of *The Duke Of Deception: Memories Of My Father* by Geoffrey Wolff. A bit of a closer reading, anyway.

The father, Wolff Sr, was a swindler who took all comers for a ride; his employers, his wives, even his own son. He liked to tell people that he was a Yale scholar who served as a fighter pilot during the war and became an aviation engineer. In reality he had dropped out of college and never served in the military.

The protagonist of the song, like Wolff's father, lies, as a matter of course, to all comers. Why does he do it? He's not sure: "I only know we're living in an unforgiving land / And a little lie can buy some real big peace of mind."

"I'm talking about people who base a whole life on lying," Randy said, "people who have cards that say 'producer' or 'CEO, Cloverdale

Music'. What does it cost to have cards printed up with anything you want? Nothing."

It's also a cowboy song with some stirring pedal steel guitar from Greg Leisz, Randy acting his socks off with little "aw shucks I'm a jerk but I know you'll forgive me" chuckles, a key change for the final chorus, but, disappointingly, still no coconut shells.

'Better Off Dead' is a sly, lounge-lizard rumba that returns squarely to the *Bad Love* theme. It warns of the debilitating pain that comes from unrequited love; how you're "better off dead / Than living with someone / Who just doesn't give a shit what happens to you."

It's *Gilda* music with ravishing choir and shrill strings, and it ends with a lonesome trumpet drifting into the hot night air with the cigarette smoke and the stench of surplus testosterone.

In concerts, Randy has been known to describe the next track as "an interesting exercise to see how many people I could hurt with one piece of music."

It's a touchingly straightforward tribute to Roswitha, his ex-wife, and it's called, simply, 'I Miss You'.

Glenn Tilbrook[*], in an interview with Randy for BBC Radio 2, asked him how his current wife, Gretchen, felt about the song. Randy replied saying that though he had always been obedient to his wives in most things there was one area in which he did as he chose, "I write what I write."

"I love my ex-wife," he said. "My boys told me I better warn her that this song was coming. She knows me, though – she knows I'd sell anyone out for a song. We were married 18 years and I never wrote a song about her in all that time. Actually, I've never written a song about anyone in my whole life."

"I wanted to write you one / Before I quit," he sang, "And this one's it."

Which sentiment further fuelled speculation that this would, indeed, be his last album and he was about to retire to a life of whittling or viniculture or make salad dressing like his namesake Paul or maybe go back to college and train to be a history professor.

---

[*] Tilbrook subsequently wrote a song about the experience called 'Interviewing Randy Newman'.

Feelings for an ex are among the most secret thoughts a person can have. 'I Miss You' makes you fear for all those people who, hearing it, thought, "Maybe it's okay to mention that I still have feelings for my ex." And 20 minutes later found themselves in Accident and Emergency howling, "Help, the bleeding won't stop."

'Going Home' is a low-key ballad set in the First World War, "the stupidest event in history. A war where they fought to gain a few hundred yards of land for months, costing thousands and thousands of lives – a senseless and shocking waste."

It's about a young man who's survived and is looking forward to returning to his country and his girl.

"This is one of those songs that I just can't sing – it's right in one of the cracks in my range," Randy said. "So we did it to approximate what a recording of that era would sound like. I know Mitchell's going to get blamed in some review for using all these effects, but we did it because I simply can't sing the thing."

The last track, 'I Want Everyone To Like Me', is an upbeat number about the all too human propensity for debilitating insecurity.

"I do want everyone to like me. That's why people get into show business. There have been times in my life where I wondered whether I was saying things I really thought or felt or meant, or whether I was saying things to make people like me. I first started worrying about it when I was in the sixth grade, and I still don't know the answer."

"I wanna earn the respect of my peers," he sings, "If it takes 100 years / I'd like to find out where they are by the way / I would run to embrace them / I'm only kiddin'."

When asked who those peers were, he mentions James Taylor, Paul Simon, Peter Gabriel, Prince, Chrissie Hynde. And among the younger stars?

"I like Sarah McLachlan and Bjork and Alanis Morissette. A lot of people thought that album [*Jagged Little Pill*] was bullshit, but I believed it; I believed absolutely that she was pissed off. And I liked that rapper who died, The Notorious B.I.G. Every once in a while something seeps through to me, but not much."

The album came out on June 1, 1999 and languished in the marketplace.

"*Bad Love* sold about 30,000 copies internationally," Randy said, "so I'd better look for a better means of subsistence."

Maybe I'm Doing It Wrong

"I've always had the hope that I'd sell millions of records," he told Jon Ronson. "I know it's delusional. Basically, my career has been a disappointment to me. There are 40,000 people out there who just love me. But they may be surprised to hear I've been aiming... beyond them. I just haven't been doing it very well.

"I've always written for, unbelievably enough, a mass public. It's never been that way, but that's who I've written for."

"You make a record and keep squeezing it out and there's something to live up to," Randy told Graham Reid on the website *Elsewhere*. "Maybe it's an energy thing, there are fields like physics and chess requiring big brain power and people in those fields will do their best work early. But maybe rock'n'roll is just a young person's thing. There's no decline in Irving Berlin over a 50-year period. He had a hit in 1954 and a hit in 1908.

"I think working on movies where you have to work with music every day for three months, 10 to 12 hours a day, helped me on the last record. I look for signs of decrepitude and me slipping and I didn't really see it. Although maybe I'm the last one to see it. But I don't think its inferior to the stuff I've done before."

His sales were never in the millions, but all the same, largely as a result of *Toy Story*, he'd become a household name.

Imitation is supposed to be the best sort of flattery. Parody is proof that you've made a mark, not necessarily a good mark, but certainly one that's been noticed.

In season two of the Fox cartoon series *Family Guy*, the family find themselves wandering around in the wake of the Apocalypse (Da Boom) looking for food. They find a house with an apple tree beside it. The only problem is that Randy Newman is there at his piano all day and all night singing about everything he sees.

The parody, voiced by Will Sasso, is not a bad shot at Randy's delivery and straightforward (some might say over-literal) lyrical style: "Red-headed lady, reachin' for an apple / Gonna take a bite / uh nope nope… / She's gonna breathe on it foyst / Wipes it on her blouse-eh / She takes a bite, chews it once, twice, three times, four times."

The family get the hell out of there.

"I thought it was sorta funny," Randy told Pete Paphides of *Hidden Tracks*. "When it came on […] I was like, 'I'm not like that! I don't write about everything I see so specifically.' Then I caught my kids looking at me in that way only your kids can look at you."

A couple of years later, Will Sasso started using the same schtick on MADtv – a Fox sketch show, some of which was based on regular strips from *Mad* magazine. Seated at a piano, wearing a grey curly wig and chain smoking, Will, with sloppy diction and the 'frightened bison' voice, gurned his way through some of Randy's more familiar tropes.

"President Bush, President Bush / I love you from your nose to your tush," he drawled.

Sasso was entranced by Randy's apparent facility for writing a song for any movie, any subject, any time. "I don't even to need to *see* a movie to write a song about it!" he says adjusting his wig. And when George Lucas comes to ask for a contribution to his new *Star Wars* movie, without a moment's pause he sings: "Jedi knights are bred out of spite."

The profile got even more public with the release of *Toy Story II*.

"We had a lot of fun doing it, though because it was a sequel, we all had to pay a lot of attention to what we'd done in the past," Randy told the *Los Angeles Times*, "which was hard for me. But I like working for John Lasseter. He gave me a lot of freedom. He didn't have a lot of temp tracks that he loved, so I got to do my own thing." (Temp tracks are bits of random music put on the soundtrack as guides for the sort of thing the director thinks might be suitable. For the 1967 movie, *The Graduate*, for instance, director Mike Nichols used a bunch of Simon & Garfunkel tunes as his temp track, then basically decided he liked them so much that he stuck with them.)

Randy and John enjoyed an excellent relationship, "... and I can't say that about every director I've ever worked with."

"Our wives are good friends," said John. "The four of us went on a publicity trip down to Latin America for a little over a week, I think. It was like *¡Three Amigos!*. We went to Rio de Janeiro and every ten minutes Randy broke into the Barry Manilow song 'Copacabana.'"

Lasseter's wife, Nancy, encouraged her husband to include a strong female character in the sequel. Bo Peep, the closest the first film had come to a female lead, did not have the makings of a feminist icon.

Jessie, the cowgirl heroine of *Toy Story II*, is loud, capable and so versatile that no less than three talents had to be hired to voice her: Joan

Cusack for the speaking, Mary Kay Bergman for the yodelling and Sarah McClachlan for the singing.

Randy was fond of Jessie: "I'm not Woody. I'm not that organized. Buzz is sort of competent. It's hard to say. I think, I guess I'd say Jessie's the one I like best. I don't know, maybe I really secretly want to be a woman. I like her. I like the music I wrote. The fact that she's got some kind of story and is, you know, kind of bitter."

Jessie has the big song.

John Lasseter's brief to Randy went: "She's gonna be telling about her life and her disappointment with her relationship with her owner as a child, as they grew up."

"That was the assignment," Randy told Keith Phipps. "I knew what the length of it was, and I knew a girl had to sing it. [...] John Lasseter's a tremendous fan of Sarah McLachlan. She was terrific. She did very well.

"It was like writing for a different instrument. I have a blues-oriented voice. That's what I sound best on. She has a different kind of contralto, or whatever the hell she has. Soprano. It's a voice that can hold notes, so I can write with that in mind. I think I can sing it, but it's funny."

The song, 'When She Loved You', is Jessie's memories of the little girl who once played with her, but then cast her aside when she grew too old for dolls. There are two kinds of people: people who weep during the 'When She Loved Me' montage, and people who lie about it.

The song runs for just under two and a half minutes at a slow tempo, which, to Randy, felt like a dead spot in the middle of a fast action film. "I didn't think kids would sit still in a theatre for that long."

John disagreed and was right to. "They did sit still," Randy said. "I watched it with a bunch of children. It was a nice thing to see. 'When She Loved Me' isn't the first time Pixar knew better than I did."

"John's instincts have gotten better and better as things have gone on," Randy told Tommy Pearson on Classic FM, "but inevitably, since I have strong opinions of my own, we've butted heads on occasion, sure. And I've won a couple. Maybe two out of six. But always without rancour, and with respect for the opinion of the other. Which isn't always the case. It's kind of an authoritarian system, and if the director tells you to do something, he's not gonna listen to your opinion too often. John is wise enough to at least listen."

Toy Story II garnered the now customary clutch of awards: a Grammy, a Golden Satellite, an Annie and an ASCAP Film And Television Music Award.

At the Oscars he was once again nominated for Best Original Song, but this time Phil Collins won for 'You'll Be in My Heart' from *Tarzan*.

A pattern was beginning to form: Randy would be nominated, but some Brit – Rachel Portman, Stephen Warbeck, John Barry, Elton John, Tim Rice, Phil Collins – always beat him.

In a radio interview in 2000, Randy was asked if he thought that the Academy Awards secretly had something against him. "You know, someday I'll do the music for a movie that does Best Picture and I'll win," he said. "Or I'll have a stroke and they'll feel sorry for me and I'll win."

Randy was a member of the Academy by this time and had gleaned some insight into the rules of the game.

"It's a strange selection process. I get to vote for make-up, cinematography, and I know nothing about it. And people who don't know anything about music get to vote on that. I don't think I'll be overly overjoyed if I do win, it's not where I live."

Later in the year, *Billboard* honoured him with a *Billboard* Century Award, which is given for overall achievement in the field of music. Previous winners had included George Harrison, Emmylou Harris and Chet Atkins.

"But the reality of those things is that as you get older, you go to more and more of them; and really they're just a bunch of show people patting each other on the back," he told Jim Macnie of the *Providence Phoenix*. "Everyone applauds. We just pat each other's back 'til we roll into the grave. I don't like any of the ceremonies I've been to, really. And when I've had to make a speech of some kind, I've been absolutely out of control. I forget to control my language and stuff. People laugh, but there's bound to be those who don't want to hear the word 'shit'."

"It is nice. But I'm not comfortable. They should wait 'til your dead."

In his acceptance speech, Randy confessed to handing over a $423,000 bribe to Timothy White – *Billboard*'s the editor-in-chief.

Randy got his 2001 Oscar nomination for 'A Fool In Love', the song he'd written for the Jay Roach/Ben Stiller/Robert De Niro film, *Meet The Parents*.

Maybe I'm Doing It Wrong

It was a relief to be back on live action films after the rigours of animation: easier, he maintained, in that they're not as fast-paced, which means fewer notes and less work. "It's like having to lift fewer bricks."

He was echoing his forbears, back in the golden age, when orchestrators were paid $5 a page, with four bars to the page. Foggy landscapes and broken hearted wide shots – lots of whole notes and half notes (semibreves and minims) – always mean faster money than car chases and anything set in Paris (tiddly dee dee dum dum on xylophone and woodwind, and trying to remember how to score for an accordion), or, God forbid, Ireland (diddly diddly diddly diddly on everything), which always meant dense eighth notes and triplets.

At the Academy Award ceremony, Randy and Susanna Hoffs of the Bangles performed the song. Randy wore a tux and was surrounded by showgirls.

Mr Dylan won for 'Things Have Changed', his song from *Wonder Boys*. He didn't bother with showgirls or even to show up. Instead he sent a video of himself shot inside what looked like a small cupboard where he was hiding along with two men in black shirts and a selection of Fender guitars.

Chapter Twenty-Two

*A*lly McBeal was a comedy/drama, aired on Fox, set in a legal firm peopled almost exclusively by hip, beautiful, shiny, wealthy, thin people who were also – because plots are difficult to manufacture from nothing more in the way of material than fabulous skin and dress-size – emotional casualties, insecure and/or ruthless.

The show made heavy use of music, either as background or featured – often sung by Vonda Shepard who (it's like an extended Randy family) later appeared in the concert version of *Faust* and married *Bad Love* producer, Mitchell Froom.

In the finale of Season 3, broadcast in May 2000 and titled *Ally McBeal: The Musical – Almost*, the characters' angst reaches such a pitch that it can only adequately be expressed through the medium of song: and not just song but Randy Newman song – that's how rough things were.

Several of Randy's finest were quoted in full or truncated version including, 'Relax, Enjoy Yourself', 'You Can't Keep A Good Man Down' (sung by Jane Krakowski in a fine Bob Fosse-style chairs and hats dance routine), 'I Want You To Hurt Like I Do', 'Falling In Love', 'Real Emotional Girl' and 'Forever', a straight love song never before heard.

Randy even put in an appearance himself towards the end, singing 'There's A Party At My House'. "He showed up at 7:30, left at 10:30," the director said. "When he was saying goodbye, he stepped up and said, 'Thank you. It's been a long and difficult season.'"

"I was probably the fattest person ever on their show," Randy said. "They told me, you're the fattest person we've ever seen."

And the catering wasn't up to much.

"There's food," he said. "Parsley, watercress, all the legumes."

"I've admired them from afar for years," Randy said, "and the singing I've heard was really professional, so I'm looking forward to seeing it.

"I met Alicia Witt. She was a concert pianist, and I talked to her for a while, and I liked her."

Alicia Witt played Hope Mercy in the show. She is a redhead, although insufficient evidence prevents the passing of definitive judgement about her qualifications as a 'nasty' redhead. "And my wife is getting all worn out, so I'm looking around. She probably plays better than I do, too."

Back in February, a planned revival of *Faust* at the Kennedy Center had fallen through but Michael Roth, who had worked with Randy on the original *Faust*, approached him with another theatre project – this time based on his own life story told through his songs.

Randy agreed and the show was slated to open the South Coast Repertory Theatre in Costa Mesa, Orange County. Jerry Patch, the in-house dramaturg worked on the script. Randy and Michael worked on the music.

The title of the show, *The Education Of Randy Newman*, was derived from *The Education Of Henry Adams,* the nineteenth century autobiography of the grandson of President John Quincy Adams and great-grandson of President John Adams.

The link between the two was more than just a pretext for a snappy title. Rather than being a straightforward account of his life, Adam's book records his meditations on the social and political changes in his lifetime. It's also narrated entirely in the third person, a device Randy often employed. And many passages in the book almost sound like a nineteenth century version of Randy: with a little vernacularisation, for instance, Adams' line, "Politics [...] had always been the systematic organization of hatreds," could slide easily into, say, 'Rednecks' or 'Roll With The Punches'.

"We developed a piece that Randy was very much a part of," Michael Roth wrote in his blog. "And I got to play two hours of rock'n'roll piano every night."

The Education Of Randy Newman starts with a prologue, then, skating over the fact that Randy was raised primarily in Los Angeles rather than New Orleans, showcases his songs of the South – 'Dixie Flyer', 'New Orleans Wins the War', 'Louisiana 1927', 'Kingfish'.

Act I ends with Randy's fictional arrival in California, and turns 'I Love LA' into a rip-roaring production number.

Act II sees the start of his successful career. His first marriage follows ('Love Story'), and then a nasty little cocaine habit ('Miami') and general debauchery ('You Can Leave Your Hat On').

After his first divorce ('I Want You to Hurt Like I Do'), Randy matures and sees the error of his ways. He falls in love again and remarries ('Days of Heaven' from *Guilty: 30 Years Of Randy Newman* and 'Feels Like Home').

More songs providing the appropriate Henry Adams political and intellectual taste of the times are included to fill in some historical and sociological background – 'Song For The Dead', 'It's Money That Matters' and 'My Life Is Good'.

Scott Warra, a 42-year-old with rosy cheeks and wide eyes, played Randy. Some critics wondered whether 'wide-eyed and rosy cheeks' accurately captured one's mental picture of the inner Randy Newman.

The sets used scrims that flew on and off above the stage with projected images providing the potential for a sort of Brechtian commentary on the songs, although, in the event, the images chosen were more *Key Words With Peter And Jane* than *Der Gute Mensch Von Sezuan:* a huge pair of spectacles for 'Four Eyes'; a police parade for 'Jolly Coppers On Parade' and a litany of every landmark mentioned in 'I Love LA' – "Sixth Street" and there it is, "Imperial Highway" – bang.

The show opened on June 2, 2000. The reviews weren't great.

Steven Leigh Morris of *LA Weekly* described with horror the way in which 'Louisiana 1927' was performed as, "a school lesson, with the narrator-teacher twanging her suspenders and chirping to her brightly costumed wards."

"There are endless examples of these kinds of perky intrusions," the review goes on, "and the way they subvert Newman's original textures of menace and irony."

Steven Oxman in *Variety* thought that, for the show to gel, "Newman would almost certainly need to write a couple of songs that would bridge some holes, especially the gaping one that sucks the energy out of the

Maybe I'm Doing It Wrong

show with a good half-hour remaining. But it would be worth it for Newman to do so… there's phenomenal potential here."

The potential, if it existed, never got a shot at fulfilment. The show ran for 43 performances in Costa Mesa, then lay dormant for a while.

Back pains are an occupational hazard of piano players, especially ones who hunch a lot. At the start of 2001, Randy needed surgery to sort out a few problems. It took a while for him to recover, but as soon as he was up and about again, he started work on the project that would win him his first Oscar.

The Pixar technical people had figured out how to animate really authentic-looking fur that bounced and shimmered. It gave them the chance to make their fluffiest film so far.

"I'm glad I get to be that cuddly, if you excuse the expression, so I get a chance to get out of myself," Randy told Roger Catlin in the *Hartford Courant*. "With my [other] stuff, you run the risk of everything coming out of the side of the mouth. And it helps me to do things that are straightforward and that children have to understand."

Monsters, Inc. is named after a company that uses the energy it generates by scaring children to power their city's grid. Trouble ensues when a monster called Sulley (a big, blue, shaggy John Goodman) accidentally lets one fearless child, Boo, escape from the world of People into the world of Monsters. Sulley, helped by his friend Mike (a single-eyed, long-legged Billy Crystal) has to catch and return her before anybody discovers his error.

"All pictures require a lot of moods, but this was a different world entirely that you had to conjure up musically," Randy explained. "It's like the real world, with people going to work, except they're monsters."

The main theme of the movie, and several other cues, draw inspiration from the Saul Bass-style title sequence and from the similarity between Monsterworld and fifties Manhattan. It's Benny Goodman big band stuff, with Lionel Hampton vibes, close harmony saxes and wild trombones.

Boo, the little girl, presented other possibilities.

"At first, I had played her as if she were a monster because that's how they perceived her," Randy told the *Animated Views* website. "In each of these Pixar pictures, I've taken the emotions of the characters seriously. In every picture, they're adults, they're not children. The film is for children primarily, in a way, but the characters have adult emotions. They felt about her as if she were something like an alien. So, I wrote some dissonant kind of frightening music for her. And yet, you're meant to laugh. But still, I wanted it full of terror, you know. Then, for the other theme, I played her just as a little girl going to sleep. There's one scene when Sulley begins to feel something for her as she finally goes to sleep in his bed: then she begins to appear differently to him."

The hit song from the movie, 'If I Didn't Have You', is another lazy shuffle with a nod – some might say more than a nod – in the direction of Hoagy Carmichael's 'Rockin' Chair'. It has a "Look ma I'm dancing" choreography opportunity, a lot of Hope/Crosby banter, an Inkspots talk section and Billy Crystal even obliges us with a couple of bars of Jolson. Anybody who asks for more from a song is just plain greedy.

This is what happened on the big night. Jennifer Lopez lists the nominees. Usually any passing Brit was enough to crush Randy's hopes and dreams and this year there were two big, big guns – Paul McCartney and Sting – in the running.

Paul McCartney gets the biggest round of applause when the nominations are announced. Then, "And the Oscar goes to…" Jennifer Lopez opens the envelope. "Randy Newman, for 'If I Didn't Have You' from *Monsters, Incorporated*.'

Randy was overwhelmed by the reaction, especially the bit that nobody got to see on TV.

It's difficult for orchestra musicians to stand up, especially in a pit where space is tight. Their instruments get in the way. They're often surrounded by bits – mutes, extra instruments they double on. If the music stand goes flying and puts their pages out of order, they'll end up playing 'There's No Business Like Show Business' while everybody else is on 'Candle In The Wind'.

But they stood up for Randy and applauded. A lot of them had worked with him, or his uncles even. He was one of them. One of their own – a proper muso – had won an Oscar.

"It really got to me," he said. "Growing up the way I did, in a family of composers, all I ever wanted was to be respected by the studio musicians and the orchestra. They're the people whose opinion matters. I was worried that I was going to cry, and I was going, 'Please, you can't do that. You'll be like Sally Field. It'll never go away.' So I blinked a lot."

The applause continued. "I don't want your pity," he eventually managed to say. "I want to thank, first of all, the music branch for so many chances to be humiliated over the years."

He also thanks John Lasseter and writer/director Pete Docter then looks down at the pit and thanks, "all these musicians many of whom have worked for me a number of times and may not again."

"I'd rather have had it for a score," he told Duncan Campbell for the *Guardian*. "But I was much more moved by the event than I ever thought I would be. You know it's not a measure of anything real, but I was up there and so was Jennifer Lopez and the orchestra stood up and it kind of got to me. I was almost embarrassed – but not quite."

"It's not one of my best songs, but that's the way those things work. When I die, it will say 'Oscar-winner' in my obit."

The Oscar did not change his life. "The impact," he said, "lasted about a day and a half."

He was at a time of life, anyway, when picking up awards almost took up more of his time than making music. As well as the Oscar, the National Academy of Popular Music and Songwriters inducted him into their Hall of Fame and the National Academy of Recording Arts and Sciences gave him their Governors' Award.

But, as always, greater even than his genius as performer, composer or songwriter was his ability to find something to *kvetch* about. He didn't feel the love. Not the sort of love Neil Diamond got.

"Neil gets that outsized kind of love some people can generate. Do I want that? That easy kind of stupid love? Yeah – are you kidding? It's the only supernatural thing I believe in."

There was also a space in his trophy cabinet where a Tony (for achievement in Broadway theatre) should go. *Faust* hadn't made it: neither had *Randy Newman's Maybe I'm Doing It Wrong*, or *The Education Of Randy Newman*.

A second chance came with the last of these when, in autumn 2002, it was revived at the ACT theatre in Seattle.

Gordon Edelstein, former artistic director of ACT and self-proclaimed "lifelong Randy Newman fan", helped rework the show into a shorter version, running about two hours.

In keeping with *Variety*'s advice, Randy supplied some new material: an opening song, 'Henry Adams'; a new father-son duet, 'Sage Advice';

and extra "stuff for each of the two wives, to flesh them out a bit and give one more of a backbone".

At one point the first wife complains, "If you don't love me tell me so / Before you tell the world in one of your stupid little songs."

"Broadway was the main thing for Gershwin, Rodgers & Hart, Harold Arlen," Randy told Misha Berson of the *Seattle Times*. "So why didn't Carole King start out writing shows? Because my generation got excited by rock'n'roll. A lot of rock songwriters just can't understand why so much Broadway stuff is so bad. Rock people don't get the appeal of something like *Cats*. I mean, what are those Andrew Lloyd-Webber things anyway?"

But now, "some of us are making the move into theatre and other things because the record business is beginning, finally, to turn its back on us geriatrics. You see Sting do a commercial, Tom Petty and James Taylor on the *Today* show. You know they're doing it 'cause they have to. In the old days, you'd just put out a new record."

Ticket sales were good. Reviews weren't bad. But still it didn't transfer to Broadway.

Randy was disappointed. His sixtieth birthday was looming. Writing for movies or, given the chance, theatre, was an increasingly attractive option, "because it's no longer easy for me to just pull songs out of the air. I'm very efficient and quick if you give me an assignment."

His next assignment, however, turned out to be what he – a man who had had back surgery, been divorced, lost both parents, been insulted by Paul McCartney and fired by Wolfgang Peterson – later described as the "worst experience of my life".

Seabiscuit was based on the true story of a drunk, depressed jockey and an over-the-hill trainer working with a horse nobody believed in during the Great Depression. If the horse had lost race after race then got drunk with the jockey, picked a fight and hoofed him to death, the movie might have had a spark of originality. But the real ending was... what do you think?

Randy had worked successfully with the director, Gary Ross, before on *Pleasantville* in 1998. But this time there was trouble.

"I wasn't happy with *Seabiscuit*," Randy told Paul Zollo, "but that was because I'm not sure what Gary Ross, the director, wanted. I did what

I thought was right. He ended up changing a lot of what I did, and that hurt my feelings, and I think hurt the picture."

The disagreement was a fairly fundamental one about the role of music in a movie. Should it pre-empt the action or let the action lead? What sort of clues should it provide, if any? In *Jaws,* the *duh-duh* music accompanies the shark's every appearance and, in at least one instance, lets you know the shark is around even though it hasn't been seen yet. The lack of music also subtly tips you off in one key scene where two kids cause mass panic by pretending to be a shark. Similarly, at the start of the shower scene in *Psycho,* the only sound you hear is water. The music kicks in only when the shower curtain is pulled back and the knife appears. So that at the start of the scene nothing, it appears, is amiss.

"Horses are racing," Randy said. "You don't necessarily do the horse race but you do the doubt about the horse race. He [the director] felt that everyone knew what was going to happen, but it isn't like everyone knows the history of *Seabiscuit.* Even if they had, you play fair with them. You don't give away any surprises with music. I hate it when that happens. When you know that, oh Jesus Christ, this is gonna happen now."

William Goldman – the best screenwriter in the history of cinema – when asked what makes a successful movie, sensibly replied, "Nobody knows anything". *Seabiscuit* got seven Oscar nominations and took $147m at the box office.

In the fifties and sixties, Verve had released a series of LPs – known as the *Songbook* albums – on which Ella Fitzgerald showcased the work of Great American Composers: *Ella Fitzgerald Sings The Cole Porter Songbook, The Rodgers & Hart Songbook, The Duke Ellington Songbook* and so on.

In 2003, Bob Hurwitz, boss of Nonesuch records, a label owned by Warners, decided to give the Randy *oeuvre* the same sort of treatment.

"I think Bob takes me seriously as an important American songwriter so he wanted a songbook type thing for people to have when I'm... I don't know... gone."

Nonesuch was a classy label that had originally specialised in orchestral and chamber music. It had flirted with spoken word records then branched out into world music. Ry Cooder's association with a bunch of elderly Cuban musicians resulted in the label's biggest hit, *Buena Vista Social Club,* an album which right-thinking people embraced almost as a basic principle of human decency.

"It is an artier label," Randy said. "I was speaking to some group and they said, 'I think you have to learn the lute to be on Nonesuch.' But the thing is I believe they'll do a better job for me commercially. They'll pay more attention and sell more records for me."

In January 2003, he went to Conway Studios on Melrose Avenue with producer Mitchell Froom and engineer David Boucher, sat down at the piano and recorded 18 tracks, revisiting songs and tunes spanning a 33-year period, from 'I Think It's Going To Rain Today' and 'Living Without You' to 'The World Isn't Fair', an instrumental version of 'When She Loved Me' and themes from *Avalon* and *Ragtime*.

"It wasn't something I would have thought to do necessarily – memorialize my own songs. It's kind of interesting to me to do this project because it does play to history in a way, but in truth that's not as interesting to me personally as new stuff. I like writing new songs, though frankly I don't do that too much either."

The Randy Newman Songbook, Vol. 1 was released the following September.

"There isn't much to *The Randy Newman Songbook, Vol. 1*," said Mark Deming on *Allmusic*, "just a guy playing piano and singing his songs... but it's just enough to make you laugh, wince, and almost cry; it's the work of one of the few people in pop music who merits the description 'genius,' and it's a remarkable summation of his singular talent."

Randy toured Europe again at the beginning of 2004 and later in the year worked on the soundtrack for *Meet The Fockers*, the sequel to *Meet the Parents* that he'd scored in 2000. He wrote two new songs for the film, 'We're Gonna Get Married' and 'Crazy 'Bout My Baby', both Fats Domino rockers, heavy on the backing vocals, and otherwise provided a score that blended nicely with the film's toxic mix of slapstick and sentimentality.

"Maybe I helped them," Randy said, "maybe I made them an extra $320."

The following year, the wind came.

It blew in from the south, swung to the west, and lessened a little as it moved across Florida then picked up strength again as it headed north over the Gulf of Mexico, at one point becoming the fiercest hurricane ever seen.

It was blowing 125 mph when it first hit Louisiana. On the morning of August 29, it passed just south and west of New Orleans. The storm surge brought water levels in the rivers and canals up 12 or 14 feet and at the same time heavy rain fell. Bridges were destroyed. The badly designed, badly maintained flood defences fell apart, leaving 80% of the city underwater.

When the first warnings came there had been attempts to evacuate the city, but the process was slow and badly organised. About 100,000, including some of the poorest and most vulnerable citizens, got left behind. Prisoners locked in their cells at the Orleans Parish Prison were helpless as the waters rose to their chests and then their necks: the lights went out, the ventilation failed, the sewage pipes fractured and the toilets backed up. In some cases, rescue, food or water didn't come for days. Later, the Sheriff's Department dismissed the stories as the testimony of psychopaths and crackheads, "nobody died, nobody got left behind". But 517 inmates were never accounted for.

In all, 1,200 people drowned in the floods, and across Louisiana, Alabama and Mississippi, between 2,000 and 4,000 people were killed and millions were left homeless.

Government response was a dog's breakfast. There were dark accusations of corruption, of the licence given to the oil business to play havoc with the wetlands, of casual neglect because the worst hit areas were inhabited by the poor and by non-whites.

For a couple of days after the disaster had hit, the President saw no reason to cut short his vacation. It was not George W. Bush's finest hour.

Randy still had family living around New Orleans. A cousin lost his house.

Not long after the hurricane, he was touring in the area: "I stopped and saw the Ninth Ward, and there's block after block of schools and drugstores and everything, and it's over. There's never going to be the same kind of life in those houses again. And I blame that on the federal government."

'Lousiana, 1927', the song he'd written about the other flood, became a battle-cry of beleaguered Orleanians, struggling to rebuild their city and their lives.

Aaron Neville sang the song on NBC's *Concert For Hurricane Relief*. One verse in particular had a keen contemporary resonance: "President Coolidge came down in a railroad train / With a little fat man with a note-pad in his hand / The President say, 'Little fat man isn't it a shame what the river has done / To this poor cracker's land'."

Stars lined up to read their impassioned appeals off autocue, imploring viewers to give generously. Harry Conick Jr was there, and Wynton Marsalis, Glenn Close, John Goodman, Richard Gere, Leonardo DiCaprio and a host of others.

"The landscape of the city has changed dramatically, tragically and, perhaps irreversibly," reads Mike Myers, nervously. Kanye West, standing next to him, jiggles a leg and looks mad about something. When his turn comes to speak he creates panic in the studio gallery by abandoning the carefully prepared script and speaking from the heart. "I hate the way they portray us in the media. You see a black family, it says, 'They're looting.' You see a white family, it says, 'They're looking for food.'"

"George W. Bush," he adds, "doesn't care about black people."

Hurriedly, the director cuts away to Chris Tucker, who has a rabbit-in-the-headlights moment before filling the edgy silence with, "Please, please, please, please, do all you can to help, help, help, help, help. Help."

Winding up the evening, host Matt Lauer tried to paper over the cracks. "Emotions in this country right now are running very high," he says. "Sometimes that emotion is translated into inspiration, sometimes into criticism. We've heard some of that tonight. But it's still part of the American way of life."

Then the entire ensemble sings 'When The Saints Go Marching In'.

Randy played 'Louisiana 1927' on another fundraiser, *Shelter From The Storm: A Concert For The Gulf Coast* and made an orchestrated version of the song for the Katrina charity album *Our New Orleans* on Nonesuch Records.

"In New Orleans [...] there's always a little sauce on everything, and things get dressed up," Randy told *Filter* magazine, "but that was so real, what happened down there, that there's no way you can turn it into folklore. They're sick of people who are trying to do that, turn it into something charming. 'The brave heart of the Crescent City' and all that shit. It was an enormous thing that beat people up around the eyes. The song ['Louisiana 1927'] is, in a way, part of what happened. I don't know what they think of it, whether they love it or not. I assume they're tired of Spike Lee being down there making movies about it, and I assume they're tired of me, too."

Fats Domino, 77 years old and living in the Lower Ninth Ward, was one of those who decided to stay behind to look after his ailing wife and ride the storm out. His home was flooded and inaccessible. He was reported missing, presumed dead. But a couple of days later the coastguards were able to helicopter him and his family off the roof of their house.

He survived, just, and released an album *Alive And Kickin'*, donating the proceeds to the Tipitina Foundation, set up to help local musicians and music education.

A couple of years later, everybody who mattered, from Elton John to Dr John, Robert Plant, Robbie Robertson, BB King, Norah Jones and Willie Nelson, put together a Fats Domino tribute album with proceeds going to the same charity – some going to rebuild Fats' studio.

Randy contributed a version of Fats' 1957 hit – particularly appropriate given the day the hurricane hit – 'Blue Monday'.

Randy wasn't sure about *Cars*.

"That whole movie is about people who've lost their way on a journey and you miss the little towns when you're on the big freeway," he told Patrick Goldstein for the *Los Angeles Times*, "and I thought, 'OK, maybe this is the end of the Pixar streak. Who in Europe or Asia is gonna get this?'"

Cars was Pixar's seventh film. It grossed $60m on its first weekend, nearly half a billion to date. Merchandise since the franchise was launched has grossed a billion.

"Which just shows you how stupid I am. John Lasseter and his people are just wired into their audience and the public taste in a way that's really deep. And certainly in a way I'm not."

The soundtrack album went to number six in the *Billboard* 200, although the film used tracks by Hank Williams, Sheryl Crow, Brad Paisley, the Chords and two versions of 'Route 66', so Randy's music cues take up less than half the playing time.

His one song, 'Our Town', sung by James Taylor, got the by now customary Oscar nomination. Melissa Etheridge walked off with the statue.

But he did win a trip to Las Vegas. "There was a charity auction up at Pixar," he said, "and I bid for, and won, a trip to Las Vegas and tickets to see O and Ka, Cirque du Soleil shows." O happens mostly in water. Ka happens up a cliff face. Randy was profoundly influenced by both shows. "I can play several pieces from the show using only my nose and my buttocks."

It was an extended family trip. Alan, a doctor, was retiring. "My brother is the best Newman we've had so far. It was great to see him and as you may have noticed, I'm a better person because of it."

He toured Europe again in 2006 and this time kept an online journal.

In Ghent, Belgium, the morning after the show, he saw a man scraping a poster for the show off a pole.

"I said, 'Hey you son of a bitch, what do you think you're doing? The show may be over, but I think the people here in Belgium would still like to have my picture on their pole.'"

He tried out 'works in progress' he'd been writing for a new album. In Vienna he played one that was still so unfinished that, "I had to kind of improvise like they do when playing jazz. It was kind of shitty, but they took it well, much as they did when Hitler marched into the city in 1937."

In England he played a show with Dr John – Randy did the first half, Dr John the second – in a marquee erected next to the Tower of London.

"I hope it goes okay and they release me when I'm done."

He tried out another new song there – a historical treatise on the nature of leadership with particular reference to contemporary American politics. Called 'A Few Words In Defense Of My Country', it was released at the beginning of the following year – just in time for George W. Bush's State Of The Union address.

To prove that Randy Newman, though 64, was fully *au fait* with the digital revolution, the release was exclusively on iTunes and came with a YouTube video: nothing fancy – he did not swing from a wrecking ball and neither did he pour a bucket of cold water over his head – he merely sat at his piano and did the song. It's spoken rather than sung – although far too laconically to count as 'rap' – and consists of a brave attempt to think of a world leader who could be described as worse than the current US President.

The morning after the State Of The Union address, in which Bush spoke of the unstoppable march to peace, freedom and democracy his administration was leading in Iraq and Afghanistan, the *New York Times* published an abridged version of the lyric.

"I don't like to write songs about current events," Randy said. "This one, for instance, won't be relevant when this administration is no longer with us. It's such a unique administration, though, that I thought it would be interesting to write something about it. I don't think we'll ever have one like it again."

The cuts made by the paper amused him. "They have an editor, they edit. But they took out a verse about the Caesars where I say, you know, they were sleeping with their sisters, stashing little boys in swimming pools and burning down the city. What are they protecting, Tiberius?"

Randy 'Tell It Like It Is' Newman, the Voice of The People, was not a role in which he felt fully comfortable.

"I've been giving my opinions too much in interviews I've been doing. All of a sudden I've turned into, like, Warren Beatty, like an activist or something. I used to hate it when show-biz people would be commenting on issues, but the way things have gone with this administration, it's in your face all the time."

For a while there was a flurry of controversy in the dumber corners of the press about the nature of irony: about whether Randy, by saying that Bush *wasn't* as bad as Hitler or Caligula was actually implying that he *was* as bad as Hitler or Caligula, or whether he was, actually, satirising the extreme terms in which some commentators spoke of the minor lapses of the Bush administration by introducing a little historical perspective into the argument.

"Contrasting Bush's rule with that of several dictators doesn't do much in the way of clearing the president's name," said one journalist. "If anything, I think Newman is pointing a cautionary finger at those who claim 'Well, things aren't THAT bad' by saying, 'Sure, they're not that bad if you compare our situation to travesties like the Spanish Inquisition.'"

To which one can only add, "D'uh".

Rolling Stone listed 'A Few Words' as its number two best single of the year.

Randy hadn't done a full movie score for two years. *Leatherheads* was a comedy about the early days of professional American football. George Clooney was directing.

Clooney asked Randy to go easy on the Americana and concentrate on the period. Randy was not impressed by Clooney's grasp of the history of American popular music.

"I disagreed with what he wanted to do and about not being true to the fact that it was in 1925 or '27, because he wanted to use things from the forties," Randy told the *Fred – Entertainment* website. "He's really a nice guy, and he liked a lot of the stuff I did. I love those rags from that period, but he told me half way through he didn't like jazz. How else are you going to do 1925?"

In the end Randy turned in his customary mix of ragtime and shuffle with the occasional note of compromise – pairing, for instance 'Tiger Rag' (originally recorded in 1917) with Gene Krupa's tom-toms from Benny Goodman's 'Sing, Sing, Sing' (1936) (which averages out to about 1926). The score also features a lush version of Gershwin's 'The Man I Love' (1924) sung by Ledisi Anibade Young. The orchestrations, played by the 83-piece Hollywood Symphony Orchestra conducted by Randy, are huge, beautiful and packed with virtuoso detail (the trumpet on 'The Man I Love' alone is worth the price of the CD).

Randy himself appears in the film as a barroom pianist, playing ragtime as a fight rages around him, now and then taking a break to crack somebody's head with a bottle.

Apart from *The Randy Newman Songbook, Vol. I* which was new versions of old songs, there hadn't been an album in nine years. Long-term fans had started thinking that maybe, as the rumours surrounding *Bad Love* had suggested, that was it. There never would be another Randy Newman album. Then, just as the queues started growing at Beachy Head, *Harps And Angels* happened.

Just like the old days, Lenny Waronker was back in the producer's chair, sharing it with Mitchell Froom. Most of the work was done in the familiar surroundings of Sunset Sound, and the orchestral tracks were recorded at his ancestral and spiritual home, the big studio at 20th Century Fox, now renamed, in honour of Uncle Alfred, 'The Newman Scoring Stage'.

Good Old Boys was about the South. *Born Again* was about money. *Bad Love* was about bad love. *Harps And Angels* is about death – and ageing, and mortality and failing faculties.

In the title track, 'Harps And Angels', a 12-bar shuffle, the narrator seems to have suffered a heart attack, but clings to life because of a 'clerical error'. He prays and his prayer is answered by a heavenly voice, accompanied by a choir of angels, which warns him that his continued survival will depend on certain conditions: "Better keep your business clean. Don't want no back stabbing, ass grabbing – you know exactly what I mean. All right girls, we're outta here."

He rounds off the story with a moral: "So actually the main thing about this story is, for me, there really is an afterlife / and I hope to see all of you there. / Let's go get a drink."

Track two starts with slow, high strings that let you know the time for shuffles is over and this is a sad one; simple and moving. Ostensibly 'Losing You' is a straightforward heartbreak song – "I'll never get over losing you".

But the song is based on a story that Randy's brother, Alan, the now retired oncologist, had told him a long time before. Wordsworth said that poetry is "emotion recollected in tranquillity" and it had taken Randy a few years to find the tranquillity.

Alan had been treating a 23-year-old, an active sportsman, for a brain tumour. The tumour was inoperable. Alan had to speak to the boy's parents. The parents had been through the Holocaust. "They said, 'We made it, we were able to get over the fact that we lost both of our families, but we don't have enough time left to get over losing our son.'"

You might need a moment.

After which, 'Laugh And Be Happy' seems frighteningly manic. Like 'Roll With The Punches', the song provides insensitive advice for those less fortunate – in this case America's immigrant population.

As he said in an interview in *Village Voice*, both composition and performance owe something to 'The Bare Necessities' from *Jungle Book*, and particularly to Phil Harris' performance as the voice of Baloo the bear. Randy had had the song laying around for some time and wrote it originally for the ill-fated 1997 project *Cats Don't Dance*, but not for the film itself: "I wrote that for the animators because they were having such a hard time.'

The song takes a musical journey through many tempi and styles. "And it goes a lot of places harmonically I wouldn't go ordinarily."

'A Few Words In Defense Of Our Country' – the internet sensation of the year before – was treated to a Nashville arrangement with Randy doing his best Floyd Kramer piano and Greg Leisz on pedal steel, segueing into a more conventionally patriotic arrangement towards the end. "I don't think the stuff on it hurts the song," he said. "Maybe it didn't help it much, but it didn't hurt it."

Following 'A Few Words In Defense Of Our Country' with 'A Piece Of The Pie' suggests that, despite previous assertions to the contrary, Randy was developing a taste for writing "songs about current events".

This one could have come straight from Theatre am Schiffbauerdamm. The lyric is Brechtian, the music – jagged, blaring and bitonal – could have arrived via musical Ouija board direct from the brain of Kurt Weill.

"It's an old-time sort of Industrial Workers of the World, socialist thing. The fact that you can work real hard and do all the country says you're supposed to do, and still not make it is a little surprising, you know what I mean?"

"The rich are getting richer, I should know," he sings. "While we're going up / You're going down / And no one gives a shit but Jackson Browne / Jackson Browne."

"Only Jackson Browne has stayed interested," Randy told the *Pitchfork* website. "Really, all that fervour and good will of the late sixties and early seventies, it went away. Things were left to remain the same. My kids just went to a camp where they worked with Hispanic and African-American kids in shelters. I mean, they come from another world. It was a fantastic experience, but, boy, their experiences were very different. And the black kids had it worse than the Hispanic kids. A lot of the Hispanic kids had cohesive families, at least a little bit. The black kids didn't. It's the saddest thing going. But people get so scared. When the Republicans say the Democrats are going to tax and spend… I mean, things look shitty! I don't know about where you are, but the roads are shitty, the schools are shitty. It's because we're not taxed like other Western countries are. They lowered my taxes! How can a country countenance lowering taxes on the upper income? I can't believe it!"

'Easy Street' reinforces the message, lazy and elite, with clarinets and saxes sliding around like fine wines in the gullet of a plutocrat. On top of the world is a grand place to be, as long as you "don't look down".

'Korean Parents' is a rolling beguine with Oriental trimmings. Like 'Laugh And Be Happy' and 'A Piece Of The Pie', it "goes a lot of places harmonically I wouldn't go ordinarily".

The idea that Asians had a knack with parenting that Americans and Europeans had lost was increasingly borne out by exam grades and general levels of attainment in music, medicine and commerce. In 2011 Amy Chua's book, *Battle Hymn Of The Tiger Mother*, became, for the sharp elbowed over-achievers, what Dr Spock had been for the repression-phobic mums and dads of the fifties.

Using the same sort of guise as he'd used in 'Sail Away' to sell slavery, the narrator in 'Korean Parents' introduces the problem of kids being out of control and suggests that instead of adopting Asian babies, he has been importing the ideal solution "guaranteed to satisfy": "Korean parents" will "whip you into shape / They'll be strict but they'll be fair."

The narrator of 'Only A Girl' is trapped in the same ignominy as the sleaze-bag in 'Shame', the *Bad Love* song. Viagra, which had come onto the market in 1998, had made this sort of thing only too commonplace. To give him his due, though, the 'Only A Girl' guy seems to be motivated more by dew-eyed infatuation than base lust, or at least he's fooling himself he is.

He's a man of a certain age who's met someone much younger and calls a friend to ask his advice. "Why would someone beautiful as she / Love someone old like me?" When the friend suggests, "maybe it's the money", the narrator is truly amazed. "Gee, I never thought of that, God damn it."

"You wonder at all these guys," Randy told Brian Braiker of *Newsweek*. "You think some 19-year-old wants some 50- or 60-year-old guy all on top of them? I tell you, there's a lot of women who married old guys and when Viagra got invented it was a bad break for them."

'Potholes' is a consideration of the potholes one encounters "down memory lane" and starts with a full and frank examination of his relationship with the women in his life. He declares his love for his mother, his wife and even his teenage daughter: "No accounting for it, apparently I don't care how I'm treated. My love is unconditional or something."

Often in concerts, Randy tells the story of how he once went to a restaurant with the family. In restaurants, he likes to sit with his back to the other diners, but, on this occasion, Alice took that chair.

"So my wife told her, 'Daddy likes to sit in that chair.'

"She gave this look and said, 'Oh, Daddy, you're not *that* famous.'"

The song goes on to describe a deeper humiliation, this one at the hands of his father Irving, who had died in 1990. When Irving first met Gretchen, he took great delight in telling her about the time Randy, as a child baseball player, pitched so badly that in the end he walked off the field in tears.

"Within minutes of meeting Gretchen, my father told her that story," Randy said. "Of all the stories, he could have told her about me, this was the first piece of information he volunteered. I mean, where is the punchline to a story like that?"

The album closes with 'Feels Like Home', the button-pushing song from *Faust*.

"'Feels Like Home'," he said, "will end up being the most popular song throughout the years. Little Newmans will be earning something from it 30 years from now."

The reviews were filled with gratifying nuggets like "classic Randy" and "America's most urbane angry old man is still making sublime, beautifully arranged music." And "you're still the boss".

The *Los Angeles Times* said: "Lyrically, every one of these ten songs in 34 minutes raises questions, reinforced by the quietest and most casual singing of Newman's mush-mouthed career."

The critic Robert Christgau marvelled at it: "Never have his arrangements exploited his soundtrack chops so subtly, changeably or precisely. You say you want the failure of the American Dream? Try a marching band put through its paces by a dyspeptic Kurt Weill."

"It's difficult to imagine any other musician," Jay Ruttenberg in *Time Out (New York)* wrote, "so nimbly addressing contemporary America, the crumbling empire, without hiding behind the abstraction that plagues so many songwriters. 40 years after his debut LP, Newman remains in a class of his own [...] now as before, no one can touch him."

When he signed with Nonesuch, Randy had hoped they would "do a better job for me commercially. They'll pay more attention and sell more records for me."

They came through. Before the album was released, he got TV exposure on, among others *The Late Show With David Letterman*, and he did a concert at the small but very select Largo At The Coronet cabaret club, performing the entire album with a four-piece band. The show was transmitted as a webcast. Video extras were provided to promote the album on Amazon, Borders and Barnes & Noble websites.

Perhaps most significantly, the album got into the supermarkets.

Maybe I'm Doing It Wrong

It went to number 30 in the *Billboard* album chart, beating his previous best, *Trouble In Paradise*, by 44 places.

He did a 15 date tour of the US and then another tour of Europe, including a special concert at St Luke's, a converted eighteenth century church just north of the City of London used as a music venue and as rehearsal premises for the London Symphony Orchestra.

He was accompanied by the BBC Concert Orchestra, conducted by Robert Ziegler, and the whole show was televised and shown that June on BBC. Later the performance was released as a DVD and, three years later, as a CD, *Randy Newman Live In London*.

He had the good sense not to pack the set list with "material from my new album". In fact, he just did three songs from *Harps And Angels*, one of which, 'Feels Like Home', wasn't new anyway and instead comforted his audience with the old favourites, opening with 'Love Story', from 1968. Some of the patter between the songs had stood the test of time.

"I want to say a little something here, Maestro," he says, before 'The World Isn't Fair', the song about Marxism in late twentieth century LA. "Some domestic details before I do this song. I have five children, four boys and a girl with two different wives: surprisingly my second wife was younger than the first, it's crazy."

"Finally," he says when the song is ended, "one to get me in *The Guardian*'s top 100 songwriters of all time."

The audience participation on 'I'm Dead (But I Don't Know It)' goes well, in a restrained British way. There's an equally British spattering of applause and a slight cheer of recognition over the intro of 'Simon Smith' – not so much the roar of recognition that used to greet Sinatra when he went into 'My Way', more the response you might get for a well-played cover-drive during a Sunday game at a Sussex county cricket ground, but the thought's there.

He closes with 'I Think It's Going To Rain Today'. He seems almost in tears. Maybe he was moved by the occasion. Or maybe, by this time, he's just bored with the song.

Disney was updating the Grimm fairy tale *The Princess And The Frog* and asked Randy to provide a score and seven songs. The new version was to be set in New Orleans in the 1920s, which meant that Randy could have done it standing on his head with his eyes closed and his ears stuffed with cotton wool.

"I've been dredging those 30 months I spent in New Orleans for all I could all my life," Randy told Jon Burlingame in *Variety*.

Mac Rebennack aka Dr John aka The Night Tripper, a human repository of New Orleans piano styles, sang the opening title song of the movie, 'Down In New Orleans'.

"There was a lot going on with that project, with me doing a lot of rewriting," Randy said. "but I'm just happy I did it, because I had Mac Rebennack singing 'Down In New Orleans'. Whenever Mac is anywhere, I'll go see him play. We both have real New Orleans roots and he talks a language almost no one understands. We were once doing a session years ago with Lenny Waronker producing, and Lenny was trying to get a special sound that was hard to get. Mac finally says, 'Lenny, don't you think it oughta sound a little more diphthereal?' He meant ethereal, but that's his own language. I love it. I use that one all the time now."

Chapter Twenty-Three

Experience had shown by now that Randy Newman and the theatrical stage were somehow chemically imbalanced.

Although ostensibly the songs seem inherently theatrical – many of them 'performed' as they are by 'characters' – there is a problem of nuance, or register. They don't work if they're in your face. They need to be thrown away. The listener needs to discover them rather than have them spelt out. Randy, when he performs them, allows you to share a world that is very much his own. He doesn't exactly invite you in. He doesn't in fact seem to care whether you come in or not. He leaves the door just a little bit ajar and the rest is up to you.

The Brits had had several goes at a Randy Newman juke-box show, one called *Trouble In Paradise*, at the Theatre Royal, Stratford East, in 1985, and another, in 1996, called *Roll With The Punches – The Songs Of Randy Newman* at the Tricycle Theatre. Neither made it to the West End.

In 2010, writer, artistic director, producer, impresario and dramaturg Jack Viertel, the man who had helped *Hairspray*, *Angels In America* and *Smoky Joe's Café* hit the heights, thought he'd have a crack at the Randy Newman conundrum.

A company was assembled with Jerry Zaks directing. The show, it was decided, would be called *Harps And Angels* and would have no narrative structure. Instead the songs would be performed like sketches in a revue with cast members acting the stories they told. Viertel was convinced that this in itself would constitute a coherent dramatic experience. He called it "a journey". Jack Zaks agreed, "It just felt like it had a natural flow to it."

There was a minimal set, projected images including a couple of film clips in which Randy appeared and an onstage eight-piece band. Michael Roth, who had worked with Randy on *Faust* and *The Education Of Randy Newman*, did the musical arrangements.

Randy kept his distance. "I had nothing to do with the creation of this show at all," he said. "Sometimes I know enough to shut up and defer to experts."

After a visit to rehearsals, he told the *Los Angeles Times*: "I don't have a face that's got a smile painted on it in any sense. [...] But I was happy on the inside. Some things I loved, and I think it'll be an entertaining evening."

It probably was an entertaining evening, albeit one that ended with an actress dying alone in a hospital bed singing 'You've Got A Friend In Me'.

The performances, by all accounts, were magnificent. Direction, sets, musicians, arrangements all came in for high praise. But still, Randy Newman and the theatrical stage remained somehow chemically imbalanced.

It opened on November 21 for a run of a month or so. The run was not extended. It did not transfer. Maybe, some day, somebody will figure out how to do it.

Pixar had become a major industry, with a turnover measured in billions and several projects in various stages of production at any time. While John Lasseter was busy with *Cars 2*, Lee Unkrich took over the *Toy Story* franchise.

He'd been co-director on *Toy Story 2*, *Monsters, Inc.* and *Finding Nemo*. *Toy Story 3* would be his first full director credit.

There is a long tradition of film composers kvetching about directors, or, more frequently, about producers who try to have their two cents' worth. Tony Thomas, in his book *Film Score*, mentions producers "who suggested that since the film was set entirely in France, the composer should use a lot of French horns". And another who said, "The strings should play an octave higher." "That would destroy the orchestration." "How about half an octave?"

True to the tradition, Randy kvetched.

"Lee Unkrich had the film temped with my music from other scores," he told Patrick Goldstein in the *Los Angeles Times*, "not just *Toy Story* stuff, but *Parenthood* and even *Air Force One*, a score I did that got thrown out. I can't say I liked it because there really wasn't much room for me to do anything. I'm not complaining, but I think I could've helped a little more on the score if I'd had more freedom to do my thing."

Looking back on the experience in a 2015 interview with Tommy Pearson for Classic FM, he said: "I'm not so sure I don't have a reputation for being a little trouble. Lee Unkrich isn't going to use me again, I don't think. The movie did great and everything, and maybe I'm wrong and if I look back on it I won't know the difference – but it didn't fit hand in glove the way I would have tried to do it."

Nevertheless, the film moved him. He told reporters that the last time he cried was the first time he watched *Toy Story 3*. The time before that was the death of Ray Charles. "I've just got to be nicer to directors. I just don't like them, because they don't leave you alone. Really it's their picture, their name's on it so if they want you to use a kazoo and a bath tub and a whisk or a broom to do something, you've got to do it."

Pixar have clearly forgiven him, or he's forgiven them. At the time of writing, *Toy Story 4* is in production, directed by John Lasseter and Josh Cooley, with music – by Randy Newman.

'You've Got a Friend In Me' featured in all three of the *Toy Story* films, performed by various artists in various styles and languages including, in *3*, a Spanish version, 'Hay Un Amigo En Mi', sung with passion by the Gypsy Kings.

The big new song in *3* is 'We Belong Together' a rollicking, horn-heavy twist number. It was nominated for an Oscar and he was asked to perform it at the ceremony.

"I suggested that I should do my song with someone really inappropriate. My first idea was me and Lady Gaga. I could see us together, with her in a big way, and me in not such a big way. I thought it would get some attention. But the Academy never goes for any of my trashy ideas.

"To be truthful, they have me on too often. I can't imagine why they'd rather have me than Brad Pitt or Angelina Jolie. The whole experience is so strange that I guess it's fun. I don't get nervous too often when I perform, but I do at the Oscars. If you make a mistake, everyone knows it."

In the end he did 'We Belong Together' by himself, at the piano, looking dapper in black tie, tux and silk shirt, while scenes from the movie were projected behind him.

Then Jennifer Hudson came on with the Gold Envelope. "And the Oscar goes to... Randy Newman."

"I'm very grateful for this and surprised," he said in his speech. "My percentages aren't great. I've been nominated 20 times and this is the second time I won. At the Academy, at the lunch they have for the nominees, they have, like, a Randy Newman chicken by this time."

"Getting an Oscar really has nothing to do with the quality of anything," he said afterwards, wearing his ingratitude like a proud badge of honour. "You'd like to think that. But it certainly isn't the best work I've done, what I ended up getting rewarded for [...] The things I won for, to my mind, were some of the least impactful things I ever did for pictures. I wrote a better song for *Babe: A Pig In The City* than I did for those two things. I wrote what was called for. But that's my opinion – which is worth almost nothing."

He was becoming a sort of US equivalent of Alan Bennett: a National Treasure. They hadn't yet named a battleship or an airport after him, but all the same his work was revered and his liberal views, so out of step with the neo-con times, affectionately tolerated as lovable quirks. It did not sit easily with him.

"I've never felt completely like I've been part of something," he told Peter Paphides for *Hidden Tracks*. "Sure, I'm American, but a feeling remains that they could turn on me at any moment. Oh, I'm under no illusions. The first two lines of my obituary will mention the Oscars and the Grammys. They'll refer to me as the composer of 'Short People'. And they'll probably mention *Family Guy*."

His 'fan club', called 'Little Criminals' had, by 2005, reached the milestone of 1,000 members. They like to perform cover versions of favourite Randy songs and regularly (twice) release CDs. The first, *Mamma Told Me Not To Sing – The Songs Of Randy Newman Sung By His Fans*, even included a 'thank-you' bonus track sung by Randy himself.

In May 2011, the plaudits continued when Nonesuch brought out *The Randy Newman Songbook, Vol 2*: 16 more tracks of the man's finest work – just voice and piano. All the tracks are good and some of them a good deal better than the original versions. 'My Life Is Good' stripped of the ominous 1980s synths, for instance, is less bullying, more self-delusional and funnier.

The voice has lost some of its power, and some of the flexibility is gone. The high E and F, for instance, in "few more nights on the street, that's all" from 'Same Girl', taken comfortably 30 years earlier, now showed understandable signs of strain. But 30 or 40 years of singing the songs live had put more detail into his performance, too – a little extra stress on "A *most* unsightly man" in 'Birmingham'; an implied sigh of despair in the phrasing of, "it's hard... just to live... just to live," in 'Baltimore'.

If anything, the playing has improved, though that might be a product of the difference between being part of a band and being a solo player: there's more freedom with tempi and, with the piano exposed, more care taken with dynamics and the shaping of phrases.

Some of the reviews carped a little about the material, suggesting that all the best stuff had been put on *Vol 1*, leaving the *Vol 2* selection weak in places, but none found fault with the performance or interpretation.

Randy, cautiously optimistic, also hoped that the progress of civilisation might mean that the songs, 30 and 40 years after they were written, might fall on more receptive ears.

"Before shows like *The Simpsons*, irony was not very well understood in the States," Randy told Tim Lewis in the *Observer*. "But I don't want to sing everything out of the side of my mouth. I want people to understand what I mean."

"This last record was interesting, more fun than I thought it would be. Now there's something you can use: 'More fun than I thought it would be!' End on something positive, OK?"

For a man now approaching 70, he seemed to be working harder than ever.

He toured extensively in 2011, all over the US, up into Canada, even to Australia where he hadn't played for 28 years ("His body of work proves yet again that on the big questions, all too often the artists can illuminate the truth better than the essayists, the journalists and, perhaps less surprisingly, the politicians." – *Sydney Morning Herald*.)

And the movies kept on coming.

"I think that for me, it got to be too much. I was down on myself by the time I finished *Toy Story*. I was doing *Princess And The Frog* for like a year, and then doing both at the same time for a while."

Multi-tasking bothered him. "I did my worst live show ever when I was working on the film [*Toy Story*]. I played Royce Hall [the imposing 1,800-seat concert hall on the UCLA's Westwood campus], and you just use different muscles when you're writing for an orchestra than when you're doing your own songs. My fingers just wouldn't go where they were supposed to. I wish I'd been in Oklahoma City rather than my hometown. For whoever was there, I owe 'em one."

There were plans for a new musical based on the 1982 Dustin-Hoffman-in-drag movie *Tootsie*. "It's a bad idea," Randy said, "so we'll see." Unsurprisingly it came to nothing. Neither did another musical based on the 1957 Elia Kazan movie *The Face In The Crowd*.

But, in 2012, he came across something he reckoned actually was a good idea.

Barack Obama was standing for re-election and Randy, like never before, put his weight behind the campaign.

By 2008, George W's unpopularity and the economic crisis initiated by the crooks and sharks of Wall Street had generated a taste for change. Barack Obama embodied change and the opposition from John McCain and his running mate Sarah Palin was a shambles. McCain could not remember how many houses he owned and Palin exhibited a stunning lack of general knowledge or understanding of pretty much anything every time she opened her mouth.

Four years on, there was an inevitable degree of disenchantment with Obama; and the Republican candidate, Mitt Romney, looked like a movie star cast as The President and knew exactly how many houses he had, not to mention the really clever stuff like where Poland was and how many beans made five.

Furthermore, many states, in the name of preventing voting fraud, had changed the registration rules in ways that coincidentally had a tendency to disenfranchise the poor. There was a battle to be fought.

In such circumstances, it is usual for wealthy rock'n'roll stars, like the topless heroine in Delacroix's *Liberty Leading The People*, to take their place on the barricades among the desperate and the dying, or to pop down to Sunset Sound and cut some pithy tracks, whichever is nearer.

Ry Cooder, who'd never managed to cultivate much affection for rapacious capitalism, released an album, *Election Special*, on which tracks like 'Mutt Romney Blues' and 'Guantanamo' revived the spirit of Woody Guthrie.

Maybe I'm Doing It Wrong

Mr Dylan and Mr Springsteen also threw their hats into the ring and vented a little spleen about Mitt Romney.

Randy released a YouTube video of a song called 'I'm Dreaming' that he'd been saving for some future album, but brought out early for the occasion. It is based very loosely on the Irving Berlin/Bing Crosby Christmas perennial 'White Christmas'. "I'm dreaming of a white President," it goes, "Just like the ones we've always had / A real live white man, who knows the score / how to handle money or start a war."

It goes on to discuss matters like the number of potential Albert Einsteins the world has lost thanks to racism and shitty education policies and even throws in a few Crosbyish 'ba ba booms'.

"The Civil War was a long time ago but there are aspects of it that remain unsettled, I think," Randy told the *Philadelphia Enquirer* the day after the song was released. "Early on in Obama's term, there was heat generated by issues that you wouldn't think would cause such passion. Even the term 'Obamacare', the way it's spit out, like he was some kind of witch doctor. Maybe I'm overly sensitive to the issue, but I don't think so. There's an edge to things that normally wouldn't have an edge."

"'I'm Dreaming' is less nuanced in its politics [than 'Rednecks'] and doesn't give voice to as complex and rich a character," said the *New Yorker*, "but it fits into Newman's songbook of first-person songs that make you wince while humming along."

Randy offered the song for free online, but encouraged listeners to make a donation to the United Negro College Fund. On his own website, he posted: "I think there are a lot of people who find it jarring to have a black man in the White House and they want him out. They just can't believe that there's not a more qualified white man.

"No European country would have elected a black man. I can't believe it happened. I think it's fantastic, like a step on the moon."

The song didn't result in mass riots in the streets or bonfires with Mitt Romney effigies on them, but Barack Obama was re-elected.

So, job done.

Safe in the knowledge that he had saved his country, Randy started his seventh collaboration with Pixar on the next in the fluffiest of all their franchises.

Monsters University, a prequel to *Monsters, Inc.*, took us back to the time Sulley and Mike first met. "The fraternity part of the film I loved,"

Randy said. "I thought it was the funniest scene in any film ever." He seems finally to have realised that, when promoting work, outrageous hyperbole is better than shuffling humility. "I looked at it 623 times," he said, "I looked at the back of the scene and I saw all these characters!" The scenes are action packed with background gags."

"The best four days of my life," he said – once you start on the hyperbole it's hard to stop – "was when I was with the orchestra. Just being with those phenomenal musicians."

Then he seems to realise he may have overdone it and reverts to his default self-deprecation. "I have a lot of room to get better. I have lists of things I need to improve; I've made those lists from the age of 15. If I would just practise this for 20 minutes or follow this for 20 minutes I could get better at certain aspects."

"I don't play for fun much. I don't like to hear myself that much," he said. And he seems to have learned, too, the virtue of finishing with the big laugh. "I guess that makes it easy for people to say 'We don't either!'"

Apart from a few references back, the score bears little relation to the *Monsters, Inc.* score. There's a lot of big college themes, marching brass and The Blue Devils Entertainment precision drummers impressively clattering. There is however, no big song. The film picked up a couple of Annies, but not even a mention in Oscar's dispatches.

Elsewhere the awards kept coming thick and fast. PEN New England, part of the international writers' organisation, gave him their Song Lyrics Of Literary Excellence Award. "Wow. I'm really touched by that," Randy said, adding that he was "just enough of a snob" to relish receiving an award from a literary group.

Then, in 2013, he was inducted to the Rock And Roll Hall Of Fame.

The ceremony, at the Nokia Theatre in LA, kicked off with Randy, Jackson Browne, Tom Petty and John Fogerty with full band and honking horn section tearing the clothes off 'I Love LA'. They trade lines. They harmonise. They punch the air like they'd been hanging out together since Randy's dad's garage back in the day. Their combined ages easily topped the double century.

Don Henley comes on and gives Randy his award pointing out that it's "shamefully overdue", and that the man "has been making extraordinary music for five decades. No one has written better about greed and shame and the family dynamic."

Henley mentions a gig Randy once did in Texas. "When you can get 2,000 people to applaud a song like 'Rednecks' in a state that's elected Rick Perry three times, you are a hell of an artist!"

Accepting the award, Randy leans into the mike and looks at his trophy.

"I thought I'd have to die first," he said.

After his speech Randy sang 'I Think It's Going to Rain Today'. Then did the line about how many grey-haired thick-set rockers were still on the road and pointedly invited Don Henley back on to the stage to join him in 'I'm Dead (But I Don't Know It)'.

"You've really got to watch the old-fogey syndrome," Randy told *Microsoft News*. "Just because more people from the seventies are out touring now, it's not necessarily that the music was better. [...] People with some kind of talent are definitely out there now."

"I once got a letter from my daughter saying that she wouldn't want a regular dad who fixes things and all that stuff," he told *Hidden Tracks*. "I was more like a dad who knows who Morrissey is; who plays Devendra Banhart. Oh yeah! I love The Smiths. Morrissey knows he's funny. It's not like he's doing comedy and he doesn't know it. In my head, I imagine Johnny Marr meticulously arranging these backing tracks so that you have this pristine ready-made hit, then Morrissey comes in and 'Punctured bicycle/On a hillside desolate.' It's irresistible!"

Gloria Cheng was a concert pianist who, after studying at UCLA, in Paris and Barcelona became a champion of contemporary music.

In 2012 Bruce Broughton, who scored *Silverado*, *Harry And The Hendersons* and *Young Sherlock Holmes*, composed for her a five-movement suite. Then John Williams (*Jaws*, *Star Wars*, *Harry Potter*) wrote her a four-movement piece after which she began to commission works from other film composers. Her aim, she said "was to find out what contemporary [film] composers think about when they go home at night? What melodies, what harmonies, what cadences haunt their private dreams?"

Don Davies (*The Matrix* series), Alexandre Desplat (*The King's Speech*), Michael Giacchino (*Ratatouille*, *Cars 2*) and Randy Newman all contributed. The works were released as a CD, *MONTAGE: Great Film Composers And The Piano*, at the beginning of 2015. Randy produced a five-movement piece, each movement of which, he explains in the liner notes, was in some way related to memories of his uncles. The notes are worth quoting at length.

'The Follies: Young and Beautiful': "Three of the Newman brothers married Goldwyn Girls and Lionel married an Earl Carroll Girl," Randy says. "Everybody seemed pretty happy to me."

'Emil Teaches Sonja Henie How To Skate': "For a while Sonja Henie was the biggest movie star in the world. She was surprised too."

'Carmen Miranda': "How Many Times Do I Have To Tell You I'm Not Mexican!"

'Lionel Teaches Marilyn Monroe How To Sing': "He did teach her to sing. [...] He said that she ate more than anyone he'd seen."

'Outdoors But Not The Red River Valley': "I remember Al saying in every film, John Ford wanted to hear 'The Red River Valley' which is a great tune, but you don't want to hear it in every picture. It bothered Al."

The sons and daughters, the nephews and nieces and grandchildren of Al, Lionel, Emil and Irving had, by this time, quietly taken over the entertainment industry. Alfred's sons Thomas (*Finding Nemo, The Shawshank Redemption, Skyfall, Spectre*) and David (*Ice Age, Scooby Doo, Daddy Daycare*) are both film composers. Alfred's daughter Maria is a renowned violinist and concert hall composer. Lionel's daughter Jenifer danced with the New York City Ballet and her son Joey is a composer, orchestrator and conductor. Randy's son Eric is a producer (*Children Of Men, Slither, Narcos*), Amos is a big shot agent... and so on.

It has been estimated that if some terrible disease struck LA, one that wiped out everyone whose name wasn't Newman, the entertainment industry would survive untroubled.

At the Max Steiner Film Music Achievement Awards in Vienna, Randy stood shoulder to shoulder with his cousin David as a couple of opera singers belted out a selection of his movie songs.

"There probably is something that flows through the blood of the Newman family, other than whisky," he said in his acceptance speech. "You can write down a note, but you have to know what the music *is*. David and his father Alfred, they knew what the music was, and I hope I know that sometimes."

At the time of writing, he's promised that another album is in the pipeline. "I'm happy with the last three albums I made; *Faust, Bad Love* and *Harps And Angels*," Randy told John Mosser on *Morning Call*. "I thought they were as good as anything I've ever did, so I'll continue until I don't think that."

Maybe I'm Doing It Wrong

The new songs include an Irish ballad, 'Where Is My Wandering Boy Tonight', that could have been recorded by John McCormack in 1927.

"I might call the album that," he told the *Telegraph*. "I don't know. I also have a song about Vladimir Putin and a song about a wife dying before her husband, cheerful stuff like that. There is a song about a guy who stayed on the beach all his life and never got off after leaving school. I'm also doing a version of 'It's A Jungle Out There', the theme tune for the TV series *Monk*. I've also done a song about a guy who is in a big arena talking about what troubles America, about questions of dark matter and global warming. He has true believers on one side and scientists on the other. He tilts it in favour of the true believers. It's a gospel song and it's long, the longest song I have ever written. It's good if you can hang in for it."

He previewed the Putin song ("When he takes his shirt off, it drives the ladies crazy") and the Irish one on his European tour in the autumn of 2015.

At the Royal Festival Hall in London, the place he first played 43 years earlier, the audience had come not exactly to worship but definitely to say thank you.

He still looks awkward as he lopes on to the stage – self-conscious. He sits, glances at the keyboard as if he's never seen one before, then launches into 'I Love To See You Smile'. The introductions – the "you're not *that* famous" story about his daughter, and the "God is going to speak to you through me" line he does before 'God's Song' – are as familiar to the faithful as Ronnie Scott's gags used to be at his club on Frith Street, but still he delivers them with Woody Allen hesitancy, as if they're fresh minted.

He encourages the audience participation for the backing vocals on 'I'm Dead (But I Don't Know It)' then chides them for chanting "You're dead, you're dead" with too much conviction.

Half way through he takes a break. In the bar, strangers talk to each other, still feeling they're members of a select club. "I thought he did 'Baltimore' ever such a lot better this time than he did at the Dominion in '84," they say.

At the end, they line up in front of the stage, their hands extended. Randy bends down to shake them, the seasoned pro.

Verdi, he's pointed out, wrote his opera *Falstaff* when he was 79. Richard Strauss was pushing 85 when he wrote his, appropriately titled, *Four Last Songs*.

Randy, a 72-year-old stripling, intends to ape them: to keep on writing, keep on recording, keep on touring.

"Musicians do," he said. "There is nobody applauding at home."

Sources and References

The authors are indebted and extend their gratitude to the many distinguished journalists, critics, scholars and artists listed below. Wherever possible, we have sought permission for quotations.

Special thanks to Sara Burns and to Chris Charlesworth and David Barraclough at Omnibus Press.

BOOKS

Baran, Stanley and Davis, Dennis, *Mass Communication Theory: Foundations, Ferment, And Future,* Wadsworth, 2012

Beech, Mark, *All You Need Is Rock,* Thistle Publishing, 2014

Black, Cilla, *What's It All About?,* Ebury, 2004

Brook, Vincent, *Land Of Smoke And Mirrors: A Cultural History Of Los Angeles,* Rutgers University Press, 2012

Buck, Paul, *Performance: The Biography Of A 60s Masterpiece,* Omnibus Press, 2012

Buhle, Paul, *From The Lower East Side To Hollywood: Jews In American Popular Culture,* Verso, 2004

Burt, Rob and North, Patsy, *West Coast Story,* Hamlyn, 1977

Conot, Robert, *Rivers Of Blood, Years Of Darkness: The Unforgettable Classic Account Of The Watts Riot,* Morrow, New York, 1968

Cornyn, Stan with Scanlon, Paul, *Exploding – The Highs, Hits, Hype, Heroes And Hustlers Of The Warner Music Group,* Harper Collins, 2002

Courrier, Kevin, *Randy Newman's American Dreams,* ECW Press, Canada, 2005

Crosby, Alfred W., *Ecological Imperialism: The Biological Expansion Of Europe 900–1900,* Cambridge University Press, 1986

Doctorow, E.L., *Ragtime,* Random House, 1975

Doll, Susan, *Understanding Elvis: Southern Roots vs Star Image,* Taylor & Francis, 1998

Donner, Frank, *Red Squads And Police Repression In Urban America,* University of California Press, 1990

Fein, Art, *The LA Musical History Tour: A Guide To The Rock And Roll Landmarks Of Los Angeles,* 2.13.61 Publications, 1998

Figner, Vera, *Memoirs Of A Revolutionist,* Northern Illinois University Press, 1991

Friedrich, Otto, *City Of Nets: A Portrait of Hollywood In The 1940s,* University Of California Press, 1997

Gaines, Steven, *Heroes And Villains – The True Story Of The Beach Boys,* New American Library, 1986

Gavin, James, *Is That All There Is? – The Strange Life Of Peggy Lee,* Atria Books, 2014

Gray, Beverly, *Ron Howard: From Mayberry To The Moon… And Beyond,* Thomas Nelson, 2003

Hartman, Kent, *The Wrecking Crew: The Inside Story Of Rock And Roll's Best Kept Secret,* Thomas Dunne Books, 2012

Henderson, Richard, *33⅓ – Song Cycle,* Continuum International Publishing, NY, 2010

Hoskyns, Barney, *Waiting For The Sun: Strange Days, Weird Scenes And The Sound Of Los Angeles,* Bloomsbury, 2003

Howes, Paul, *The Complete Dusty Springfield,* Reynolds and Hearn Ltd., 2001

Hull, Stephen Wayne, *A Sociological Study Of The Surfing Subculture In The Santa Cruz Area,* San Jose State University, 1976

James, Etta and Ritz, David, *Rage To Survive – The Etta James Story,* Perseus Books, 2003

Kaplan, Erin Aubry, *Black Talk, Blue Thoughts, And Walking The Color Line: Dispatches From A Black Journalista,* Northeastern Library of Black Literature, 2011

Karlin, Fred, *On Track: A Guide To Contemporary Film Scoring,* Routledge, 2004

Kastin, David, *Song Of The South: Randy Newman's Good Old Boys,* Turntable Publishing, 2014

Kelly, Michael, *Liberty Records: A History Of The Recording Company And Its Stars 1955–1971,* McFarland & Co. Inc, 2014

Leeson, Edward, *Dusty Springfield: A Life In Music,* Robson Books, 2001

Leiber, Jerry, Stoller, Mike and Ritz, David, *Hound Dog – Leiber And Stoller Autobiography,* Omnibus Press, 2009

Levant, Oscar, *A Smattering Of Ignorance,* Doubleday, 1940

Levant, Oscar, *Memoirs Of An Amnesiac,* Putnam, 1965

Levant, Oscar, *The Unimportance Of Being Oscar,* Putnam, 1968

Lichtenstein, Grace and Dankor, Laura, *Musical Gumbo: The Music Of New Orleans,* W W Norton & Co. Inc, 1993

Ligeti, Andrew Ernest, *The Search For Hallowed Ground In The City Of Angels: Spatial Empowerment Of The City Of Los Angeles Counter Culture 1965–1967,* California State University, Northridge, 2012

Macdonald, Paul (ed.) and Wasko, Janet (ed.), *The Contemporary Hollywood Film Industry,* Wiley-Blackwell, 2007

Malamud, Bernard, *The Natural,* Farrar, Straus, and Cudahy, New York, 1952

Marcus, Greil, *Mystery Train: Images Of American In Rock'n'Roll Music,* E. & P. Dutton & Co., 1975

Marmostein, Gary, *Hollywood Rhapsody – Movie Music And Its Makers,* Schirmer Books, 1997

Martin, George with Hornsby, Jeremy, *All You Need Is Ears,* St Martin's Press, New York, 1994

McFadden, Cyra, *The Serial,* Knopf, 1977

Morris, Christopher D., *Conversations With E.L. Doctorow,* University Press of Mississippi, 1999

Newman, Randy and others, *Guilty: 20 Years Of Randy Newman,* Booklet accompanying the 4 CD box set, Rhino Records, 1998

Plasketes, George, *B-Sides, Undercurrents And Overtones,* Ashgate, 2009

Pollock, Bruce, *In Their Own Words,* Macmillan/McGraw-Hill School Division, 1975

Radsinzkii, Edvard (translated by Schwartz, Marian), *The Last Tsar – The Life And Death Of Nicholas II,* Hodder & Stoughton, 1992

Raeburn, Bruce Boyd, *New Orleans Style And The Writing Of American Jazz History*, University of Michigan Press, 2009

Ronstadt, Linda, *Simple Dreams – A Musical Memoir*, Simon & Schuster, 2013

Sacks, Oliver, *Awakenings*, Duckworth, London, 1973

Schatz, Thomas, *The Genius Of The System: Hollywood Filmmaking In The Studio Era*, Simon & Schuster, 1989

Schneidhorst, Amy C., *Building A Just And Secure World: Popular Front Women's Struggle For Peace And Justice In Chicago During The 1960s*, A&C Black, 2011

Schultz, Bud and Schultz, Ruth, *The Price Of Dissent: Testimonies To Political Repression In America*, University of California Press, 2001

Sheeley, Sharon, *Summertime Blues*, Ravenhawk Books, 2010

Shipton, Alyn, *Nilsson: The Life Of A Singer-Songwriter*, OUP USA, 2013

Snow, Mat, *Randy Newman In Person*, Kindle Books, 2011

Solnit, Rebecca and Snedecker, Rebecca, *Unfathomable City – A New Orleans Atlas*, University of California Press, 2013

Stegmann, Leonard, *California Dreaming*, Kindle Books, 2014

Thomas, Tony, *Film Score – The Art And Craft Of Movie Music*, Riverwood Press, 1991

Thompson, Douglas, *Cilla: 1943–2015*, Metro Books, 2015

Various, *Rolling Stone Album Guide, The (New)*, Rolling Stone, Simon & Schuster, 2014

Waterman, J. Douglas (ed.), *Song: The World's Best Songwriters On Creating The Music That Moves Us*, David & Charles, 2007

White, Timothy, *Long Ago And Far Away: James Taylor His Life And Music*, Omnibus Press, 2001

Wilson, Karen (ed.), *Jews In The Los Angeles Mosaic*, University of California Press, 2013

Wolff, Geoffrey, *The Duke Of Deception: Memories Of My Father*, Hodder & Stoughton, 1969

Zanes, Warren, *Revolutions In Sound: Warner Bros. Records: The First 50 Years*, Chronicle Books, San Francisco, 2008

Zollo, Paul, *Songwriters On Songwriting*, Writer's Digest Books, 1991

PRESS

Addicted To Noise, October, 1995

The Aquarian, Mike Greenblatt, November 19, 2014
The Australian, Rosalie Higson, July 12, 2011
BAM (Bay Area Music), Mark Leviton, January, 1982
Beat International, Steven Turner, February, 1972
Billboard, July 8, 1972, August 12, 1995, November 28, 1998; Phil Gallo, July 25, 2003; Timothy White, September 15, 1979, December 16, 2000
Boston Globe, Michael Blowen, December 18, 1981
Chicago Sun-Times, Roger Ebert, December 12, 1986
Chicago Tribune, February 6, 1978, May 7, 1978
Creem, Clive James, June, 1973
Daily Express, October 19, 1974
Daily Telegraph, Chrissie Illey, February 16, 2012; October 23, 2015
Dallas Observer, Robert Wilonsky, November 5, 1998
Entertainment Weekly, Chris Willman, October 13, 1995; Owen Gleiberman, April 19, 1996
Filter, Martin Sartini Garner, July 5, 2011
Guardian, Dorian Lynskey, May 9, 2013; Duncan Campbell, October 2, 2003; Jon Ronson, July 31, 1999
Hartford Courant, Roger Catlin, October 15, 2000
Harvard Ukrainian Studies (Vol. 11, No. 1, 2 (June 1987) – The Pogroms of 1881, Omeljan Pritsak, June 1, 1987
Houston Chronicle, October 11, 2013
Life, August, 1956
The Listener, Richard Gregory, June 28, 1973
Los Angeles Times, Erin Kaplan, November, 2001; Kristine McKenna, October 9, 1988; Laurie Winer, September 27, 1995; Richard Cromelin, November 3, 2001
Melody Maker, October 15, 1977; October 22, 1977; November 5, 1977; December 3, 1977; December 10, 1977; Chris Welch, May 20, 1975; Ray Coleman, June 3, 1978; Robert Partridge, June 8, 1974
Mix Magazine, David Gans, May, 1983
Mojo, Barney Hoskyns, August, 1998
New Musical Express, June 1, 1974; Paul Rambali, December 7, 1979
New York Journal-American, Dorothy Kilgallen, March 28, 1964
New York Times, Jamie Diamond, March 21, 2002; Joe Queenan, June 20, 2004; Robert Shelton, May 26, 1968
New Yorker, September 18, 2013

Newsweek, Brian Braiker, August 13, 2008

Observer, Tim Lewis, May 14, 2011

Offbeat, Scott Jordan, November 1, 1998

People, Arthur Lubow, May 2, 1983; Michelle Green, September 25, 1995; Susan Toepfer, December 5, 1988

Philadelphia Enquirer, Dan DeLuca, October 17, 2013

Playboy, October, 1974; January, 1987; Robert Christgau, October 1995

Providence Phoenix, Jim Macnie, June 22, 2000

Rolling Stone, Bruce Grimes, April 16, 1970; Charles M. Young, November 17, 1977; Christopher Connelly, January 28, 1983; March 31, 1983; David Felton, August 31, 2014; August 31, 1972; Jerry Hopkins, June 22, 1968; Michael Goldberg, August 11, 1988; Stephen Holden, July 6, 1972; October 7, 1979; Steve Pond, October 20, 1988; Timothy White, November, 1971; October 12, 1978; November 1, 1979; Charles M. Young, November 17, 1977

Seattle Times, Misha Berson, October 23, 2008

Spectator, Rod Liddle, October 12, 2013

Stereo Review, Rex Reed, March, 1969

Tampa Times, Sean Daly, November 12, 2014

Time, December 19, 1963

Time Out (New York), Jay Ruttenberg, July 29, 2008

The Times, Geoffrey Wansell, August 1, 1968; Michael Wale, March 23, 1972; June 4, 1974; Richard Williams, February 14, 1983

Toronto Globe & Mail, November 20, 1981

Toronto Star, Margaret Daly, October 8, 1977

Variety, Jon Burlingame, November 16, 2009; Todd Everett, September 27, 1995

Village Voice, September, 2008

Words & Music, Mark Leviton, September, 1972

ONLINE

A.V. Club – *www.avclub.com/article/randy-newman-56302* – Keith Phipps – May 19, 2011

Ally McBeal – *www.romanization.com/personal/randy/randy_mcbeal.html*

All Music – *www.allmusic.com/album/the-randy-newman-songbook-vol-1-mw0000316084* – Mark Deming

American Songwriter – www.americansongwriter.com/2012/08/randy-newman-louisiana-1927/ – Jim Beviglia
American Songwriter – www.americansongwriter.com/2006/05/randy-newman-why-music-matters-in-film/ – Paul Zollo
AV Animated Views – animatedviews.com/2009/monsters-inc-s-composer-randy-newman-i-score-because-i-care/ – Jérémie Noyer – November 13, 2009
Billboard – www.billboard.com
Billboard Hot 100 – www.billboard.com/charts/hot-100
The Cabin.net – thecabin.net/stories/052100/sty_0521000086.html#.VkmsBcq6PeE – May 22, 2000
Dawn Eden – dawneden.blogspot.co.uk/price.html – Dawn Eden
Deadline Hollywood – deadline.com/2014/12/michael-weller-milos-forman-doctor-zhivago-1201335934/ – Jeremy Gerard – December 29, 2014
Discogs – www.discogs.com
Elsewhere – www.elsewhere.co.nz/absoluteelsewhere/485/randy-newman-interviewed-whats-the-buzz-1999/ – Graham Reid – February 6, 2008
Entertainment Weekly – www.ew.com
Fred – asitecalledfred.com/2008/09/11/interview-randy-newman/ – September 12, 2008
Fretts On Film – frettsonfilm.com/2013/05/02/the-fretts-on-film-interview-three-amigos/ – Bruce Fretts – May 2, 2013
Geni – geni.com
Hiddentracks – hiddentracks.org/articles/interview/i-m-under-no-illusions-the-first-two-lines-of-the-obituary-will-mention-the-oscars-and-the-grammys/ – Pete Paphides – 2011
Library of Congress – www.loc.gov/today/cyberlc/feature_wdesc.php?rec=6375 – Mark Horowitz – November 11, 2013
Library of Congress – www.loc.gov/item/jsmith000199/ – Joe Smith – April 15, 1986
Michael Roth – Composer, Musician, Sound Designer – rothmusik.wix.com – Michael Roth -
Moon Thief – pedrocerillos.blogspot.co.uk/2014_01_01_archive.html – Peter Burg – January, 2014
Movies.com – Movies.com – 2011
Music Radar – www.musicradar.com/news/guitars/session-giant-waddy-wachtel-on-11-career-defining-records-582673 – Waddy Watchel
National Review – www.nationalreview.com/article/210171/jan-dean-alan-reynolds – Alan Reynolds

Performing Songwriter – *performingsongwriter.com/randy-newman-songs/* – Lydia Hutchinson – November 28, 2014

Pitchfork – *pitchfork.com/artists/15999-randy-newman/* – Joshua Klein – October 27, 2008

Popdose – *popdose.com/uncovered-randy-newman-born-again/* – Mike Salisbury – September 13, 2010

Randy Newman – *randynewman.com/category/biography/*

Randy Newman – *randynewman.com/category/articles/journal/* – Randy Newman

Robert Christgau – *www.robertchristgau.com/get_album.php?id=14157* – Robert Christgau

Robert Christgau – *www.robertchristgau.com/xg/rock/newman-89.php* – Bunny Matthews, quoted by Robert Christgau

Songfacts – *www.songfacts.com/blog/interviews/randy_newman/* – Bruce Pollock

Superseventies Rocksite – *www.superseventies.com/spnewmanrandy.html*

Superseventies Rocksite – *www.superseventies.com/ssrandynewman.html*

Support For The Short – *supportfortheshort.org/*

The Big Picture – *latimesblogs.latimes.com/.m/the_big_picture/patrick-goldstein/* – Patrick Goldstein – February 17, 2011

Intelligent Life – *intelligentlifemagazine.com/taxonomy/term/1105* – Tim De Lisle – August 18, 2015

The ELO Network – *theelonetwork.weebly.com/jeff-lynne-interview.html*

The Morning Call – *www.mcall.com/entertainment/music/mc-randy-newman-state-theatre-easton-20141115-story.html* – John Mosser

Theatermania – *www.theatermania.com/off-broadway/shows/randy-newmans-faust-the-concert_302614/* – David Gordon – July 2, 2014

UK Charts Archive – *uk-charts-archive.wikia.com*

Variety – *variety.com/*

Wildcelt.com – *wildcelt.com* – Marleen M. Quint

BROADCAST

30 Rock, Season 3, Episode 8, Created by Tina Fey, written by John Pollack, NBC Universal Television, January 15, 2009

Costas At The Movies, Bob Costas, MLB Network, February 11, 2013

Desert Island Discs, Kirsty Young, BBC Radio 4, October 18, 2008

Hearts And Minds, directed by Peter Davis, BBS Productions, 1974

I Am, Unfortunately, Randy Newman, Jon Ronson, BBC4, November 21, 2003

Little Criminals And Good Ol' Boys: The Randy Newman Story, Glen Tilbrook, BBC Radio 2, August 7, 1999

The Dick Cavett Show, Dick Cavett, ABC Television, December 18, 1970

The Old Grey Whistle Test, Bob Harris, BBC2, June 6, 1978

The Old Grey Whistle Test, Bob Harris, BBC2, June 4, 1974

The Thing About Harry, Stuart Grundy, BBC Radio 2, February 15 & 22, 1977

Tommy Pearson, Tommy Pearson, Classic FM, February 14, 2015

Index

12 Songs 83–9

'A Few Words In Defense Of My Country' 238–9, 241–2
'A Fool In Love' 224–5
'A Piece Of The Pie' 242
'A Wedding In Cherokee County' 114
Albert, Elliot 118, 120
Aldon Music 26
Alexander II, Tsar 1–2
Ally McBeal (TV show) 226
Altman, Al 22
Altman, Robert 145, 146
America (60's and 70's)
   "Born again" claims 134–5
   cultural and racial segregation 40–2, 104–5, 115
   Frank Sinatra's reign 43–6
   hippy era, start and end 48–50, 75–6
   pop music grew up 42–3
   Presidential failings 96, 110
   self-obsession era 135
   Southern resurgence 101–3
   war and protest 42, 43, 76, 109–11
Asher, Peter 190–2
'Ask Him If He's Got A Friend For Me' 25–6
Avalon (film) 181–3
Awakenings (film) 184

Babe: Big In The City (film) 208–9
Bacharach, Burt 36, 38
'Back On My Feet Again' 114–15
Bad Love 212, 213–20
'Bad News From Home' 173
Bagdasarian, Rostom 21
'Baltimore' 124–5
Band, The 103
Bart, Lionel 179–80
Beach Boys, The 41, 47
Beatles, The 32, 43, 47, 72, 120–1, 168
Beaumont, Sascha 7
Bennett, Alvin 21, 22
Berlin, Irving 2, 5
Berry, Jan 15, 16, 44, 45

'Bet No One Hurt This Bad' 61
'Better Off Dead' 219
'Big Hat, No Cattle' 218–19
'Birmingham' 109–10, 251
Black, Cilla 35
Black Dyke Band 208
Blaine, Hal 24
Booker, James 71
Boone, Pat 27–8, 215
Born Again 135–43
Botnick, Bruce 56
British Invasion 32
Buckingham, Lindsey 153
Bugs Life (film) 206–7
Burdon, Eric 51, 84
Buried Treasure 25–6
'Burn On' 96–7
Burns, George 97
Bush, George W. 235, 237–9, 252
Butler, Jerry 36
Byrds, The 43, 102

Cammell, Donald 72
Campbell, Glen 23, 24, 27
Capitol Records 45, 81
Carazo, Castro 112
Cars (film) 237
Castelnuovo-Tedesco, Mario 20
Cats Can't Dance (film) 203–4
Cavett, Dick 104
Cecil, Malcolm 114
Chaplin, Charlie 6–7
Charles, Ray 94
Chase, Chevy 165–6
Cheng, Gloria 255
Chipmunks, The 21
'Christmas In Capetown' 154
civil rights movement 85–6, 109
Clooney, George 239–40
Cochran, Eddie 21, 23
Cocker, Joe 98, 216

Cold Turkey (film) 74–5
Collins, Judy 48
Colson, Chuck 134
Cooder, Ry 67, 73, 83, 109, 117, 120, 190, 233, 252
Cornyn, Stan 58, 59, 65–6
Costello, Elvis 67
'Country Boy' 28
'Cowboy' 62
Crystals, The 37, 41

Dahl, Roald 204
Dale, Dick 41
Daly, William 4–5
Dana, Vic 26, 43
Davis, Sammy Jr. 46
'Davy The Fat Boy' 63, 67–8
'Dayton, Ohio-1903' 97
De Bruyne, Kris 118
De Caro, Nick 110
De Laurentiis, Dino 144–5, 146
DeShannon, Jackie 21, 23, 28–9, 30
'Dixie Flyer' vi, 170–1
Doctorow, EL 144, 146
Domino, Fats 27, 71–2, 236
Dr John 238, 246
Dylan, Bob 2, 43, 47, 84, 85, 102, 168, 215, 225, 253

Eagles, The 120, 125–6, 127
'Easy Street' 242
Edwards, Gus 4
Einstein, Albert 124
ELO 136–7
entertainers' Jewish heritage 2
'Every Man A King' 112–13
'Every Time It Rains' 216

Fairfax High alumni 15
'Falling In Love' 172–3
Faust (album) 189–96

Faust (theatre shows) 196–9
'Feels Like Home' 193, 244
Figner, Vera 1–2
Fleetwoods, The 21, 24–5, 26
'Follow The Flag' 174
Forman, Miloš 146–7
'Four Eyes' 170–2
Fox, James 72, 74
Franklin, Erma 30, 41
Freddie & The Dreamers 43
Freud, Sigmund 123–4
Frey, Glen 109, 112, 120, 140
Froom, Mitchell 213–14, 234, 240

Garrett, Snuff 21–2, 29
Gates, David 23
Gelfman, Gesya 2
Gershwin, George 5
'Ghosts' 138
'Girls In My Life, Part 1, The' 139
'God's Song (That's Why I Love Mankind) 98–9
Goffin, Gerry 26
'Going Home' 220
'Golden Gridiron Boy' 27–8
Goldman, William 187
Good Old Boys 108–16
Gordon, Jim 83
Gordon, Mack 86
Great Film Composers And The Piano 255–6
'Great Nations Of Europe' 216–17
Greif, Michael 190, 198
'Guilty' 110
Guilty: 30 Years Of Randy Newman 209–10

Haggard, Merle 101
'Half A Man' 139–40
'Happy New Year' 38
'Happyland' 50

Harper's Bizarre (The Tikis) 48–50
Harps And Angels 240–5
'Harps And Angels' 241
Harps And Angels (revue) 247–8
'Have You Seen My Baby' 84
Hayes, Jack 182
'He Gives Us All His Love' 74, 95
Henley, Don 109, 112, 140, 152, 158, 190, 192, 254–5
Herman's Hermits 43
Howard, James Newton 169
Howard, Ron 178–9
Hull, Stephen Wayne 41
Hurricane Katrina aftermath 234–7
Hurwitz, Bob 233

'I Don't Want To Hear It Anymore' 36
'I Love LA' 153–4
'I Love To See Your Smile' 179–80
'I Miss You' vi, 164, 219
'I Think He's Hiding' 62
'I Think It's Going To Rain Today' 48, 51, 63
'I Want Everyone To Like Me' 220
'I Want You To Hurt Like I Do' 175–6
'If I Didn't Have You' 230
'If You Need Oil' 88
'I'll Be Home' 125
'I'm Dead (But I Don't Know It)' 216
'I'm Different' 157
'I'm Dreaming' 253
'In Germany Before The War' 122–3
'It's Money That I Love' 136
'It's Money That Matters' 174–5
'I've Been Wrong Before' 35, 38

J&M Recording Studio 70–1
Jackson, Michael 203, 216

Jagger, Mick 72–3, 76
James, Etta 98
James And The Giant Peach (film) 204–5
John, Elton 187, 189, 192
'Jolly Coppers On Parade' 122
Jones, Tom 98
'Just One Smile' 37–8

'Kathleen (Catholicism Made Easier) 126
Keenan, Barry 44
Keep, Ted (Theodore) 21, 22
Kelly, Gene 203–4
Keltner, Jim 109, 127, 190
King, Carol 26
'Kingfish' 113
Kirshner, Don 26
Kiss 133–4, 140, 141
Knopfler, Mark 169–70, 173, 174–5
'Korean Parents' 242–3
Koskoff, Rossa 2–3
Koskoff, Yale 2–3
Kutner, Beverley 38

La Rue, Grace 4
Laine, Frankie 29–30
Land Of Dreams 169–76
Landis, John 165–6
Lapine, James 189–90
Lasseter, John 200–1, 206, 207, 222–3, 237
'Last Night I Had A Dream' 92, 95
'Laugh And Be Happy' 241
'Laughing Boy' 63
Lear, Norman 74
Leatherheads (film) 239–40
Lee, Brenda 23
Lee, Peggy 80–2
Lehrer, Tom 96
Leiber, Jerry 15, 26, 35, 80–1

'Let's Burn Down The Cornfield' 84
Levinson, Barry 161–2, 181–3
Liberty Records 14, 20–1
'Linda' 61
'Lines In The Sand' 184–5
LiPuma, Tommy 169
'Little Criminals' 121
Little Criminals 121–7
Little Criminals (fan club) 250
Little Richard 27, 71
'Living Without You' 61, 91
London, Julie 20
'Lonely At The Top' 90–91, 95
Long, Huey 10, 111–12
'Losing You' 241
'Louisiana 1927' 110–13, 235–6
'Love Story' 60–1, 89
'Lover's Prayer' 84
'Lucinda' 85
Lynne, Jeff 137, 170, 172, 215
Lynryd Skynyrd 103

Maddox, Lester 104, 117–18
'Make Up Your Mind' 186–7
'Mama Told Me Not To Come' 51, 84, 89
Mamet, David 197–8
Manson, Charles 76
Marcus, Greil 118–19, 127
Margouleff, Robert 114
'Marie' 110
Marino, Pete 99
Marshall, Penny 184
Martin, Bill 77
Martin, George 34–5
Martin, Steve 164–5
'Masterman And Baby J' 174
Matassa, Cosimo 70
Maverick (film) 187–8
'Maybe I'm Doing It Wrong' 91
McCartney, Paul 77, 125, 168, 215

McDaniels, Gene 29, 41
McGhee, Brownie 94
McGuire, Barry 43
McVie, Christine 153
Meet The Fockers (film) 234
Meet The Parents (film) 224
Melcher, Terry 30
'Memo To My Son' 97
Metric Music 22, 23–4
'Miami' 156
Michaels, Lorne 164, 189
'Mikey's' 155
Minnelli, Liza 89
Mitchell, Joni vi, 75, 168
Mojo Men 48
Monkees, The (TV series) 32–3
Monsters Inc. (film) 229–30
Monsters University (film) 253–4
'Mr President (Have Pity On The Working Man)' 110
'Mr Sheep' 138
'My Country' 214–15
'My Life Is Good' 155–6, 250–1

'Naked Man' 113–14
Nelson, Ricky 22–3, 37
Nevins, Al 26
New Orleans 69–70, 111, 171, 234–5
'New Orleans Wins The War' 171
Newman, Adele (nee Fox) 10, 11, 13, 14, 176–7
Newman, Alan 12, 14, 20, 27, 238, 241
Newman, Alfred Alan 3–6, 9, 20, 34, 121–2, 146, 189, 256
Newman, Alice 183, 243
Newman, Amos 53, 97, 132–3, 150–1, 176, 256
Newman, David 256
Newman, Emil 8–9, 94, 117, 256
Newman, Eric 53, 97, 256

Newman, George 8
Newman, Irving 9–14, 16–17, 25, 55, 95–6, 99, 139, 142, 177, 243–4
Newman, John 53
Newman, Lionel 8, 9, 20, 34, 146, 256
Newman, Luba (nee Koskoff) 3, 10
Newman, Michael 3, 4
Newman, Patrick 183
Newman, Randy
  Ally McBeal contribution 226–7
  awards 163, 204, 213, 224, 230–1, 250, 254–5
  billboard promotion 141–42
  birth 11
  British artist's 60's hits 35–8, 51–2
  Bugs Life score 206–8
  career hopes 210, 220–1, 258
  coping with fame 75, 131–2
  digital age 238
  Dreamworks move 210–11
  drug taking 53, 55
  early songwriting 18, 24–31
  eyesight problems 14, 16–17
  Family Guy parody 221–2
  Fats Domino album 71–2
  Faust (album and theatre shows) 189–99
  film scores 162–3, 179–80, 182–3, 184, 186–8, 205–9, 232–3, 234, 237, 239–40, 245–6, 251–2, 253–4
  film soundtracks 73–4, 161–2, 164–5, 204
  first live performances 90–3
  first songwriting contract 22
  Greil Marcus's critique 118–19, 127
  gun incident 158
  Harry Nilsson collaboration 78–80

ill-health 166–7, 229
Jewish snub 14
Johnny Cutler, creation of 105–8
Lenny Waronker, friendly critic 14–15, 19, 24, 26, 27, 35, 169
Lenny Waronker production 83, 91, 94–5, 108–9, 114, 126–7, 240
Lenny Waronker's professional role 47, 53, 55–6, 59–60, 63–4
London shows 100, 107–8, 131, 188, 245, 257
low self-esteem 94
marriage to Gretchen Preece 180–1, 183, 202–3, 219, 243–4
marriage to Roswitha Schmale 52–3, 132, 149–50
Monsters Inc. score 229–30
music studies at UCLA 19–20, 33
musical family members 146, 256
musical influences 7, 62, 96, 162–3
New Orleans and Hurricane Katrina 234–6
New Orleans memories 69, 171, 245–6
Obama endorsement 252–3
Oscar nominations 148, 163, 180, 183, 187, 202, 208, 209, 224–5, 230–1, 237, 249–50
peer ratings 77, 152, 220
Peggy Lee collaboration 80–2
personal legacy 250, 254–5
Ragtime score 145–6, 147–8
recording style 63–4, 113–14
relationship with children 132–3, 150–1, 176, 214–15, 243, 255
relationship with father 13, 25, 95–6, 142, 177, 214, 243–4
residences 149–50, 202–3
school days 14, 172

segregation riots (1965) 42
separation from Roswitha 163–4, 176
'Short People', reaction to 128–30
singing abilities 27–8, 109, 212–13
song for Roswitha 219
songwriting, mid 60's change 47–8
songwriting breaks 103–4, 119–20
songwriting style 151, 159–60, 179, 213, 216
Southerners, attitude towards 104–9
teenage years 15–18
tours 117–18, 118, 159, 188–9, 238, 251
Toy Story film scores 201–2, 222–4, 248–9
tribute show 149
TV adverts 118
TV appearances 89, 107, 115, 118, 152–3, 159, 175, 244
Uncle Alfred's influence 7, 163, 186–7
Van Dyke Parks collaboration 54–5, 57–8
Warner Brothers' ethos 66–7
Warner-Reprise albums 59–64
Warner-Reprise deal 53, 66–7
work in progress (2015) 256–8
working for 20th Century Fox 34–5
Newman, Robert 7, 8, 10
Newman, Thomas 256
Nilsson, Harry 33, 77–80
Nitzsche, Jack 30, 73
Nixon, Richard 96, 110
'Nobody Needs Your Love' 37, 38
Nonesuch Records 233–4, 244

Obama, Barack 252, 253
'Old Kentucky Home' 87

'Old Man' 95–6, 177
'Old Man On The Farm' 126
'Only A Girl' 243
Ostin, Mo 45–6, 71, 210
'Our Town' 237

Pallenberg, Anita 72–3
'Pants' 140–1
Parenthood (film) 178–80
Parks, Van Dyke 33, 48, 53–7, 83, 186
Parsons, Edward A. 3
Parsons, Gene 83
Patience and Prudence 21
Performance (film) 72–4
Perry, Richard 46, 71
Pitney, Gene 36–7
Pixar 200–1, 206–7, 229, 237, 248
Pleasantville (film) 209
'Political Science' 96
Porter, Cole v
'Potholes' 243
Preece, Gretchen 180–1, 202–3, 219, 243–4
Presley, Elvis 70–1, 101
'Pretty Boy' 137
Price, Alan 51, 52
Proby, P.J. 23–4, 27

Rafelson, Bob 32–3
Ragtime (film) 145–9
Raitt, Bonnie 190, 192–3
Randy Newman 60–6
Randy Newman Live In London 245
Randy Newman Songbook Vol.1 234
Randy Newman Songbook Vol.2 250–1
'Real Emotional Girl' 156–7
'Red Bandana' 174
Redford, Robert 162
'Rednecks' 105, 106, 109
Reprise Records 45–6

Reynolds, Alan 16
Richards, Keith 72–3
'Rider In The Rain' 125–6
Roberts, Oral 13
Rock 'n' Roll origins 70–1
'Roll With The Punches' 173–4
'Rollin'' 115
Rolling Stones, The 72, 76, 215
Ronstadt, Linda 158, 190, 192, 194
'Rosemary' 87–8
Ross, Gary 209, 232–3
Roth, Michael 198, 227, 248
Russell, Leon 23, 49

Sacks, Oliver 183–4
'Sail Away' 94
Sail Away 94–9
Salisbury, Mike 115, 141
'Same Girl' 155, 251
Sasso, Will 221–2
Schmale, Roswitha
    childhood stories 122, 124
    marriage to Randy Newman 52–3, 132, 149–50
    separation from Randy 163–4, 176
Schneider, Bert 32–3
Schoenberg, Arnold 19
Schroeder, Aaron 38
Seabiscuit (film) 232–3
Selick, Henry 204–5
'Shame' 215
Sheeley, Sharon 22–3
'Short People' 126–7, 127–30
'Sigmund Freud's Impersonation Of Albert Einstein In America' 123–4
Silver, Joan Micklin 149
Simon, Paul 154, 158, 168
'Simon Smith And The Amazing Dancing Bear' 50, 51, 52, 77, 95

Sinatra, Frank 43–6, 90
Sinatra, Frank Jr. 15, 44
Sinatra, Nancy 15, 46
Sloan, P.F. 15, 43
Smiths, The 255
'So Long Dad' 61–2
'Somebody's Waiting' 29
'Something Special' 173
Sondheim, Stephen 149
Song Cycle (Van Dyke Parks) 56–8
'Song For The Dead' 157
Spector, Phil 15, 24, 30, 37, 41
'Spies' 138–9
Springfield, Dusty 35–6, 38
Springsteen, Bruce 156, 215, 253
Stills, Stephen 33
Stojowski, Sigismund 3
Stoller, Mike 26, 80–1
'Story Of A Rock And Roll Band, The' 136–7
Streisand, Barbra 91
surf culture 40–1
'Suzanne' 84

'Take Her' 29–30
'Take Me Back' 157
Taylor, James vi, 64, 67, 190, 237
Terry, Sonny 94
'Texas Girl At The Funeral Of Her Father' 121–2
'The Beehive State' 62–3
'The Blues' 154
The Education Of Randy Newman (theatre show) 227–9, 231–2
The Natural (film) 161–2
'The One You Love' 217
The Paper (film) 186
The Princess And The Frog (film) 245–6
'The World Isn't Fair' 217–18
'There's A Party At My House' 157

'They Just Got Married' 139
'They Tell Me It's Summer' 24–5
Thomas, Irma 30–1, 41
Three Amigos! (film) 164–6
Three Dog Night 89
'Tickle Me' 91
Titelman, Russ 24, 46, 73, 91, 94–5, 97, 105, 109, 112, 114, 115, 120, 126, 169
Torrence, Dean 15, 16, 44–5, 77
Toy Story (film) 201–2
Toy Story II (film) 222–4
Toy Story III (film) 248–9
Tracey, Robert 6
Trouble In Paradise 152–8
Trueblood, Mark 91

'Uncle Bob's Midnight Blues' 88
'Underneath The Harlem Moon' 85, 86–7
University High alumni 15–16
Unkrich, Lee 248

Vee, Bobby 21, 28, 37
Viertel, Jack 247–8
'Vine Street' 57–8
Voormann, Klaus 120–1, 127

Walker, Jimmy 8
Walker, Scott 36, 37
Walker Brothers 36
Wansall, Geoffrey 51–2
Warner-Reprise 48, 53, 58, 59, 65–7, 127, 176, 195, 210
Waronker, Lenny
  Dreamworks move 210–11
  Irving Newman's stories 139–40
  Liberty Records 22
  peer ratings 152
  producer role 83, 91, 94–5, 109, 114, 120, 126–7, 169, 240

Randy's friend and critic 14–15, 19, 24, 26, 27, 47, 169
Randy's professional promotion 35, 48, 53, 59–60, 63–4, 108
university studies 20
vocal part 112
Warner-Reprise appointment 46, 48–50, 53, 67
Waronker, Simon (Si) 14, 20–1, 22
Was, Don 191
'We Belong Together' 249
Wexler, Jerry 36
White, Clarence 83
'William Brown' 140
Wilson, Brian 44, 54, 55, 100
'Wrecking Crew' (studio musicians) 24, 41, 60

'Yellow Man' 87
'You Can Leave Your Hat On' 97–8
'You Can't Fool A Fatman' 121
Young, Neil 103
'You've Got A Friend In Me' 202, 249

Zaks, Jack 247–8